Parallel Visions, Confluent Worlds

Parallel Visions, Confluent Worlds

Five Comparative Postcolonial Studies of
Caribbean and Irish Novels in English, 1925–1965

RICHARD McGUIRE

THE UNIVERSITY OF THE WEST INDIES PRESS
Jamaica • Barbados • Trinidad and Tobago

The University of the West Indies Press
7A Gibraltar Hall Road, Mona
Kingston 7, Jamaica
www.uwipress.com

© Richard McGuire, 2017

All rights reserved. Published 2017

A catalogue record of this book is available from the
National Library of Jamaica.

ISBN: 978-976-640-612-7 (print)
978-976-640-613-4 (Kindle)
978-976-640-614-1 (ePub)

Cover illustration: Mainie Jellett, *Achill Horses* (1938).

Cover and book design by Robert Harris
Set in Adobe Garamond Pro 11/14.5 x 27
Printed in the United States of America

To my mother and father

Contents

Acknowledgements **ix**

Introduction **1**

1. "Dis Yard Is a Battle Ground": Alfred Mendes's *Black Fauns* and Liam O'Flaherty's *The Informer* **15**

2. "Two Tunes": Jean Rhys's *Voyage in the Dark* and Elizabeth Bowen's *The Last September* **44**

3. Matriarchal Economies: C.L.R. James's *Minty Alley* and Patrick Kavanagh's *Tarry Flynn* **70**

4. "A Missile without Provenance or Target": Sam Selvon's *The Lonely Londoners* and Samuel Beckett's *Murphy* **99**

5. Shadow Kings: George Lamming's *In the Castle of My Skin* and Michael Farrell's *Thy Tears Might Cease* **124**

Conclusion **154**

Notes **163**

Selected Bibliography **173**

Index **187**

Acknowledgements

I AM THANKFUL TO THE DEPARTMENT OF Literature, Film, and Theatre Studies at the University of Essex, Colchester, for its part in the development of this project. In particular, I express gratitude to Professor Peter Hulme, a scholar without peer and a key figure in the development of Caribbean and postcolonial studies. Professor Maria Cristina Fumagalli and Dr Jak Peake at Essex are exceptional academics who were also key players in the shaping of this work.

I am grateful to Professor Alison Donnell at the University of Reading, Professor Evelyn O'Callaghan at the University of the West Indies at Cave Hill, Barbados, and Professor Maria McGarrity at Long Island University Brooklyn for their invaluable suggestions and advice throughout the course of my research for this book.

Special, personal thanks are extended to my good friend Dennis Bull. I owe so much to my wife, Julie Ann McGuire, and my stepdaughter, Wiley Bowen, for their unwavering support and enthusiasm during these years of study. To all, I extend my most sincere acknowledgement.

Introduction

POST-1922 IRISH LITERATURE IS BY DEFINITION POSTCOLONIAL. Since the late 1980s, there has been a healthy growth of critical scrutiny of the complex situation of Irish history, cultures, society and literature within postcolonial debates. Nonetheless, this book is the first dedicated major study specifically of the postcolonial dimensions of the comparatively neglected post-1922 Irish novel in English. This text attempts to establish a postcolonial Irish novelistic tradition by closely examining five novels that employ formal and thematic attributes of realism to narrate processes of disengagement from British colonial rule. Ireland is, after all, a prime example of a country with a long colonial history: it was the first overseas location colonized by the English, from 1169, after the Norman landings in England a century previous. From this point in history, wave after wave of colonial encounter, settlement, commercial exploitation of indigenous peoples and various forms of oppressive legislation took place. The impact of colonialism persisted in Ireland long after the country was absorbed largely unwillingly into Britain, in the Act of Union 1800, as part of the United Kingdom of Great Britain and Ireland. It arguably continued long after Irish independence and partition in 1922.

Bill Ashcroft, Gareth Griffiths and Helen Tiffin's 1989 survey *The Empire Writes Back* sees postcolonial literatures as texts that work in dialogue with, and often at variance with, the dominant colonial discourses of "English literature". Postcolonial societies, they argue, are those that work to establish difference from the totalizing, imperialistic representations of their peoples, customs and cultures as imposed by their rulers. Postcolonial societies ordinarily develop "through several stages which can be seen to correspond to stages both of national and regional consciousness and of the project of asserting difference from the colonial centre".[1] The term "postcolonial", as employed in the above gloss, is more descriptive than definitive. Indeed, Bart Moore-Gilbert remarks that when applied as a definitive concept, the term "postcolonial" has such "elasticity" that it has been regarded as some as progressively "imploding as an analytic construct".[2] While there is and should be thus no clear consensus as to a definition of the adjective "postcolonial", I choose to accept Peter Hulme's proposition that it at least "refers to a *process* of disengagement from the whole colonial syndrome". Hulme's italicized noun is decisive here, as it means that the prefix "post" does not (or should not) mark some historical point *after* independence from colonial rule.[3] Hulme's remark is echoed by critics ranging from Ania Loomba to Alison Donnell, who agree that the term "postcolonial" refers to processes of detachment from the apparatuses of colonial hegemony. While three voices do not a broad consensus make, I concur with them, and propose that Irish texts and writers were in many respects postcolonial, in that they operated within processes of intellectual, historical, cultural and political dissolution from the once-dominant discourse of the colonial age. Ireland experienced the best part of eight hundred years of British occupation in one form or another before it became partially independent in December 1922.

Given that much Irish literature, most particularly poetry and drama, has already been read in terms of its perceived postcoloniality, it is perhaps surprising that the post-independence Irish novel has not been given similar attention: after all, the novel is usually seen as the literary form that pays particular attention to its sociohistorical contexts. For instance, critics outside of the frame of Irish literary studies, from Kenneth Ramchand to Sandra Pouchet Paquet, have indeed read the fictional output from other former British colonies, such as islands of the Caribbean, as postcolonial in that it articulates and reflects disengagement from the mindset and infrastructures of British power. Such critics, by virtue of the focus of their study, evidently regard the Caribbean novel of the 1920s to the 1960s as a key example of literature that utilizes the form of longer prose fiction to portray and analyse the lives of a vast range of people from different socioeconomic backgrounds, all living during a period of intellectual detachment from colonial ideology and power systems. However, postcolonial attributes of the post-independence Irish novel have heretofore been understated, if not overlooked. This book will therefore make an original contribution to scholarly research by examining the extent to which these

Irish novels might constitute a postcolonial canon equivalent to their Caribbean correlatives. This examination will be conducted by taking five canonical postcolonial novels from the former British West Indies as an exemplary series alongside which to set five Irish novels, paired based on a number of at least apparent formal and thematic parallels, without losing sight of the specificities of the different historical contexts.

The ways that Caribbean literary texts have grown in public profile, and have come to be regarded as seminal creative expressions of what is now called postcolonial thought, are as complex as they are various. The role of the BBC Overseas Service's radio series *Caribbean Voices* in this process cannot be understated, as week after week from 1943 to 1958 it demonstrated the capacity to introduce a global listening public to the works and literary concerns of West Indian writers such as Una Marson, Sam Selvon, Derek Walcott and V.S. Naipaul. The international scope of readership of West Indian writings and their preoccupations was clear when, in 1953, Richard Wright wrote an introduction to the first US edition of George Lamming's *In the Castle of My Skin*. Wright saw strong links between the white-controlled society of Lamming's novel and his own native Mississippi.[4] African-American writers such as Wright and James Baldwin met with Caribbean writers including Lamming, Aimé Césaire and Frantz Fanon at the First International Congress of Black Writers and Artists in Paris in 1956. The Congress's aim was "that each country and group of countries draw up an inventory of the needs expressed by citizens, individually and collectively, and of cultural resources that might meet those needs in an equitable way".[5] The following years saw artistic movements, writers, academics and publishers pursuing the objectives of the Congress. By the 1960s, the Black Arts Movement in the United States and the Caribbean Arts Movement in Britain showed similar trajectories regarding how writers and intellectuals in each region sought to draw up inventories of black art and culture. By 1970, the efforts of African-American intellectuals to introduce black writers to US academic syllabi had led to Kent State University in Ohio selecting Ralph Ellison's *Invisible Man* as a thesis topic. Academies began to review centuries of black literature for assimilation into their teaching and research platforms, inclusive of the Harlem Renaissance which had also featured Caribbean figures such as Claude McKay and Marcus Garvey. Then, the 1970 republication of Lamming's *In the Castle of My Skin* by Collier Books offered a timely reminder of the importance of Paris in 1956 and those pioneers who had convened to compile a body of black culture that was now tentatively influencing the academy. The republication of Lamming's novel, which towards its conclusion shows the protagonist's friend Trumper returning to Barbados from a long spell experiencing the racial politics of the United States and speaking about Black Consciousness, acknowledged and reinforced the text's canonical place in the origins of a modern black intellectual movement of the Americas.

In Britain, Heinemann's establishment of an African Writers Series from 1962, featuring works by Chinua Achebe and Ngũgĩ wa Thiong'o, and that same London publisher's 1964 launch of the *Journal of Commonwealth Literature* opened up new vistas for academics and publishers to rediscover works by writers from across those countries colonized by the British Empire. Even though the University of Leeds – the site of the first Conference of Commonwealth Literature – appointed Sierra Leonean academic Eldred Jones to its first fellowship in 1965, it did not directly follow that Commonwealth literature, inclusive of works from the British West Indies, was automatically a contender for assimilation within this, or any, British literary academy.[6] New Beacon Books, an independent bookstore and publishing company founded by John La Rose and Sarah White in 1966, originated in a Hornsey, North London, flat – hardly at its time (or at any time) an obvious contender for cultural primacy with the grand English publishing houses.

New Beacon Reviews, first published by La Rose and White in 1968, was originally intended only as an occasional periodical. In spite of its inauspicious beginnings, this British Caribbean journal constituted the first effort to revisit the Caribbean literary works of the Harlem Renaissance and *Beacon* era, and to carry such analysis further into understanding these writings' implications for a new period of black British arts and letters. If the *Beacon* era was a period where there was a swell of cultural activity among a progressively self-aware West Indian intellectual society, then the New Beacon project would constitute a renaissance of such thought for the 1960s and beyond. Its first edition did indeed feature essays on Claude McKay, Eric Williams, Wilson Harris and Jean Rhys: all four writers are now regarded as central to Caribbean studies.[7] The 1970s constituted the high point of Commonwealth literature studies; the 1980s saw in the infancy of postcolonial criticism. Over this period, academics such as Kenneth Ramchand analysed West Indian novels in English written from the 1920s onwards. Ramchand's 1970 monograph *The West Indian Novel and Its Background* was published a good fifteen years or so prior to the point at which Commonwealth literature switched to the new theoretical and critical practice of postcolonial studies.[8] However, Ramchand's book anticipates some of the methodology and concerns of postcolonial scholarship in focusing on how early Caribbean writers singled out the novel form as an optimum way to narrate, in a realist mode, the lives of West Indians in the socioeconomic, political and cultural contexts of their late-colonial era.

The widespread acceptance among scholars and readers of the importance of *Beacon* authors such as C.L.R. James and Alfred Mendes, and writers such as Rhys, did not therefore happen overnight or by a clear, programmatic effort. Over the course of the next few years, from 1968, New Beacon Books published intermittently: the first *Beacon* novel to be republished was James's *Minty Alley* in 1971. In 1970 Heinemann's new Caribbean Writers Series began to republish, and in the process facilitate, the reappraisal of older Caribbean novels such as Guyanese writer Edgar Mittelholzer's 1941 *Corentyne Thunder*. Yet it would be another thirteen years before New Beacon saw to the 1984 republication of one of Caribbean literature's most groundbreaking novels, Mendes's 1935 *Black Fauns*.

Eventually, around the end of the 1970s and the early 1980s, as the study of Commonwealth literature morphed into postcolonial studies, a broader range of publishers and academics began to take interest in older Caribbean novels and thus between them established a Caribbean postcolonial novelistic canon.[9] For example, London publisher Longman – a well-known company dating from as early as 1724 and an imprint of Pearson's Schools since 1968 – launched its Drumbeat series, dedicated to African and Caribbean writers, in 1979. Key Caribbean novels of the 1950s featured in this series: Kenneth Ramchand provided a skilful introduction to a 1985 Longman Drumbeat republication of Sam Selvon's 1956 novel *The Lonely Londoners*; David Williams gave a critical 1986 introduction to George Lamming's 1953 *In the Castle of My Skin*. Many critics and scholars became involved in providing introductions to volumes in this series, which had the effect of at least introducing the developing body of West Indian literature into schools, colleges and universities.

In focusing their interest on longer prose fictive works produced decades prior to the main wave of island independence from Britain, academics such as Ramchand and Rhonda Cobham effectively acknowledged that the early

Caribbean novel was seminal in the development of an intellectual movement of decolonization from the sociocultural and ideological constructs of British rule. They investigated ways in which early Caribbean writers such as Mendes and James discovered the advantages of using the novel's narrative elements of story, characterization, setting and voice, or its generic modes of social realism and naturalism, to hold a mirror up to the nature of societies who for too long had been neglected or misrepresented by imperial authors.

In his 1985 Longman Drumbeat introduction to Selvon's novel *The Lonely Londoners* (1956), Ramchand went on to draw comparisons between the Trinidadian Selvon and Dominican writer Jean Rhys, author of *Voyage in the Dark* (1934), in their construction of the migrant novel as a means by which to articulate postcolonial themes of dislocation, passage, limbo and statelessness.[10] Jean Rhys was therefore another Caribbean writer who, after her death, was assimilated into a West Indian and postcolonial literary canon. It was not until the 1970s that Rhys's work began to be examined closely for its West Indian dimensions and tentatively find its way into a postcolonial canon. In light of the growth of postcolonial studies in the 1980s, new scholars focused more and more on the Caribbean aspects of Rhys's life and work.[11] For example, Sandra Pouchet Paquet, another early postcolonial scholar, devotes a book-length study to an exploration of the work of Barbadian novelist George Lamming (b. 1927). In *The Novels of George Lamming*, Paquet is particularly focused on discussing how Lamming uses his creative imagination to produce literary texts embodying decolonizing processes in the Caribbean.

How and why texts become canonical may often be a matter of accident, and a protracted process, rather than the result of any clear design or manifesto. With West Indian literatures in English, the former is very much the case. It is over the course of the past five decades that a consensus has slowly evolved among Caribbeanists for the justifiable canonicity – or literary, cultural and historical importance for research and teaching – of novels by Mendes, Rhys, James, Selvon and Lamming, among others.

The early postcolonial academics wrote about Caribbean writers largely because they were from the same general geographical area and knew their works and sociocultural contexts intimately.[12] Since the late 1980s, the geographical scope of postcolonial studies – and with it, the postcolonial canon – has expanded considerably to incorporate new regions, new critics and new postcolonial readings of older literary texts.[13] Ireland was one such region of literary production to attract postcolonial studies. In 1988, Edward Said, Fredric Jameson and Terry Eagleton contributed to separate volumes of the Derry-based journal *Field Day*, with seminal essays attempting to situate discussion of any literary, creative product of Irish culture within the scope of postcolonial studies rather than within the constraints of British literature. These essays were later republished in 1990 as a book, *Nationalism, Colonialism and Literature*. In the introduction to that volume, Seamus Deane offered a mission statement for *Field Day*, to show that its assessment of the situation in Ireland "derives from the conviction that it is, above all, a colonial crisis".[14] Later, the first three volumes of *The Field Day Anthology of Irish Writing* (1990–91) were part of a deliberate attempt by postcolonial Irish writers and editors (inclusive of Seamus Heaney, Deane, Tom Paulin, Luke Gibbons and Declan Kiberd) to compile a canon of Irish writing in Gaeilge and English, from medieval poetry to the present day.[15] Yet it is at this point that attempts by postcolonialists to select – or rather, elect – an Irish canon ran into difficulties and controversy. The perceived androcentric bias of the editors' selection of literary texts raised the question of the problems inherent in intentional canon-forming by committee: one can take a revisionist approach to literature, but one still risks marginalizing other texts, other voices, in creating a new canon. Opposition from Irish feminist literary scholars finally brought about the additional publication of two new *Field Day Anthology* volumes in 2002, dedicated to Irish women writers, but these were seen by some detractors as tokenistic and too little, too late for *Field Day*.[16]

The innovative but incomplete achievements of *The Field Day Anthology* were followed by new, more sharply focused monographs proposing to evaluate, expand and fine-tune understanding of the role of Irish literature within postcolonial studies. I have noted Declan Kiberd's editorial role in the first three volumes of *The Field Day Anthology*. Following *Field Day*, Kiberd's major 1995 work, *Inventing Ireland: The Literature of the Modern Nation*, was the first dedicated book-length postcolonial critical survey, rather than anthology, of Irish literature.[17] Kiberd looks back at male and female writers of Irish poetry, drama and prose since the end of the nineteenth century and argues that Irish literature can be read in a postcolonial context, where "a native writer formulates a text committed to cultural resistance".[18] He believes that Irish writings, whether written prior to or following independence, have an intellectually postcolonial dimension if they seek in their moment of production to work against colonial hegemony. In its wide-ranging study, *Inventing Ireland* investigates how modern Irish writers have formulated literary strategies to interrogate and resist the ways in which Ireland, over centuries of British colonial domination, was portrayed as Other, as the not-England and as the antithesis of an imperial "England of the mind". Kiberd writes chapters with largely thematic postcolonial bases, such as "Ireland: England's Unconscious?", "The Periphery and the Centre" and "Post-colonial Ireland: A Quaking Sod", and examines a broad number of authors and texts in this light. However, Kiberd is engaged in a broad survey of Irish writing and thus does not look closely at the novel genre for its decolonizing potentiality.[19]

Kiberd's *Irish Classics* (2000) proposes another selection of canonical Irish writers, inclusive of Samuel Beckett and Patrick Kavanagh: given that Kiberd is engaged in a survey and not a generic comparison, he again does not single out the novel for its decolonizing potency.[20] Kiberd certainly improves upon the shortcomings of *The Field Day Anthology* in his two acclaimed volumes. In the two decades since *Inventing Ireland*, Irish studies has become more comparative in its increasingly sophisticated postcolonial research ambition to understand how the forces of colonial capitalism and power in Ireland can be understood by cross-reference to other colonized societies. Conversely, analysis of colonial economics and rule in Ireland, and the impact of British hegemony on Irish society and culture, continues to facilitate an illuminating context for comparative postcolonial studies of other former British colonial regions and cultural practices. Maria McGarrity's 2008 book *Washed by the Gulf Stream* is highly original in perceiving and investigating Irish and Caribbean literary, historical and geographical crosscurrents.[21] McGarrity clearly considers Irish literature, inclusive of the Irish novel, as postcolonial. In 2015, McGarrity – together with noted Caribbeanists Alison Donnell and Evelyn O'Callaghan – co-edited a multidisciplinary book, *Caribbean Irish Connections*, which acknowledges a wide range of enlightening parallels, if not confluences, between aspects of Irish and West Indian histories, literatures and societies.[22]

In spite of such developments in postcolonial Irish studies, there has been very little, to date, in the way of dedicated analysis of the Irish novel in the first four decades after independence to compare with postcolonial readings of the Caribbean novel. There has been no concerted effort to try to understand how Irish writers used the novel form to investigate and critique processes of intellectual decolonization from the many still largely intact political and ideological structures of British rule. A strong reason for this is that scholars and critics have tended to write about the literary genres that had greater visibility and circulation from the 1920s. By the time of the birth of the Irish Free State, the poetry of the Irish Literary Revival was recognized and celebrated by the new Irish government. Abroad, W.B. Yeats received the Nobel Prize for Literature in 1923; he was now such an establishment figure at home that he was appointed a senator of the Irish Free State. Yeats's Abbey Theatre constituted part of a drive towards a national culture. It is easier to look back at those literary genres that, in their time, were being read in relation to a parting of ways from British national culture, than to the more obscure post-independence Irish novel, which did not have the public exposure or impact granted to the dramatic form, or poetry, in Ireland. This is because, even if specific Irish novels were not banned by the authorities, they still were not very likely to be distributed by Irish booksellers. In the current climate of comparative study of Irish literature, it is timely and right to return to the much-neglected Irish novel of this period – to resituate it within Irish and postcolonial studies, and to find out the extent to which its apparent formal and thematic parallels with Caribbean novels of the time are due to similar processes of disengagement from the ideological constraints of British rule.

In Ireland, the independence year 1922 brought insularity, sociocultural fragmentation and the censorious influence of a Catholic-led state hegemony upon the country's literary output. One of the first decisions of the twenty-six-county, partitioned and overwhelmingly Catholic-orientated Irish Free State government was to set up a Committee on Evil Literature. Its intention was to "protect" the ill-educated and the vulnerable from allegedly immoral mass-produced art and literature. The 1929 Censorship of Publications Act, under W.T. Cosgrave's Cumann na nGaedheal government (1923–32), had a most deleterious effect on the development of the novel in Ireland. (Films were also frequently banned in Ireland. Likely as a consequence, there was no Irish film industry of any note before the Film Act of 1970.) Other cultural genres, such as poetry and theatre, tended to escape these measures.

Poets, for instance, could escape censorship and get away with writing about most themes by applying ambiguity to mask their content behind elaborate allusions, tropes and obfuscations. W.B. Yeats's poetic collection *The Tower*, written a year before the censorship act, was not banned, even though its poem "Leda and the Swan" depicts an act of sexual violence. The event of rape in this poem is mitigated thematically in its origins in Greek mythology: it is a story long taught as a staple of a "respectable", Classics-based education. Yeats's dexterity in using symbolism in this poem allows for any number of readings of the text, including political ones. Yet the poem is careful not to spell out a single contentious meaning against which censors could protest. It avoids the directness of a prose utterance, and thus escapes the threat of being silenced for clearly spreading immoral ideas beyond an educated elite. The Irish theatre, though hardly confining itself to "safe" topics either, also escaped the censors, for different reasons. Debates regarding audience interruptions of early performances of Sean O'Casey's *The Plough and the Stars* (1926) at the Abbey Theatre became so high-profile and political – with Yeats wading in to give his opinion – that calls to censor Irish plays on the grounds of their themes decreased in the face of opposition.[23] By contrast, the socio-realist novel has a potentially far greater audience than the modernist novel, the limited-circulation poetry anthology or the play. Its forms and themes are also generally more accessible to mainstream audiences. In the main, this type of novel is a popular literary medium usually foregrounding a straightforward story over any elaborate discourse. In the realist mode, the novel is understood quite easily, even by the "vulnerable" audiences whom Irish authorities claimed to protect.

Maud Ellmann discusses the tyrannical hold of the Catholic Church on the Irish novel in the first few decades after independence. She remarks that author Benedict Kiely had three novels banned during the 1940s and the 1950s. She adds, "Although Irish writers managed to find publishers abroad, the Irish public was deprived of the finest writing of the era; the only books available in libraries and bookshops were religious works, or those which celebrated Irish life and culture."[24] Irish novelists of any serious social import simply did not have an audience, unless they published abroad. The five Irish writers discussed in this book – Liam O'Flaherty, Elizabeth Bowen, Patrick Kavanagh, Samuel Beckett and Michael Farrell – all had novels published in Britain rather than Ireland. Consequently, critics outside of Ireland, and indeed outside of postcolonial studies, have tended to approach certain of these texts in relation to various other aspects of their forms and themes. The reception of Beckett's *Murphy*, published in London in 1938, is a case in point as it tends to be read in relation to late modernism, philosophy, absurdism and comedy rather than in the frame of fictive representations of the migrant experience at the heart of the British Empire.

The method of this study is thus to use a comparative approach in order to understand the ways in which Caribbean *and* Irish writers used similar literary strategies, via the novel form, to give voice to a range of themes and issues concerned with social, political and ideological detachment from Britain. Naturally, this is hardly to deny the crucial historical, cultural, political, linguistic and geographical differences between the British West Indies and Ireland. To over-conflate, or not be mindful of such differences in pursuit of a comparative postcolonial grammar, would of course risk gross essentialism. In fact, as this text will demonstrate, is often *because* of the distance between the specific contexts in which Caribbean and Irish texts are produced that comparisons between them, carefully scrutinized for their nuanced similarities, can appear all the more revelatory to Caribbeanists, Irish studies scholars, postcolonialists and comparative scholars alike.

The reason for beginning in chapter 1 with a comparison of *Beacon*-period Trinidadian writer Alfred Mendes's barrack-yard novel *Black Fauns* (1935) and Irish writer Liam O'Flaherty's slum novel *The Informer* (1925) is that the two novels are early attempts by writers to find a new expressive medium – socio-realist, longer prose fiction – to depict the lives, struggles, hopes and inner worlds of previously under- or misrepresented individuals in the poorest communities of societies set up by colonial economic systems. Thus, the novels also match in that they are, even on the surface and prior to closer study, promisingly compatible in theme. This renders them worthy of closer postcolonial comparative analysis to see how far these corollaries continue. *Black Fauns* explores the midtown slums and barrack yards of Port of Spain and, with a careful and sociological eye for naturalistic depiction, investigates the lives and trials of people who live hand-to-mouth. Mendes tries to convey in novelistic format what happens when the Trinidadian poor are suddenly confronted by the apparent good luck of a financial opportunity or windfall achieved by chance or ill-gotten gains. *The Informer* suggests corollaries with *Black Fauns* in that it holds a microscope to the struggles of a poor Irish slum area, founded on the basis of British colonial economy, where people cannot determine the source of their next meal. Just as in *Black Fauns*, when the chance of money, however questionable its provenance, enters the domain of the poor and the hungry, people will betray those closest to them just to get hold of even a small sum of ready cash. This chapter will test the strengths of such apparent parallels.

The reason for comparing Dominican author Jean Rhys's *Voyage in the Dark* (1934) with Anglo-Irish Ascendancy writer Elizabeth Bowen's *The Last September* (1929) is that they are two similar tales of eighteen-year-old female orphans born into declining estates and facing uncertain futures. The corresponding postcolonial dimensions of the novels are to be investigated throughout the course of chapter 2. *Voyage in the Dark* portrays a young colonial Dominican woman in the declining years of her caste's plantocratic dominance, trying to cope with the experience of psychic dislocation from the sureties of the past. Jean Rhys, born in Dominica of a white Creole colonial background in 1890, was well positioned to analyse the effect that the crumbling of colonial power had on its latter generations and their damaged sense of identity, place and purpose. In many respects, *Voyage in the Dark* is semi-autobiographical, although Rhys does not merely translate her life into fiction. Rather, Rhys imagines a particular state of anxiety prevalent among young women of planter-settler heritage just as their socioeconomic and cultural status slips close to irreversible collapse. Similarly, *The Last September* is a semi-autobiographical novel about a young girl who is seemingly lost for identity and place at the end of her forebears' colonial age. Bowen's novel examines the psychology and society of the Anglo-Irish Ascendancy in its last throes of dynastic planter-settler power. Dublin-born Bowen, writing in 1929, used her advantage of several years of distance from the last weeks of true Ascendancy power in 1920–21 to look back on her caste in its final throes. Chapter 2 will take into account numerous textual similarities and historical specificities of the texts, in order to gauge how they compare in postcolonial terms.

Trinidadian author C.L.R. James's *Minty Alley* (1936) is compared with Monaghan writer Patrick Kavanagh's novel *Tarry Flynn* (1948), since the novels' portrayals of female-headed families and matriarchal economy reflect similar contexts of late-colonial or residual-colonial society and economy, worthy of closer postcolonial comparative scrutiny in order to gauge how strongly these parallels withstand analysis. *Minty Alley* is in many respects a socially prescriptive novel. It uses the form of longer prose fiction to reveal in an unfolding narrative how women in ordinary and often menial occupations are responsible for maintaining many of the key comforts and privileges of late-colonial society. C.L.R. James, as one of the *Beacon* generation of writers in Trinidad along with

Mendes, endeavours to present to the reader a depiction of Trinidadian women as a specific and crucial part of Trinidadian society and economy. The protagonist Haynes, a twenty-year-old male, discovers over the course of the events of the novel just how much he is truly dependent on women of less advantaged socioeconomic status. Patrick Kavanagh's *Tarry Flynn* works correspondingly as a satirical, novelistic social commentary: the protagonist is a young male, who fancies himself a young dreamer and poet, living on his family farm in rural Cavan, Ireland. Over the events of the novel, the true heroes of the narrative are shown, however, to be the shrewd, hard-working and ingenious women of the farming community. This chapter tests how strongly a reading of parallel representations of matriarchal economy in these novels stands up to a comparative reading of their texts and postcolonial historical contexts.

Chapter 4 compares Irish writer Samuel Beckett's *Murphy* (1938) with Trinidadian author Sam Selvon's *The Lonely Londoners* (1956) to investigate how the novels parallel one another as depictions of a key phenomenon of colonialism: the early- to mid-twentieth-century migrant experience in London. *The Lonely Londoners* has become enshrined in the canon of Caribbean and black British writing as a seminal masterpiece in the evolution of a West Indian migrant narrative voice. *Murphy*, however, has had little in the way of postcolonial reception. It has usually been read in terms of its philosophical or comic attributes, rather than as a depiction of Irish migrant life in London in the mid-1930s. By comparing the two novels textually and contextually in relation to their representations of dislocation, passage, limbo, settlement and psychic alienation from the location of arrival, I shall test the extent to which *Murphy* can be read comparatively.

In chapter 5, I read Carlow writer Michael Farrell's sole novel, *Thy Tears Might Cease* (1963), alongside Barbadian author George Lamming's *In the Castle of My Skin* (1953) to test their comparability in postcolonial terms as *Bildungsromane* set in periods beset by political violence. The latter novel is foundational in anticipating postcolonial studies, while the former has been out of print since 1999. We shall never know all the reasons why Farrell so jealously clung to his sole, semi-autobiographical novel *Thy Tears Might Cease* up until his 1962 death, and withheld it from the eyes of almost everyone, even though it was mainly drafted in multi-volume format by 1937. The chapter looks at thematic parallels between the novels – the formation of identity in the postcolonial *Bildungsroman*; the representation of political violence; and the corruption of nationalist ideology by capitalist interests – and seeks to probe their postcolonial comparability to the fullest extent.

The five Caribbean authors discussed in this book, though in date of birth spanning a broader period, from 1890 to 1927, all played a decisive part in the cultural production of the pre-independence period of British Caribbean history. Their work spans the groundbreaking *Beacon-* and *Windrush-*era periods of Caribbean literature, a revolutionary period of emergence in Caribbean literature and thought, which took place between the 1920s and the 1960s. The five Irish authors were born between 1896 and 1906 and were at least sixteen years of age by the time of Irish independence. They were therefore old enough to remember themes and circumstances surrounding independence and its repercussions. It could be argued that all of the writers in this study devised a means to capitalize upon the potentiality of the novel genre. They used it as a way of giving a new and sophisticated voice to their own generations' unprecedented, decolonizing changes in perceptions of identity, community, class, nationhood and culture. This book examines how Irish and Caribbean novelists employ parallel literary strategies to highlight moments of intellectual, social, cultural and political disengagement from the British Empire.

1.

"Dis Yard Is a Battle Ground"

Alfred Mendes's *Black Fauns* and Liam O'Flaherty's *The Informer*

FROM THE FIRST PUBLICATION OF THE PERIODICAL *New Beacon Reviews* in 1968, writers and publishers began to reassess and clarify the contribution of Trinidadian periodicals such as *Trinidad* (1929–30) and the *Beacon* (1931–34), as well as novels produced by Caribbean authors in the 1930s, to the emergence and growth of non-colonial, self-representative Caribbean writings in English.

The 1971 republication by New Beacon Books of C.L.R. James's 1936 novel *Minty Alley* was part of this widespread resurgence of critical interest in texts written around the *Beacon* era of the late 1920s and 1930s. Such activity precipitated the eventual establishment, by the end of the century, of many *Beacon*-era texts as canonical West Indian and postcolonial literary works.[1]

Kenneth Ramchand, the author of a 1970 study, *The West Indian Novel and Its Background*, wrote an introduction to *Minty Alley* that emphasized the groundbreaking role of Trinidadian *Beacon* writers such as C.L.R. James (1901–89) and Alfred Mendes (1897–1991) in formulating a new, self-representative voice for the Trinidadian and, by extension, Caribbean people.[2] Mendes had begun privately to experiment with writing prose before meeting James in the early 1920s. The friendship between Mendes and James led to their deciding to create a new Trinidadian literary society that would interrogate the social values in a country ruled by Britain. The Trinidad group was the first anglophone Caribbean movement, large or small, dedicated to discussion or production of arts and letters. In 1929, Mendes and James devised and edited the magazine *Trinidad*: its first number was published that December. Ramchand, in his introduction to *Minty Alley*, relates that the great innovation of the *Beacon* era was its authentic rendering of the lives of the lower classes, the dispossessed, and the inhabitants of Trinidad's impoverished barrack yards and slum areas, hitherto excluded from literary depiction. The daily lives of the poor were documented in *Beacon* texts, uncompromisingly, without euphemism or circumvention. The people's customs, their attempts at maintaining pride and dignity in adversity, and the violence and bloodshed resulting from their financially precarious existence were all treated in vivid detail.

The republication of the old *Beacon*-period works in the 1970s and 1980s was thus part of an effort by Caribbean and black British intellectuals to recognize and celebrate the *Beacon* writers' seminal role in the shaping of Caribbean literatures in English. The "New Beacon" era also ushered in an increasingly sophisticated understanding of the original *Beacon* period's formulation and evolution of writing that challenged dominant modes of representing peoples of the British Empire.[3] According to Rhonda Cobham, by the 1980s, the *Beacon* writers of the 1930s had received "the lion's share of this new critical attention" to Caribbean literatures.[4] In 1984, New Beacon republished Trinidadian writer Alfred Mendes's 1935 novel of barrack-yard life, poverty and social unrest, *Black Fauns*.

Reinhard W. Sander has called the *Beacon* period the crux of the "Trinidad Awakening", where writers worked towards a faithfully socio-realist detailing of the environment, customs, internal politics, and linguistic and cultural codes of the lower urban classes as a means of voicing the concerns of their people.[5] *Beacon* authors tried to place a section of marginalized Trinidadian society at the centre of their narratives by introducing common settings and elements of society previously largely ignored in literature of the West Indies. These tales spoke of hidden urban slums created by the social injustices of colonial economics. Stewart Brown remarks how authors in this period, such as James and Mendes, wanted to show how the poor could still be portrayed as dignified, proud individuals in spite of the squalor and adversity of their living circumstances.[6] The slum settings of the Trinidadian barrack yard provide the background for stories in which petty crooks, tricksters, and poor and working-class women, living on their wits in a colonial man's world, struggle day-to-day to maintain human self-respect and overcome their reduced financial and social lot.[7]

This chapter identifies many of the characteristics of *Black Fauns* – a novel whose characters struggle against the authority of colonial capital – which make it relevant to postcolonial studies. It also examines the text as the product of a period where writers were just beginning to find a means to convey the lives and inner worlds of the poor in British territories. It then sets out to illustrate how Liam O'Flaherty's well-known 1925 novel of post-independence Irish slum life, violence and betrayal, *The Informer*, accords with many attributes of Mendes's novel and can be read extensively in a postcolonial comparative context. O'Flaherty's imaginary construction of the slum – a south-side Dublin maze of streets – is, like Mendes's Laventille, Trinidad, a microcosm of urban colonial-expansionist exploitation. There are suggestions of a very sophisticated political awareness on the part of some of the people of the slum, which might reflect the author's own politics. From a postcolonial perspective, both novels thus encapsulate beginnings in the development of a body of literature seeking to understand the contradictory motivations, impulses and aspirations of an impoverished community pursuing social status under the shadow of hundreds of years of British colonial capital. The narrators of the two novels give slum characters a political voice, but are just beginning to work out how to present to the reader these characters' inner worlds and thoughts. Thus, they are texts in the burgeoning stages of an effort to represent the lives of characters on the margins of colonial power.

Black Fauns is a novel about the economically deprived community of an urban Trinidadian barrack yard in the 1930s. The main characters in the novel are poor Port of Spain women; most do laundry work in order to make the meagre amount to pay their rent, and thus often find themselves in debt to the rent collector, Mr de Pompignon. They live in constant threat of eviction and find themselves constantly trying to stay in de Pompignon's good favour. Drunkenness, disputes and fights are rife as these characters compete for space and status in a cramped midtown slum. Mendes thus introduces the reader to the brutal truths of a broken island. Trinidad in the 1930s was as affected by the Depression as anywhere else. Overproduction of sugar, cocoa and coconuts led to low prices and decreased trade, and thus mass unemployment. Workers in the burgeoning oil industry complained of poor wages. Captain Arthur Cipriani attempted to mediate with workers, yet a mood of frustration against the ruling classes was becoming more widespread.[8] In the Port of Spain barrack-yard environment of *Black Fauns*, Mendes illustrates a society for whom social mobility is not possible except by migration to America. To remain in the yard is to be near the lowest socioeconomic stratum of the urban population (bar homelessness). Some characters seek to maintain pride and social and individual dignity under poor conditions.

Mendes's conscientious appreciation of the previously unexplored lives of the Trinidadian poor, who assert self-regard in the midst of squalor, dates back to early in his literary career. Before *Black Fauns*, Mendes was a contributing editor of the *Beacon* (owned by Portuguese Creole writer Albert Gomes). Mendes remarked in his autobiography,

> I am not saying that the *Beacon* by itself was responsible for what has been happening in Trinidad over the past forty-five years; what I *am* saying is that its antennae caught all the winds of change blowing from every corner of the world and translated them in terms of Trinidad's social, economic, moral and cultural life, which gave the people an understanding of what had been mysteries to them before.[9]

If there was a wind of change blasting a new energy of intellectual, decolonizing thought in Trinidad, then it can also be said to be well represented fictively in Mendes's imagined space of the Trinidadian barrack yard. In a 1973 interview, Mendes explained that the exact yard in which he stayed while researching for *Black Fauns* was "at the bottom of Park Street just before you came into Richmond Street" (p. xi). This area is at the heart of the capital: a hidden Trinidad perilously close to the visible, supposedly respectable version. Within walking distance of the seat of colonial rule, the marginal yard community of the novel is shown in the opening scene subversively questioning its rulers' fitness to govern. From the outset of the novel Mendes appears keen to point out the ready intelligence and political awareness of at least some of this community, so that readers are under no illusions that this is merely a bourgeois, condescending sketch of lower-class local colour. At the start of the novel, the character Miriam – the most progressive in her thinking of all the residents of the yard– argues with the religious, obeah-practising Ma Christine and the pugnacious Ethelrida about the hierarchy of power between colonial whites and the rest of the island population. Irrespective of the façade of a black middle class and the illusion of a society free to enjoy the comforts of modernity, Miriam proposes that one should be in no doubt about who is really in control on the island:

Miriam drawled: "We have tram-car in Port-o'-Spain. We have train in the country. We have all them teeayter with picture in it. Who make all this, Miss Et'elrida? You ever see nigger Governor in the colony? We have black magistrates, it's true; but who put them there? The sun ain't got nothing to do with it. If the white man does get pale when he come here, that don't prevent him from sitting in the seat of the mighty, my child. I say it once, I say it again; this is white man's land. Slavery abolish? They only *write* that. I look an' see slavery still stalking the land like it never leave it. Black people does dig an' sweat like mule. You ever see white man working like mule in Trinidad? The white ladies does sit down 'pon their behinds all day long, giving orders; an' giving orders to who, Miss Et'elrida, to who, I ask you? You ever see white ladies give 'pon orders to white ladies? An' look at the Red House, where the Governor does sit with his council. It have nigger there; yes; but who does stand up for our rights? You call Capting Cupriani a black man when all the time he white like water? The negro in the Council 'fraid their own shadow, my child! An why? I ain't have to ask you that!" (pp. 13–14)

It is significant in postcolonial terms that Mendes would give Miriam such an articulate voice of social criticism to illustrate the political thoughts of everyday people in Trinidad. In many ways, Miriam's viewpoint is very like, and thus implicitly as sophisticated as, Mendes's own. For instance, in his autobiography, Mendes remarks that by about 1932, he found it odd that his friend C.L.R. James, who was moving to England, began to lose interest in Trinidadian politics. James refused to critique the Trinidadian trade union leader and Port of Spain representative on the Trinidad and Tobago Legislative Council, Captain Arthur Cipriani, in spite of Cipriani's opposition (as a Catholic) to a new Divorce Bill on the island. Mendes, interestingly, chose his words with some weight when arguing that "James greatly admired this white man who introduced trade unionism to Trinidad's workers".[10] Mendes's phrase "this white man" is particularly telling here. So, it would appear that Miriam is refracting the author Mendes's own sense of wariness of Cipriani, on the basis that Cipriani is ultimately white (and thus reflects the views of the colonial hierarchy).

Miriam, criticizing the hierarchical structures of Trinidadian life, alludes to the Red House, "where the Governor does sit with his council" (p. 14). The Red House was the official colonial parliament building in Port of Spain. The original building was painted red to commemorate Queen Victoria's Diamond Jubilee in 1897; it was burned to the ground in the 1903 water riots. A new, grandiose Red House was built and opened in 1907: it appeared as a defiant statement of British colonial control and imperial self-awareness in its impressive mass and Greek-style architecture. It was still an iconic and symbolic signifier of British colonial power in the 1930s context of *Black Fauns*. The class struggle that Miriam discusses – a struggle often racially divided between whites in power (including Cipriani) and non-white, poor Trinidadians – is one of pre–labour riot Trinidad, where the ideology and administration of colonial rule is just beginning to be seriously questioned. Mendes and his character Miriam are already vocal about their reservations concerning colonial figures whom they suspect will proclaim themselves to be acting in the interests of the working classes but in the end will serve only their own ambitions.

Miriam evidently seeks to maintain social and individual dignity under poor conditions. Mendes is very careful to show from the start of the novel that life for the Trinidadian poor is far from some naive, prelapsarian idyll that can only be wrecked over the course of events by the sudden arrival and intervention of some troublemaker. On the contrary, here is clearly an already quite fundamentally damaged society in which its members have little realistic political representation. It might be ideal if the yard people worked together to achieve a strong sense of social cohesion and political identity, but the reality of life, as presented by Mendes, is that people have so few choices for improvement that they must fend for themselves and make the best of whatever comes their way, even if that sometimes means betraying another's trust or breaking the law. Since they are among the most vulnerable of society, they have no opportunity to organize collective resistance for change and must instead live on their wits within the system, or perish. Due to the sheer desperation and lack of ready capital in the Port of Spain slums, they risk violence every day by having to deceive others for individual fleeting comfort or advancement.

So, due to competition for sparse available money and opportunities for self-improvement, some characters degenerate into theft, inter-community violence and murder. Mendes appears to use a popular method of European naturalist novel writing in detailing the collapse of an already unstable poor community due to the evils of an antagonistic factor such as money. While Mendes does not allude to Émile Zola in his writings, one could reasonably argue for the influence of a Zola-esque naturalism in Mendes's work, as there is much of the basic *fabula* of classic naturalist novels such as *Germinal* in *Black Fauns*.[11] *Germinal* is a quasi-scientific experimental novel that takes certain characters with predispositions towards madness, violence or subversive behaviour and drops them into a flashpoint situation to see what will happen.[12] Mendes uses this novelistic convention and applies it to his story, but with the important added factor of using a Caribbean setting with Caribbean characters. Mendes thus uses the naturalistic novel to analyse the conditions of the Trinidadian poor. For example, Port of Spain characters with evident predispositions, needs and vulnerabilities are cast in an environment where competition for any kind of advancement is naked and aggressive. In *Black Fauns*, that setting is the barrack yard, a scene of constant quarrel. The arrival of an unexpected amount of cash is the point of *peripeteia* in the story that triggers the more unsavoury and destructive propensities of certain members of the community.

Mendes wishes to demonstrate the harshness of these slum economics. He points to how even very agreeable and likeable members of the yard find themselves on the wrong side of the law just for trying to take some initiative to improve their financial lot. One member of the yard, Ethelrida, reveals to her neighbours what has happened to her partner, Mannie. Mannie is a calypso-singing, rabble-rousing rum drinker. He is raucous but utterly loyal and deferential to Ethelrida; he may have some vices but he betrays an essential moral goodness. His worst flaw is that he takes wild chances when inebriated to chase the opportunity of acquiring some extra money. Mannie has allowed himself to be led into an opium deal in the back room of a large local Chinese store by the wharf. The deal, of course, has been staked out by police, and Mannie has been arrested and thrown in jail. However, Ethelrida reveals with delight that the likeable rogue has been a little too smart for his superiors:

> "An' de money?" Aggie asked.
> "That's de joke", said Ethelrida, chuckling. "In de dark an' confusion Mannie get hold of it an' put it in a secret pocket he have in his jacket what he use for gambling. The police search him, but they ain't find it." (p. 124)

It is precisely this money that changes the fortunes of the yard community. Ethelrida then surprises her peers:

> She put her hand down into her bosom and extracted a roll of notes. "Look it here!" she said triumphantly.

> The eyes of the women standing around popped out of their heads and they gasped. Ma Christine's pipe fell out of her mouth and broke.
>
> "Don't fret, old lady", said Ethelrida. "This going to buy all de pipes you wants." (p. 124)

At least in the short term, crime pays, as the yard benefits from the brief ease and benedictions that Ethelrida's windfall bestows upon them. It does not take long for Mr de Pompignon, the rent collector, to hear about Ethelrida's good fortune. Ethelrida not only pays her rent arrears but those of Miriam and Ma Christine, and forestalls the perils of homelessness.

In such desperate conditions, some women of the yard react to Ethelrida's spoils with the hunger and lust of the starved and deprived – particularly those who have tasted a suggestion of life outside the slum, such as a newcomer, Estelle. Estelle is no helpless waif or stray who is prepared to fade away silently in the shadows of Ethelrida's ascendancy. She is instead a street-wise Trinidadian slum dweller who has little choice but to fight, steal and betray in order to take a share in the first bit of money to have found its way into the yard in a long time. Mendes's representation of Estelle is subversive in many aspects. Estelle challenges the dominant social codes of imperial British patriarchy in being an unmarried, pregnant, bisexual woman. From her first arrival, Estelle is no weak figure of pathos. She is not the broken, barefoot and pregnant archetype straight out of an English novel, such as Fanny Robin in Thomas Hardy's *Far From the Madding Crowd* (1874). Mendes shows how Estelle uses her unusual physical beauty to seductive effect. He creates her character as powerfully subversive in the way she exploits her physical attractiveness to manipulate people around her, male and female, emotionally and sexually, for her own material gain. Estelle will not acquiesce to subjugation, for if there is a short supply of money to be had, she will have it and transcend her poverty.

Estelle is a floating signifier, able to code-switch between communities rather than find herself ostracized from any one community. Estelle moves into the social sphere of the yard quite readily, as she already knows one person in its community from her complex past: Martha, a psychologically vulnerable young woman with whom Estelle has previously had a physical relationship. Prior to the arrival of Estelle in the yard, Martha is shown in the novel to be attracted to people of ambiguous gender. Martha is especially attracted to Estelle, who destabilizes the binary of male/female. Before the arrival of Estelle and then Snakey in the yard, Martha dreams of making love to an androgynous hybrid of Snakey with Estelle's face (p. 58). Estelle also deconstructs the gender opposition of feminine and masculine in being a mother but also a sexually active lover of men and women. She exploits the perceived exoticism of her physical beauty for personal and financial gain. The narrator of *Black Fauns* identifies Estelle as a "*dougla*": a person of mixed Afro- and Indo-Trinidadian heritage (p. 141). Estelle destabilizes racial types in a way that is appealing at least to Martha:

> Martha couldn't get over her surprise at finding Estelle her neighbour after all these months of absence. . . . [Estelle] was a young woman of twenty-two, and anybody could see that she wasn't a pure negress, that one of her parents was East Indian. Her hair was thick and glossy, her nose was high-bridged: it was only her mouth that gave her negroid ancestry away, her mouth and that pronounced blackness of skin so often found in *douglas*. Perhaps it was this very mixture of bloods in Estelle, the negro and the East Indian, that made her attractive to Martha. (p. 141)

Estelle makes the most of the allure of her perceived exoticism and racial difference, procuring Martha as the agent of her schemes to acquire money from their neighbours by deception and stealth. It is too easy to read Estelle as the novel's principal antagonist. After all, she seems even to lack a maternal instinct for her mortally sick child, let alone any care for other people around her. It is true that she seduces the psychologically vulnerable Martha to look after the child and steal Ethelrida's money for her. Estelle is instrumental in driving an already unstable young woman into irreversible mental turmoil. Martha even attempts to kill Estelle as a result of the latter's constant, alternating manipulation and abuse of her. Yet it is hardly the case that Estelle has had a full gamut of alternative opportunities for self-sufficiency at her disposal. Mendes shows her at the very bottom of a socioeconomic hierarchy in Trinidad, from which it is nigh-on impossible to climb upwards but by stealth and morally questionable guile. Mendes is showing that Estelle is hardly greedy in seeking to get Martha to take Ethelrida's money; greed would require a prior surfeit. Estelle has nothing, and thus has nothing to lose by stealing to have something for nothing. She might manipulate Martha, but although she is somewhat self-pitying, she does not lie when she summarizes her chaotic personal life as one of trouble: "I have only trouble, trouble, trouble and I can't get a little pleasure when I feel like it!" (p. 172). Estelle's sense of the world as one of chaos and moral nihilism might well be a product of being so poor as to not even afford the luxury of the white, civilizing colonizer's faith in redemption from her plight:

> "God!" said Estelle testily. "That is white people's god, an' if He can't take care of me, if I seeing trouble, trouble, trouble, I can't fall down 'pon my knees an' worship Him. Can you worship anyt'ing dat don't treat you right? Can you worship that kind of God if he make you like he say he make you – an' then leave you to starve?"
> "I didn't t'ink of that," Martha murmured.
> "I know you didn't, my child. You can't see more furder dan your nose, much less your eyelash." (p. 147)

Mendes in many ways allows Estelle as much social insight into the failures of the promises of British colonial rule as demonstrated by Miriam at the start of the novel. Estelle might have taken a less righteous path than Miriam in response, but that is because she has utterly lost belief in the moral, political, religious, economic and ideological authority of the British on her island. Mendes constructs Estelle as a counterstructural figure whose antagonism towards her rulers is a grievance that spurs on her refusal to comply with living obediently in the filth and misery of the yard. She may be morally flawed, but she is the product of a broken society, and she has had little opportunity to rise above it and turn out otherwise.

Another subversive yard resident whose fortunes are changed by Ethelrida's money is Mamitz. Mamitz's apparent, relative affluence in satins and silks, and her affected middle-class haughtiness, are over the course of the novel treated with suspicion, rumour and contempt; the community believes that Mamitz's luxuries must have been ill-gotten gains. Ethelrida confides her theories to the confused Martha:

> "You mean she have a man, Miss Et'elrida?"
> "I ain't saying nothing, Miss Mart'a. All I'se asking is: where she does get her silk an' satin from? Where she getting her fowl from on a Sunday? Where she be now? Where she go when she leave this yard at eight o'clock at night? An' all you want to know somet'ing?" The women drew a little closer and Ethelrida lowered

her voice: "Look; all you remember las' week Saturday night before she leave here at nine o'clock at night? All you remember? All right. I goin' tell you somet'ing now. She didn' come back till five o'clock in the morning!" (pp. 23–24)

The women may find Mamitz's activities incorrigible, yet that is hardly to say that Mendes is encouraging the reader to think the same. In fact, Mendes does not solely characterize Mamitz through the mediating perspective of her scornful yard neighbours. He also takes time to present scenes in which Mamitz characterizes herself, in her spoken words, as a woman of self-assurance and ambition. Mendes reveals that Mamitz, like Estelle, will not simply put up with living hand-to-mouth in the slums under British rule. For instance, when Ma Christine's son Snakey returns to the yard on a visit after years in Harlem, he arrives with full ceremony including ironed-out hair, Americanized talk, an affected city slicker's amnesia at the sight of a humble Trinidadian plantain and, most importantly, wads of dollars. What more can Mamitz do to improve her fortunes but ingratiate herself into Snakey's company? There was no large-scale women's labour movement on the island to protect the interests of the Trinidadian poor in the early 1930s. Mamitz is a woman who seeks to make the most of whatever expendable wealth might find its way into her hands, by any means necessary. She is very honest and self-aware about this. If Snakey wants to sleep with Mamitz, he has to wine and dine her in downtown Chinese restaurants and pay for their hotel rooms. Mamitz is shrewd enough, from their second date, to gauge the extent of Snakey's finances, suggesting that he has – like many other men who returned from Harlem – "Hundreds of dollars" (p. 287). Snakey, who has brought just seventy-five dollars with him, informs Mamitz that his "dough nearly done". Mamitz unceremoniously drops Snakey's arm there and then.

Mamitz, like Estelle, is able to use the perceived attractiveness of her mixed race to her advantage. Unlike Estelle, however, Mamitz has mixed *European* and African heritage. Mamitz aims to profit from her particular type of appearance, and so for material benefit she sleeps with members of the very colonial class who hold power in Trinidad. Mamitz is frequently a figure of envy and disingenuous moral scorn for the other women in the yard, yet she knows that she has at least a relative power over them – and even Snakey – in being able to choose generous partners of more prestigious social and financial status on the island:

"What you t'ink I is?" she said with quiet irony. "You t'ink I going wit' you for love? You don' know I have a lot of rich white men I can go out with? You t'ink I have time to waste wit' you?"

Snakey was taken aback. "But I give you all my dough", he protested. "You take every cent of it!"

"And wasn't I worth it, eh?" Mamitz said quietly, with not a touch of anger. "Who want me got to pay." (p. 293)

Perhaps Mamitz is coldly business-like with Snakey here, but she has a livelihood to think of. The alternative to dining, making love and having fun downtown like any person of self-worth and social visibility is the dark, inhospitable pit of loneliness in a small shack in a neglected corner of Port of Spain's hidden places of near-destitution. Mendes shows how someone who has tasted another life cannot simply go back, financially or psychologically, to a meagre existence on society's margins. At least the socially astute Miriam, if not the envious Ethelrida, can well appreciate Mamitz's attempts to better her circumstances with the apparently flush, prodigal Snakey:

"Miss Mamitz have to have big hook to catch Snakey, my child", said Miriam. "An' the man see life. He come from big city. If Port-o'-Spain girl can catch New York man – good for her, I say!"

"Must be she t'ink he have money," said Ethelrida, her lips in the shape of a sneer.

"I can't find it in my heart to condemn her for that."

"No, but I can find it in my *head* to condemn de bitch for dat!" was Ethelrida's retort.

"Miss Et'elrida, put your head outside. You don't see how de sun is shining happy! Go outside. Drink some of it. Let it put happiness in your spirit, my child." (pp. 277–78)

Miriam's advice to Ethelrida to put her head outside means here for her to venture beyond the claustrophobic, soul-destroying parameters of the barrack yard and to see how Mamitz is merely trying to drink in the sun of a happiness denied to the yard people in the drudgery of their daily lives. For Miriam, Mamitz should not be admonished but understood. If, as I have claimed, Miriam is to an extent reflexive of Mendes's authorial position, then it is reasonable to infer that Mendes wishes the reader to accept Miriam's sensitive and insightful empathy with Mamitz, rather than Ethelrida's posturing aggression towards Mamitz, as a view we should share.

The situation between Snakey and Mamitz is far from straightforward. Snakey is not only sleeping with Mamitz but also the unstable and obsessive Martha. Martha has already stolen Ethelrida's money at the behest of Estelle; now, when Snakey asks Martha for money, she steals it from Estelle's room to give it to him. In a case of dramatic irony, Martha does not realize that this money is to pay for Snakey's liaisons with Mamitz. On discovering Snakey and Mamitz's affair, Martha stabs Mamitz to death. This tragic turn of events carries neither the moral prescription of a providential English novel nor the Zola-esque result of a social experiment into what happens when money is dropped irresponsibly and quickly into a poverty trap. *Black Fauns*, rather, shows that when people are hungry and desperate enough for change in their lives, they have little choice but deception and violence to either defend or grab some happiness. Where colonial government officials ignore the poor, who can turn their lives around? Mendes might not produce long passages of focalization in which we can plunge deeply into the minds of characters such as Estelle and Mamitz to show their motivations. Yet their spoken dialogue says so much about their attempts to escape the horrors of the yard, and says it so articulately, that one cannot help but feel some degree of empathy with them, even though they so are quick to turn to crime or betray their neighbours to get what they want. It is easy to have scruples when one has options. Estelle and Mamitz are beautiful, intelligent women in a man's world who have an advantage over their less fortunate female peers in that they can work other people to find a path out of the yard. Mamitz's tragedy is that she does not escape but is destroyed by the yard; however, she realizes at least some hope for self-improvement that, with better education and socioeconomic opportunities, might have seen her free.

As an author writing in the early stages of what we now call the postcolonial novel, Alfred Mendes faced the challenge, in *Black Fauns*, of representing the lives of the Trinidadian poor while positioning an authorial narrative voice in relation to the characters he presented. One of the most successful ways in which the characterization of the people of the yard is depicted is through mimetic renderings of spoken dialogue, with all the richness and vitality of urban Trinidadian dialectal and idiomatic phrase and tone carefully reproduced. The novel commences with Ma Christine's voice calling out in its distinctive Creole, "Miss Miriam! Ho! Miss Miriam, ho! Look; I receive a letter from Snakey. Come an' read it for me, doodoo" (p. 7). Mendes is careful to capture such grammatical idiosyncrasies as the substitution of the present for the past tense of the first-person indicative active verb "receive", as well as the elision of the end consonant in the conjunction "and". Ma Christine continues, "All boy-piccany is the same, Miss Miriam.... Their hearts is black and bitter." Again, Mendes demonstrates his ability to approximate Creole dialect. The noun "piccany" is a variant of "piccaninny", a West Indian Creolization of the Spanish word "*pequeño*", meaning black child. As employed by an Afro-Trinidadian person, this word is divested of some of its potentially pejorative overtones. Mendes is also mindful to reflect the tendency of Trinidadian Creole to substitute the singular for the plural form of the verb "to be". What Mendes does here is more than a lifelike portrayal of local colour. He portrays his characters' voices in a manner that is without stage-like caricature.

While the narrative discourse of *Black Fauns* is multi-voiced, and the characters of the novel speak in their own tongues, the narrator himself does not quite speak in the personal, idiomatic tongue of the people whom he depicts in his tale. A Creole narrator would, by his language, more clearly signify as a Trinidadian sympathetic with – if not even being one of – the people of the yard. Instead, the omniscient narrator speaks in a register and dialectal form that can be identified as Standard English. It would, however, be hasty to assume that, just because the narrator sounds like a colonial British man, he offers the viewpoint of the colonizer. Rather, the narrator's voice has decolonizing power. Take, for example, the narrator's use of free indirect discourse to plunge into Martha's consciousness. The narrator uses what narratologist Dorrit Cohn calls dissonant psycho-narration: in other words, he represents Martha's thoughts not only in the past tense and the third person, but also via the narrator's mediating Standard English, writerly language.[13] However, this notwithstanding, Mendes still shows considerable empathy with the Afro-Trinidadian Martha in reproducing, within these constraints, her anguished thought processes regarding her feelings about Estelle, Snakey and Christophine (her confidante privy to the knowledge of her theft from Ethelrida). Through Mendes's sensitive use of focalization, the narration allows Martha to represent herself, more than she is represented:

More than ever now she felt the need of [Snakey], the need of someone to whom to turn in her hour of anguish and distress. As she lay staring at the night in her room, she knew that her love for Estelle had turned into hate, almost in a flash. It had taken but a few lucid moments for it to be borne in upon her that Estelle was not what she had thought her to be; and in those few moments her love had withered and hate had taken root. (p. 210)

As this passage of focalization continues, the level of dissonance between the narrator's voice and Martha's diminishes, and there is quite apparent consonance and dialogic harmony between narrator and Martha in the exclamation, "And why, oh why had she confided in Christophine? Was she a person to be trusted?" (p. 210). Mendes shows some considerable skill in mimicking the Standard English discourse of an English realist novel but also repeating it with a difference. He allows a poor Trinidadian barrack-yard woman's most sincere and expressive voice to seize a large degree of agency over his ostensibly authoritative narrative. Here is a good example of Homi Bhabha's hybridity in play.[14] Mendes sounds like an Englishman but he uses his voice to allow Trinidadians to speak through him and destabilize the hegemonic qualities of the form of the English novel.

Rhonda Cobham, however, appears not to give a great deal of credit to Mendes for his talents in portraying the consciousness of the people of the yard:

> Because [Mendes] does not use dialect for reported speech, the language in which Mendes describes the women's soliloquies seems at times unnatural. In addition, though the dialogue of the women often implies a complex motivation for their actions, Mendes seems to feel that they are incapable of actually recognising such complexities within themselves. But when the author tries to interpret and account for his character's emotions there is a curious hiatus between what the author thinks his character can understand and what he expects us to recognize. (p. xiii)

One passage that Cobham singles out for particular debate is a long passage of focalization from Martha's perspective regarding her act of violence against Estelle, which Cobham claims to be interrupted by the narrator offering his opinion that Martha was incapable of realizing that her rage was a response to Estelle's abuse and manipulation. Cobham asks, "Why, one wonders, should Martha be unable to connect her rage with her stealing for Estelle?" (p. xiv). It is worth reproducing the extract from the novel here, so that proper attention can be paid to it in the light of the claims made about it:

> Martha recalled in detail the misunderstanding of the morning and that terrible jealous hatred that had stabbed at her when Estelle had told her she was going to the Court-House. And she remembered, too, all that time she was left alone with the baby; how her jealous hatred had grown more and more intense as the minutes went by; how the baby had had spells and spasms which had frightened her; and how, when Estelle arrived and stayed outside in the yard with the others, she had wanted to run out to her and strike her or something like that. Above all, it was the *manner* Estelle had used on her return to the room, sarcastic, accusing, whining, that had sent the blood pulsing into her head, made her seize the knife and want to commit murder.
>
> It didn't occur to Martha that Estelle's forcing her into another commission of theft after all these months of absence from each other had played a part in rousing her to a state of insane rage the night before. (pp. 196–97)

Cobham makes the error of seeing a "curious hiatus" between what the narrator believes the vulnerable Martha of the barrack yard is capable of recognizing for herself, and what the narrator presumes that the reader can work out concerning the true nature of Martha's motivations and behaviour. Such a claim suggests that Mendes deliberately denies Martha the capacity of psychological self-realization, and gives the reader more of an insight into Martha's motivations and feelings than she is ever capable of understanding. However, Cobham's reading does not see that Mendes simply adheres to a particular convention in representing consciousness in fiction that has been, in the main, a staple device of the realist novel since at least the time of Jane Austen. Anyone familiar with Jane Austen's *Northanger Abbey* (1817) will know that there are numerous examples in the text where the narrator plunges into the young heroine Catherine Morland's thought processes, via dissonant psycho-narration, and then interjects with ironic quips and assessments regarding Catherine's immaturity and lack of self-insight.[15] The matter of whether Catherine is ever capable of a moment of life-changing *éclaircissement* is a conclusion to be revealed at the end of *Northanger Abbey*. Sadly, the tragic Martha in *Black Fauns* does not realize such a moment of clarity by the end of Mendes's novel. Nonetheless, in the above passage, Mendes is clearly following a standard literary convention in his treatment of Martha's anxious mind.

By the 1950s, Caribbean writers in English such as Sam Selvon had devised a way through which a Creole-speaking narrative voice could more easily fuse with the focalized perspective of the characters in the work, and maintain an impression that the entirety of the text was a polyphony of Caribbean voices. In the 1930s, Mendes, who was Trinidadian but not Afro-Trinidadian, spent several months staying in the barrack yards of Port of Spain and becoming intimate with the speech, customs, thoughts and, more importantly, day-to-day worries and responsibilities of the people he observed. Mendes's slight distance from his subject may or not be registered in his choice of Standard English as a heterodiegetic mode of voice, yet he manages to use his writerly skill to represent the consciousness of a people previously without a voice in West Indian literature. *Black Fauns* reworks conventions of the European naturalist novel in a Trinidadian setting; the characters of the naturalistic novel have concerns that are reflective of their island's socially unequal colonial systems of finance and government. *Black Fauns* is a very early example of someone using a novel to show, in careful, realist detail, what ordinary people's lives look like in a colonial society.

Turning to Liam O'Flaherty's *The Informer*, one can immediately see a similarity of setting between it and *Black Fauns*. One observes in both novels a decrepit, poverty-stricken area of the capital of an island founded on British colonial enterprise and government. The key characters of the two novels fight, cheat one another and browbeat one another for the occasional flutterings of petty cash that spill into the alleyways and tenement rooms in which the desperate and starving victims of social inequality subsist, a matter of yards from the grand buildings of power. Even when one observes some specificities of historical and geographical setting to take into account when addressing O'Flaherty's novel, such as its banking and political setup, on inspection one begins to find similarities with elements of *Black Fauns*'s description and critique of colonial economy. *The Informer* is a novel about a poor Dublin community in the months immediately following Irish independence: the British may ostensibly have withdrawn from the capital, yet they have left behind their banks, their capitalist way of life and the inherent social inequalities.[16] Dublin's slum streets are reproduced from the start of the novel as a claustrophobic, labyrinthine "maze", with "[a]n indefinable smell of human beings living in a congested area" (p. 7). The use of the word "maze" suggests a puzzle as well as the challenge of escape. However, these unfortunate people barely notice one another; they are puzzled to the point of irreversible confusion and world-weary melancholy by their predicament, with no hope of finding an exit route: "An old woman crossed near the far end. She had a black shawl about her head and in her hand a milk-jug, with a corner of the shawl drawn across its mouth to keep out the rain. A man was singing forlornly, facing the kerb on the right-hand side, with his cap held out in front of him. He was begging, but nobody took any notice of him."[17]

These characters, forlorn and unobserved, are caught in a situation where the poor have no real representation or self-representation, and where the ruling classes only mind their own interests. Perhaps by the 1920s, Ireland was, on the face of things, different from late-colonial Trinidad in that the post-independence tricolour had been hoisted over Dublin's post-independence centres of power. The major bank in Dublin that had been created from the height of the Anglo-Irish Ascendancy in the 1780s – the Bank of Ireland, founded by Royal Charter in 1783 – became the official bank of the Irish Free State in 1922. However, it still used sterling and did most of its external trade with Britain in 1925, the year of *The Informer*.[18] The Irish Revenue Commissioners were a merger of the previous British-run Inland Revenue and HM Customs and Excise: little had yet really altered in terms of Ireland's banking and finance systems since the days of colonial rule.[19] The new Cumann na nGaedheal government of the 1920s, and in particular the agriculture minister Patrick Hogan, resolutely pushed for the Irish Free State to continue operating upon an agricultural economic platform, even though it had been a policy of pre-independence Republicanism to steer the country into greater industrial development. This was a matter of considerable consternation for critics of the new state's poor economy, who worried that a lack of industry would precipitate mass migration.[20] So, in fact, from late-colonial times to 1925, near to nothing had changed in Ireland to distinguish it as a developing, independent economy. In remaining in many respects a construction of colonial history with no immediate plans to change drastically, the Irish Free State in the 1920s was still not very much less British than many still-colonial territories, such as 1920s and 1930s Trinidad.

Similarly to *Black Fauns*, *The Informer* quickly establishes a point that is significant to postcolonial readers: in spite of the proliferation of poverty caused by a history of colonial social injustice, many characters among the poor refuse to relinquish their pride and ambition. They are politically aware and seek self-determination. Commandant Dan Gallagher, the head of the Trotskyite Revolutionary Organization that has sprung up in Ireland since the Russian Revolution, eloquently and astutely outlines his political philosophy. He espouses highly complex and articulate ideas on the revolutionary as an automaton of external social and historical forces:

> The philosophy of a revolutionary is this. Civilization is a process in the development of the human species, groping in advance, impelled by a force over which neither I nor the human species have any control. I am impelled by the Universal Law to thrust forward the human species from one phase of its development to another. I am at war with the remainder of the species. I am a Christ beating them with rods. I have no mercy. I have no pity. I have no beliefs. I am not master of myself. I am an automaton. I am a revolutionary. (p. 103)

Gallagher's political ideology is not light years from O'Flaherty's own, at least at one stage in the latter's career. At the height of civil war in Ireland, a militant O'Flaherty captured the Rotunda Hospital in Dublin for several days and hoisted the red flag above it in the name of "the Council of the Unemployed". It seems reasonable to assume that O'Flaherty felt at the time that, via this action, he was operating by the guided hand of history, since he was not operating under the sanction of his more immediate comrades. He was disciplined by the Communist Party and retired to his native Gort na gCapall for rest and recuperation.[21] So, just as Mendes's Miriam in *Black Fauns* is authorially reflexive and thus a fictive mediation for the writer's politics, Dan Gallagher voices at least elements of O'Flaherty's known socialist beliefs at some point in the 1920s.

As with *Black Fauns*, it is tempting at first to read *The Informer* as a Zola-esque, naturalist experimental novel. The latter novel's protagonist is Gypo Nolan, a man with broken, violent careers that ended in double-dealing and ignominy. The reader is told early on, "Gypo Nolan had once been a policeman in Dublin, but he had been dismissed owing to a suspicion at headquarters that he was in league with the Revolutionary Organization and had given information to them relative to certain matters that had leaked out" (p. 16). In a novel with a title like *The Informer*, one might, before even reading the remainder of the text, second-guess its quasi-scientific investigative narrative. One could presume that, over the course of the text, a man with a case history of duplicity – now starving – is placed by the novelist-as-investigator into a social situation where he is suddenly presented with the opportunity to inform on someone for gain. In many respects, this prediction is indeed borne out as the outcome of the plot. However, as was the case with Mendes in *Black Fauns*, O'Flaherty makes the point that, under an effectively still-British economic system, and in the slums created by that system's unequal distribution of wealth, people have little choice but to turn to deception and crime to survive. *The Informer*, like *Black Fauns*, shows people so desperate and deprived of hope that they have to take the ultimate risk in order to elevate their status even for a few brief hours. In 1920s Dublin, Gypo really has little chance to improve his wealth, being nearly destitute at the start of the novel. The prerequisites for his fall are decided by forces of social and economic oppression caused by centuries of British domination. Gypo only tries to reverse his misfortunes given a sudden opportunity, as unexpected as the money that lands in Ethelrida's hands in *Black Fauns*. He has little chance to weigh his options on a more moral and profitable life. He could no longer work for a non-existent Royal Irish Constabulary; his subsequent paramilitary days are also over. He has no discernible future to grasp at anything but the first chance of money to hand.

Prior to the start of the action in the novel, Gypo had recently been in the close association of another Organization member, Frankie McPhillip, who had killed a regional secretary of the Farmers' Union. Both Gypo and McPhillip had been suspended from the Organization on account of suspicion as to the unsanctioned murder. Gypo, thus disenfranchised and consequently homeless, is now alternating between living on the charity of his on-off concubine, a sex worker by the name of Katie Fox, and staying in hostels for the homeless in Dublin. McPhillip has been on the run from the police and living in the wilds, but risks coming back to the capital; he is now dying from exposure to the elements. McPhillip finds Gypo in a hostel canteen to tell him that he has returned to Dublin to take secret shelter with his parents, due to his illness. This information implants in Gypo the seed of his scheme to inform on McPhillip and earn some much-needed money. Like Estelle and Mamitz, Gypo can only ultimately follow the imperatives of survival against adversity. It is not easy to ponder on moral variables with an empty stomach. Yet, O'Flaherty is not so crudely deterministic that he wishes to depict Gypo as a mere instrument of social forces: Gypo just behaves proactively in the face of sparse chances for any advancement. Gypo, like Estelle and Mamitz, acts decisively and with full consciousness when he tries to change his financial luck. He walks purposefully and confidently, rather than like some unaware automaton, to the police station to supply his information regarding McPhillip's whereabouts:

> [Gypo] walked up the steps, steadily, one at a time, making a loud noise. He kicked the swing door open with his foot without taking his hands out of his pockets. In the hallway, a constable in a black, cone-shaped, night helmet stood facing him, pulling on his gloves. Gypo halted and stared at the constable.
> "I have come to claim the twenty pounds reward offered by the Farmers' Union for information concerning Francis Joseph McPhillip," he said in a deep, low voice. (pp. 18–29)

This point is of significance to postcolonial readers for the following reason. Gypo, like Mamitz who brings in the law to sue and secure damages against the pugnacious Ethelrida, may seem quick to use the very state apparatus that enforces class oppression. However, it would be hasty to censure these characters when they have next to nothing. O'Flaherty and Mendes are each making an important sociological point. Characters such as Gypo, Mamitz and Estelle are all at an early stage in psychological liberation from the dominant structures of colonial economics. They do not have the benefits of education or class privilege, but they have some acquaintance with life outside the slum. Consequently, they can never be ideologically contained within it, marginalized or silenced. They are ambitious at least for emancipation from the alleyways and tenement shacks of terminal hopelessness, and are intelligent enough to seize any chance for escape they get, even if they do not know what to do once the opportunity comes their way.

Gypo cannot spend his blood money too soon. He parts with his twenty pounds with frenzied abandon over the course of the next twelve hours. Gypo inwardly curses McPhillip for presenting himself when there was no time for him to make plans regarding how to manage and explain his sudden wealth (p. 40). O'Flaherty allows the reader access into Gypo's mind to encourage the question: in an environment where money is so scarce and its availability is so unpredictable, how could Gypo have formulated his plans differently? If more money were to hand, would Gypo even have had to consider risking his life and those of his friends for a few hours of handling cash? Gypo's visit to the police station to claim his twenty pounds was his own decision, but it was also his only real choice if he wanted any momentary stay from wondering when, and from whence, his next meal would come. Now, with the Revolutionary Organization on his trail, and anxious to experience a life so long denied him, Gypo dissipates his funds with fury over the course of one long night, in bars, in upmarket, out-of-slum brothels and in a fish shop.

Fuelled on drink and the ephemeral sense of power that a sudden windfall will instil in someone used to having nothing, Gypo magnanimously and ceremoniously corrals many of the local poor of Dublin's late-night street people into a fish shop to provide them with a huge feast. O'Flaherty here provides an implicit critique of how Dublin's still late-colonial financial systems work: the poor are so unused to having any money that, when it comes, it is such a shock that it passes hands as quickly as it arrives. Similarly to Mannie and Ethelrida's money in *Black Fauns*, which Ethelrida is eager to share in paying for her peers' rent arrears, Gypo's money pays to feed the stomachs of "the riff-raff and the jetsam of the slums, the most degraded of types of those who dwell in the crowded warrens on either bank of the Liffey" (p. 111).

Gypo's generosity in the fish shop is noted by watchful agents of the Organization: he is captured, tried by Gallagher, found guilty and imprisoned, pending sentencing. Gypo escapes and flees, ironically returning through Dublin's slums at top speed. The slums are the maze described at the start of the novel; Gypo has tried to escape it but now, his money gone, he is back where he started at the beginning of the novel: "It was the slum district which he knew so well, the district that enclosed Titt Street, the brothels, the Bogey Hole, tenement houses, churches, pawnshops, public-houses, ruins, filth, crime, beautiful women, resplendent idealism in damp cellars, saints starving in garrets, the most lurid examples of debauchery and vice, all living thigh to thigh, breast to breast, in that foetid morass on the north bank of the Liffey" (p. 228).

Ideals die in damp cellars and saints starve in garrets: there is no permanent escape from the maze of poverty; brief respite is almost worse than never leaving at all, because the realization of one's doom in the slum is all the more bitter for having sensed a liberating alternative. Even Mamitz in *Black Fauns* returned to her barrack-yard shack after every excursion, to sleep, and ultimately to die. A similar fate awaits Gypo, shot to death in a slum church, at the feet of the grieving mother of Frankie McPhillip and begging her forgiveness for Frankie's murder.

Liam O'Flaherty, very similarly to Alfred Mendes, employs narrative devices that strive to give a measure of agency to a section of people with a history of struggling under colonial rule. O'Flaherty avoids a tendency towards overcoding the dialects and phraseology of members of the Irish poor as a patronizing stage-Irish brogue. In *The Informer*, there is none of the exaggerated musicality or "peasant quality" or "pq" of a supposedly authentic Irish voice fetishized by Yeats and other Ascendancy writers during the Irish Literary Revival.[22] The poor are not commodified in order to promote some bourgeois fantasy of a prelapsarian, naive alternative to the drudgery of middle-class ennui. Rather, O'Flaherty aims to portray in the voices of his characters their own experience of the harshness and unpleasantness of poverty in a society in which the bourgeois classes have handed them a hard deal. Take the exchange between Gypo and McPhillip at the start of the novel:

> "Where the divil did ye come from, Frankie?" he said.
> "It don't matter where I come from," cried McPhillip in an irritated tone. "I got no time to waste passin' the compliments o' the season. I came in here to get wise to all the news. Tell us all ye know. First, tell me . . . wait a minute. How about them messages? Did ye deliver them? Don't mind that grub. Man alive, are ye a savage or what? Here I am with the cops after me for me life an' ye go on eatin' yer spuds. Lave down that damn knife or I'll plug ye. Come on, I'm riskin' me life to come in here and ask ye a question. Get busy an' tell me all about it."
> (p. 17)

There is no attempt to sell a construct of stereotypical Irish bonhomie here. O'Flaherty even gives McPhillip his own opportunity to deconstruct the notion that as a matter of formality, these two men should greet each other "passin' the compliments o' the season". Thus, O'Flaherty does not just provide a socio-realist alternative to convention; he allows his characters to critique the convention in their own words. O'Flaherty captures authentic vernacular Hiberno-Irish linguistic signifiers such as "divil" for "devil" and the archaic "ye" for "you", but he is not merely interested in local colour. The rapid-fire nature of McPhillip's torrent of imperatives – "Tell", "tell", "Don't mind", "Lave down", "Get busy an' tell me" – characterizes him as a man in mortal peril, extremely anxious for Gypo to listen to him and give him vital information upon which his life may well depend. From the start of the novel, O'Flaherty is more concerned with allowing a character to express the horrors of his individual circumstances. This has ramifications for postcolonial readers, because here, in *The Informer*, is a breakthrough attempt to give people whose lives have been conditioned and oppressed by colonial power systems a voice to relate the uncompromising truths of their misery. Such realism had not been achieved in the poetry and drama of the Irish Literary Revival, and such a critique of colonial rule had not been quite so demonstrable as via O'Flaherty's unprecedented representation of the character of McPhillip, who is clearly (by the evidence of his own voice) hunted, fearful and at the mercy of forces of a post-independence system still in many ways the same as the colonial order that preceded it.

The Informer, like *Black Fauns*, is significant as a narrative of gender politics in an economic system that is to all intents and purposes British colonial, irrespective of Irish independence in 1922. Katie Fox exhibits similarity with Mendes's Mamitz in being a woman who will sometimes sleep with men for money. Katie, like Mamitz, barracks her men to entertain her when they are in pocket: for instance, when she sees her on-off lover Gypo uncharacteristically opulent, by his standards, buying drinks in a bar, she quickly accosts him under the knowledge that that "Whenever Gypo had any money he spent it with her" (p. 37).

Katie differs somewhat from Mamitz in that she will sleep with her man even when he has no money; that said, neither woman is averse to getting what they can from men in order to try to survive the hardships of slum life, even if that entails betrayal. O'Flaherty portrays precisely the life that Katie Fox is trying to escape from towards the end of the novel. It is not dissimilar to the hard conditions faced by Mamitz in Mendes's novel. Katie shares a tiny tenement room, and even a bed, with a reclusive former sex worker by the name of Louisa Cummins. Louisa resides permanently in bed, amid "junk of all sorts, from a notched mug, out of which the old lady drank her tea, to a statue of Saint Joseph that hung on the bedpost" (p. 236). Gypo, on the run, arrives at Katie's door, where Katie is in the room with Louisa. Louisa represents the failures of the life Katie lives: she was once attacked by police and, while apparently still strong and in good physical health, she stays in bed all day and night, a broken spirit. Gypo, the focalizer of the scene, notes regarding Louisa: "She lay on her side, with her white, shrivelled head ensconced in a grey pillow, that had no case to cover it. The feathers protruded from the pillow. The old woman's white hair was strewn about the pillow and the bed-clothes, like strands of seaweed floating on the surface of a shallow sea at low tide" (p. 237).

Katie is enraged by the sight of Gypo, who has collapsed on her bed, exhausted, beside Louisa and thus occupies her space. The fact that Katie is cramped in such a small, impoverished locality, with people whose shortcomings in life remind her of her own predicament, infuriate her to act upon the only real opportunity for escape at her disposal. After fancying herself (perhaps somewhat psychotically) as descended from royalty, Katie snaps out of her strange reverie and realizes how she might realistically escape the slum, Gypo and Louisa, if only for a short while. Like Gypo, she must become an informer. She runs out of the tenement flat to find Commandant Dan Gallagher, to alert him to Gypo's whereabouts. Once again, O'Flaherty illustrates that the poor have very few ways to show initiative and improve their lives except when an unexpected chance to betray their peers comes their way. Late-colonial economics divide and rule the poor in the slum worlds of Mendes's *Black Fauns* and O'Flaherty's *The Informer*.

Many women quite cleverly have their hands on the spoils of Gypo's spent money by the end of the novel. For example, Gypo first of all buys Katie drinks in one public house; second, he entertains a higher-class brothel crowded with women including the money-minded madam, Aunt Betty; and third, he pays for the company and drink of one woman, Connemara Maggie. If money is sparse, and there is a regular life of transcendence of the loneliness of the slums to be had, Katie, Aunt Betty and her girls, and Connemara Maggie are shrewd enough to position themselves in places where men unused to sudden, good fiscal fortunes are eager to burn proverbial holes in their pockets. Their mode of business may stray into the seedier nocturnal realms of the city, but it is a living and a means to some way of life, whereas staying in a dark tenement room is no life at all.

The risks of the job have made some women harder than others if they are to be successful enough to stay out of the seediest slum brothels. The higher-class brothel proprietor Aunt Betty, in fact, operates as carefully and ruthlessly as Mamitz in making sure that her clients are under no illusions as to the price of the services she provides. She has to do so to maintain her position, only a step away from the gutter. She is extremely truculent to Gypo when he first enters her establishment. Sizing him up as a vagrant, she informs him, "You better be going somewhere else. You're wasting your time here, my good man."

However, as soon as Gypo puts his hand into his pocket, pulls out notes and offers to buy a round of drinks, "It was like the performance of a miracle" (p. 134). With sparkling eyes, Aunt Betty becomes the epitome of the charming hostess (albeit only when she has closely inspected his money to make sure that the notes are not counterfeit).

There are some nuances between the novels' narrative parallels and the power structures that determine them, which are conditioned by each novel's historical setting in relation to independence. In *Black Fauns*, Miriam explains the hierarchical order in Trinidad – including her description of the government's main building, the Red House. In the Trinidad of the novel, colonial power still controls the island. However, *The Informer*'s Ireland is displayed as a post-independence power vacuum, fraught by factionalism between pro- and anti-Treaty forces battling to attain supremacy. Within the anti-Treaty contingent are communists seeking not a nationalist but an internationalist, soviet-style socioeconomic reconstruction of a post-British, thirty-two-county Ireland. In chapter 6 of the novel, the narrator explains how the Revolutionary Organization has "spread its influence among the farm labourers and over the whole country". He reports an extract "from an article . . . in the columns of the official organ of the American Revolutionary Organization" regarding the character Commandant Dan Gallagher, Gypo's erstwhile leader, and his aims to effect a communist Ireland. I have used italics in the quotation below to emphasize that the Revolutionary Organization operates to oust the bourgeois nationalist classes who have assumed the running of Ireland following the Treaty:

> When the glorious history of the *struggle for proletarian liberation in Ireland* comes to be written, the name of Comrade Dan Gallagher will stampede from cover to cover in one uninterrupted blaze of glory . . . No other living man has given nobler service to the *world revolution* than this sturdy fighter, who rules the workers of Dublin with greater power than is wielded by *the Irish bourgeoisie*, who *are still nominally in the saddle*. (p. 76)

The narrator also reveals the International Executive of the Revolutionary Organization's frustration with Gallagher, whom it feels runs the Irish Section "purely and simply as a dictator" (ibid.). Yet the executive, mitigating somewhat Gallagher's conduct, is shown to remark that Gallagher struggles to obliterate in the working class "a romantic love of conspiracy. A strong religious and bourgeois-nationalist outlook on life and a hatred of constitutional methods" (p. 77). There is strong historical verisimilitude in this characterization of Gallagher. Roddy Connolly, the leader of the Communist Party of Ireland, had to try to adapt his internationalist ideas to a post-partition, internally fragmented Ireland, to the frustration of communists in Russia.[23] In many respects, the class struggle in *The Informer* is conditioned by the context of the collapse of British rule in Ireland and the scramble for control of the island in the months and years that followed.

This notwithstanding, very little had really changed in Ireland's economic structure since independence to make Ireland significantly different from any other territory still under British rule. Roddy Connolly's father James had predicted as early as 1897 that, "If you remove the English army to-morrow and hoist the green flag over Dublin Castle, unless you set about the Organization of the Socialist Republic your efforts would be in vain." He continued that a post-independence Ireland with British colonial financial systems left intact would be pretty much as before: "England would still rule you. She would rule you through her capitalists, through her landlords, through her financiers, through the whole array of commercial and individualist institutions she has planted in this country and watered with the tears of our mothers and the blood of our martyrs."[24]

In spite of a political power vacuum, British colonial economics still dictated the socioeconomic structure of Ireland, as predicted by James Connolly. The most vulnerable members of society were marginalized in decaying, run-down urban housing. They were to all intents and purposes ghettoized, the same in the Ireland of the 1920s as in the 1910s or the 1900s. The hand of economic oppression in the Ireland of *The Informer* was that of the landlord, the financial, commercial and individual corporate interests. This is essentially a partner to the hand controlling Trinidad in the 1930s, regardless of where Ireland and Trinidad differed in terms of their processes of independence.

A postcolonial comparative reading of *The Informer* shows that O'Flaherty, similarly to Mendes in his writing of *Black Fauns*, creates a mode of novel that, through skilful use of dialogue and focalization techniques, gives people who have long been disenfranchised by colonial economy a means to voice their own experience and point of view – whether directly via dialogue or, through free indirect thought, via the mediating presence of the narrator. *Beacon* writings in general are, as Stewart Brown says, "concerned with issues of pride and dignity among people who have little material wealth or social status", and *Black Fauns* is a just such a tale, in novelistic form, of people of the barrack yard trying to rise above the squalor and economic limitations of their living conditions.[25] Similarly, *The Informer* is a novel of Irish life in a society where the colonial economic structures founded by British rule are still in place, post-partition. Like *Black Fauns*, it shows people trying to rise above the worst poverty and degradation of life in the tenements. Mendes and O'Flaherty display a social conscience largely informed by their bitter experience of having been soldiers fighting for Britain in an imperial war, the First World War. Their heightened empathy with the poor, who often paid the ultimate price for being part of the Empire on the battlefields of war or who subsisted in the most wretched districts of colonial towns and cities, found developing expression via their early literary output. Mendes's contributions to *Trinidad*, produced in association with C.L.R. James and others, whether by accident or design innovated the expression of the life of the people of an island under British rule. Looking back at *Trinidad* and *the Beacon*, Mendes, in his autobiography, summed up how the creation of "a West Indian climate" came about through *Beacon*-era authors coming together and writing about the common peoples of the islands:

> We, not of set purpose but quite unconsciously, created a West Indian literary climate which eased the way for young men in the future who possessed the urge to write. *They* were the ones who created the literary *tradition,* an extension of the literary *climate:* Naipaul, Lamming, Selvon, Mittelholzer, all of the generation following ours. We established the norms – dialect, way of life, racial types, barrack-yards, West Indian character and poverty – and these were the postulates that brought a West Indian literature into being.[26]

Mendes himself, as part of the *Beacon* generation, is crucial to the creation of a Caribbean literary tradition that sought to understand precisely how marginalized peoples under British control, excluded from the privileges and comforts of the ruling and middle classes, lived, loved, fought and struggled to survive. *Black Fauns* is important in the development of what can be called intellectually decolonizing thought, in that Mendes took the experimental, naturalistic novel form and showed what happens when desperate people in desperate circumstances under late or residual-colonial economic and power structures have to fight for any kind of amelioration of their lives. His novel investigates what happens when poor people in a cramped space, with identified weaknesses, scramble for a few pennies thrown seemingly from above into the mire between them. Mendes adapts the Zola-esque convention of the novel by positioning his story within the frame of the precise socioeconomic conditions of late-colonial Trinidad. Characters such as Mamitz and Estelle behave as they do, betraying their yard community as they seek to leave it and live a life usually enjoyed every day by rich, white colonials. The narrative strategies of focalization and narrative voice that Mendes portrayed his barrack-yard characters may have been advanced upon by younger Caribbean writers in subsequent decades, yet Mendes established a norm for taking the time to represent the perspective, plight and problems of the West Indian poor.

O'Flaherty is a post-Joycean realist writer who is deeply important to the evolution of the Irish novel in portraying from an uncompromisingly close perspective the everyday lives of the impoverished, famished, yet nonetheless aspirant Dublin poor. O'Flaherty's Dubliners still reel from the socioeconomic structures of an only recently withdrawn British colonial power, and in many ways they are still conditioned by its effects. O'Flaherty's skill in naturalist depiction of scene and character provide him with the means to narrate a social commentary on the urban Ireland that British rule has created and left in its wake. Characters such as Gypo Nolan and Katie Fox struggle for a few hours of deliverance from the clutches of deprivation, by whatever means possible; O'Flaherty shows that they have been oppressed to the extent that, out of fear and an instinctive flinch for escape, they will betray their own people. In Irish writing, before O'Flaherty, the bourgeois and financially independent classes were the standard subject matter for novelistic representation just as in the vast majority of English novels. O'Flaherty breaks away intellectually from the trend of the classic English novel and creates a new form in Irish writing – a form of, if not for, the people whom he portrays.

This chapter has investigated the extent to which O'Flaherty established a post-Revival norm in awarding agency to people whose voices had not been clearly heard in Irish fiction. O'Flaherty, similarly to Mendes, set a new trend in a particular kind of novel that not only closely critiqued issues relating to disengagement from British rule but let the previously underrepresented subjects of colonialism critique that rule via their own speech and thoughts.

2.

"Two Tunes"

Jean Rhys's *Voyage in the Dark* and Elizabeth Bowen's
The Last September

IN JEAN RHYS'S CANONICAL POSTCOLONIAL NOVEL, *Voyage in the Dark* (1934), an eighteen-year-old female protagonist of Dominican planter-settler stock struggles to maintain a sense of identity as the colonial world of her childhood falls into decline. Elizabeth Bowen's *The Last September* (1929) also features an eighteen-year-old female protagonist fraught by crises of colonial identity and life-direction at the end of Ascendancy rule. The publication of *The Last September* precedes that of *Voyage in the Dark* by five years, but the two novels parallel one another in addressing issues of the collapse of the colonial Big House, using closely corresponding plot mechanisms and character types. This chapter considers the extent of these parallels in detail via comparative close readings of the texts in order to re-evaluate *The Last September's* significance as a postcolonial novel.

Anna Morgan, the protagonist and narrator of *Voyage in the Dark*, is an orphan, cut off from any direct link to her colonial planter heritage, especially since coming to England two years previously with her stepmother, Hester. From the fragments of information suggested in Anna's accounts of conversations with her various friends and lovers in a number of English boarding houses, it transpires that her mother was of the Costerus family, landed for five generations on the Constance Estate in Dominica.

Anna's father was Gerald Morgan, a speculative first-generation Cambro-Dominican planter-settler, whose gambling and bad debts – at least in the implied opinion of his surviving second wife, Hester – appear to have contributed to his premature death. Prior to migrating to Ilkley, Yorkshire, England, Anna and Hester had sold up their last Dominican property, the unsuccessful Morgan's Rest. Hester soon plundered Anna's rapidly depleted inheritance before Anna left to pursue a career as a chorus girl in the provincial towns of Great Britain. It is at this stage in her life, with Anna fending for herself in the unwelcoming chill of England, that the principal action of the novel commences. England, Anna's new migrant locale, is cold, inhospitable and drab. Anna works on a circuit of English towns that seem to share near-identical uninspired, uninviting layouts and characteristics, for want of a better word, of English urban planning: "There was always a little grey street leading to the stage-door of the theatre and another little grey street where your lodgings were, and rows of little houses with chimneys like the funnels of dummy steamers and smoke the same colour as the sky."[1]

The complex and lucid detail of Anna's background is largely informed as a subjective, first-person fictive construct of Rhys's own childhood experience. Rhys was born Ella Gwendolen Rees Williams in Roseau, Dominica, on 24 August 1890. At the age of sixteen and a half, Rhys left a Dominica fraught by generational tensions between older and newer colonial settlers. She accompanied her Anglophile paternal aunt Clarice to England in 1907 and undertook six months of private education at the Perse School for Girls in Cambridge before an abortive spell at the Academy of Dramatic Art (under her birth name, Gwendolen Williams). After Rhys's failure in serious drama, largely due to the academy's disapproval of her West Indian accent, her aunt Clarice first tried to encourage her niece's literary talents, but then sought to secure her passage back to Roseau. However, Rhys rebelled and found a situation as a chorus girl in a touring music hall comedy. Rhys's late-colonial background, her family's ill-fated property ventures on the island, the Anglophile pretentions of an older relative, her departure at a young age to England and her enrolment as a chorus girl in a travelling provincial music show – all this became source material for *Voyage in the Dark*, giving ballast to the novel's depiction of the complexities of late-colonial identity.

The bedsit interiors of Anna's lodgings are cold, grey and unpleasant. When she is faced with the English cold, it has a psychologically numbing effect on her, as if the grey clouds are a curtain falling, "hiding everything I had ever known" (p. 7).

Yet Anna does not try to maintain a sense of continuity with her previous life in Dominica by summoning to mind remembered facts about her colonial heritage. The only way that she can salvage a sense of self, of memory and of place is to channel remembered physical sensations and emotions relating to Dominica's Market Street: "I didn't like England at first. I couldn't get used to the cold. Sometimes I would shut my eyes and pretend that the heat of the fire, or the bed-clothes drawn up around me, was sun-heat; or I would pretend I was standing outside the house at home, looking down Market Street to the Bay" (p. 7). This Dominica is not the world of the planter-settler, but the thriving locale of the Afro-Dominican populace, as perceived by a colonial on the verge of identification with that world. Anna recalls olfactory memories first and foremost, such as the smell of the local people, the smell of smoking wood used to prepare local food and the distinctly Afro-Caribbean food itself, such as "salt fishcakes fried in lard" (p. 7). Anna uses the racial epithet "niggers" to describe the local people, a point that betrays her colonial privilege and mindset. Yet, she conjures up an Afro-Dominican world in order to invoke an impression of her own home and origins. This illustrates that her instinctive sympathy lies more with Afro-Dominican culture than with the grey world of England (to which she, as the scion of European colonialism, should putatively feel more affinity).

Anna comes closest to expressing a sense of her Dominican vitality via sparsely worded, evocative descriptions of her physical sensations. In fact, Anna distrusts the tyranny of words, which to her seem to belong to an exclusive order that works to label her, marginalize her and instil fear in her. As Anna reads Zola's *Nana* – a male writer's attempt to construct in words the experience of a woman not dissimilar in profession to Anna herself – she experiences a sense of fear and dislocation from the "endless procession of words . . . dark, blurred words going on endlessly" (p. 9).

Sylvie Maurel, a Rhys scholar and critic who is heavily influenced by the post-structuralist theoretical movements of Kristevan feminist semiotics and reappraisals of Bakhtinian dialogics, offers the idea that Anna's Dominican sensations, sense-perceptions and memories are a pre-linguistic *chora* that works to destabilize the main diegesis of the narrative. Maurel writes, "[W]hile the diegesis is set in England, constant reference is made to Anna's home island in the shape of remembrances or of a mental, silent subtext whose ceaseless surfacing seems to exert pressure on the diegetic text."[2] Maurel further argues that Dominican remembrance is a form of "West Indian *chora*", or even a "locus of *jouissance*" that operates as a means by which Anna can survive what Maurel calls sublimation to the law of English patriarchy. England is a text, an imperialistic sign system, which works to destroy Anna's felt sense of self. Anna's resistance to the hegemonic power of the British imperial-patriarchal Word takes on a specifically postcolonial significance when she reacts against the cold social niceties and codes of English people around her. When Anna arrives in England, she feels apart from the other white English chorus girls with whom she lives and works. Anna's remembered physical reaction to the smells, impressions and warmth of the Dominican market has left its imprint upon her body. Anna's blood reacts to warmth, which brings to her mind the multifariousness of experience in the Caribbean.

Anna celebrates a Dominica of the mind where "the black women sell fishcakes on the savannah, they carry them in trays on their heads. They call out, 'Salt fishcakes, all sweet an' charmin', all sweet an' charmin'" (p. 7). Anna is still to some degree part of the heat of that market. In England, however, where a veil of grey monotony and predictability is cast over towns, and in the manners between men and women of different classes and castes, Anna, once so alive, is now cold to other people's touch.

Anna has embarked on a tour of provincial theatres and a succession of brief tenancies in grey, anonymous boarding-house rooms, where she spends much time with an English girl, Maudie. Maudie and Anna meet two gentlemen, one of whom, Walter Jeffries, becomes Anna's lover. Walter touches Anna during their meeting and pronounces her "cold as ice. Cold and rather clammy" (p. 12). Anna had previously articulated the difference between her culturally ambiguous, but vitally creolized Dominican remembered sense of self and place versus her current English surroundings, via the physical plane of sensing warmth. Now Maudie, Anna's English associate, reduces Anna's physical rather than linguistic expression of complex identity to one word: a crude racial epithet. Maudie demonstrates the tyranny of words that Anna resists, but this time Maudie labels – and confines – Anna's identity according to the dominant imperialist discourses of racial stereotype. Maudie "explains" Anna's coldness to Walter: "The girls call [Anna] the Hottentot. Isn't it a shame?" (p. 12). When Anna is asked by Walter, "Why the Hottentot?", it is telling that Anna does not or cannot reply to him. Anna, as a white Dominican in England, clearly has not thought of herself in such a racialized way. Now, mainly on account of her accent and mannerisms, she finds herself referred to via a European colonial term for the Khoikhoi aboriginals of Southern Africa: the term "Hottentot" was an unsophisticated attempt by colonists to label the native – and perceived primitive – Khoikhoi people by the supposed sound of their speech.[3] In the view of Anna's English peers, whether spoken in truth or jest, to be from the colonies is to be comparatively uncivilized. In the racially binaristic context of early twentieth-century England, Anna's cultural complexity is not understood or regarded. Although Anna is white, her Creole voice and gestures mark her out in English society as somewhat Other, or socially and racially inferior to the norm.

Anna instinctively mistrusts words, to the point that she stops listening to what Walter is saying and instead focuses on his physicality. Walter's body, and the body that often belies the intent and content of conversation, is a truth that Anna can understand. Anna rejects Walter's words and reminds herself of the concrete reality of the social situation in which she deals with him: "He spoke very quickly, but with each word separated from the other" (p. 12).

What happens here is significant in postcolonial terms. Anna, a white Creole, finds herself effectively put in her place in England, even though in Dominica she would be very much part of the ruling caste. Words have been used against her in a way she does not quite understand. Anna has been placed on a lower rung on some imperial ladder of status and she is confused by this. Although Anna does not consciously formulate some complex strategy to resist being marginalized in this way, the implications of what she does in response can be read as an act that in effect (if not in design) resists the authority of Walter's language, the language of power. Anna focuses not on what Walter is saying but on Walter's mannerisms and physicality as he speaks. In many ways, a postcolonial reader can say that by doing this, Anna is reacting to the primacy of imperial language. Jean Rhys is not merely portraying Anna as a fictive version of herself here, or using her own experience as the material for Anna's characterization. Rather, Rhys is very deliberately constructing Anna's responses to Walter as a way of illustrating how a white Creole woman in the early twentieth century would, and does, react when she arrives in England and feels oppressed by the language of authoritative males. Carole Angier, in her 2000 introduction to *Voyage in the Dark*, remarks that Anna's distrust of words and valorization of feeling reflects Jean Rhys's own approach to writing. Angier comments, "Jean Rhys was a writer who distrusted words. She used the fewest and shortest ones she could, as though she were trying not to use words at all" (p. viii). Rhys's 1934 letter to Evelyn Scott, in which she describes her use of voice in *Voyage in the Dark*, qualifies Angier's argument. Rhys suggests that the point of being so economical with words in the novel is to emphasize that the protagonist forms a sense of identity at least as much in tune with the persistence of her past sensations and experience – implicitly her Dominican sense of self – as with the codes and structures of her present-day society in England.

Specifically, Rhys writes of the novel,

> It's written entirely in words of one syllable. Like a kitten mewing perhaps. The big idea – well I'm blowed if I can be sure what it is. Something to do with time being an illusion I think. I mean that the past exists – side by side with the present, not behind it; that what was – is.
>
> I tried to do it by making the past (the West Indies) very vivid – the present very dreamlike (downward career of girl) – starting of course piano and ending fortissimo.
>
> Perhaps I was simply trying to describe a girl going potty.[4]

Perhaps. Yet Anna's ability to cling to some sense of a Caribbean identity while faced with the strangeness and imposing linguistic hegemony of imperial-patriarchal England is also her saving grace. Seen from a postcolonial perspective, Anna resists total ontological engulfment and annihilation by the alien, cold, uniform sign systems of English town planning, and the attitudes to race, class and gender power structures, by constructing a dialogic narrative wherein the remembered past fuses with and adapts the present: the fire of a bedsit interior becomes Dominica's Market Street. In a 1959 letter to Francis Wyndham, Rhys describes that when she returned to London from Paris in the early 1930s, she soon felt the legacy of her Dominican upbringing calling her, "knocking at my heart". The result of this calling on the emotions manifested itself in writing: "So – *Voyage in the Dark*."[5] It would of course be a stretch to attempt to psychoanalyse Rhys's intentions for writing *Voyage in the Dark* at this time. Yet it would be reasonable to conjecture from Rhys's correspondence that Anna's resistance of British codes is in part a self-reflexive, fictive rendering of Rhys's own tendency to listen to her heart's invocation of

Dominica: a way of asserting a sense of her identity in the face of its threatened status while living in England.

Having moved to the nocturnal *demi-monde* world of London in her affair with Walter, Anna meets Hester for lunch while the latter has ventured from her house in Ilkley to lodge temporarily at "a boarding-house in Bayswater" during a shopping stay in the capital. Anna reacts against what she subjectively reads as her stepmother's assertion, from a remark about "unfortunate propensities", that her mother was "coloured". Although Anna insists in response that "she wasn't" (p. 56), she has already by this point in the text mused on a history of intimate personal relations between European settlers and Afro-Dominican slaves. Hester continues to chastise Anna on racial grounds for resembling an African in her voice and characteristics: "[Y]ou growing up more like a nigger every day. Enough to drive anybody mad" (p. 54). Although Anna is white, she recalls reading a slave-list at Constance Estate featuring her uncanny double "Maillotte Boyd, aged 18, house servant, mulatto", and Hester's perversion of Exodus 34, "The sins of the fathers Hester said are visited upon the children unto the third and fourth generation" (p. 46). Eventually, Anna seems to question her own racial identity (in terms that we might call a social construct), if not exactly her actual racial background. Rhys's narrative is often framed around the ramifications of Anna's suppositions regarding her past: Anna appears to regard herself less and less surely as a white Creole colonial. More and more, she demonstrates anxiety about her place within and between Dominican and English worlds. The fact that the bigoted Hester, an English-born woman of late-colonial heritage, appears in Anna's mind to be aggressively quick to distance herself from Anna's maternal colonial caste only serves to reinforce Anna's mistrust of aligning oneself with or against any one clear group of people, colonial or otherwise.

Unlike Anna – who belongs on her maternal side to a society in which the caste divisions between European settlers and Afro-Dominicans have over centuries become somewhat complex – Hester Morgan represents a first-generation English influx of wives of speculative late-colonials who, in actual historical fact, arrived in Dominica in the last years of the nineteenth century as part of a campaign of imperial road-building and greater colonial penetration of the island under Henry Hesketh Bell. Bell is not fictively rendered in *Voyage in the Dark*, yet Rhys creates Hester as an embodiment of the mindset and prejudices of Bell-era colonial wives in Dominica.

Hester's late husband and Anna's father, Gerald Morgan, represents a generation of speculative new English planter-settlers in Dominica such as those described in Symington Grieve's *Notes upon the Island of Dominica (British West Indies)*. These settlers risked losing any money invested on new lands if they made "the mistake of taking up more land than they [could] properly develop with the capital at their disposal", particularly if they were not prepared to make the effort to cultivate lands over a course of years.[6] Cocoa plantations, according to Grieve, required as many as thirteen years of preparation before the crop yielded adequate dividends; a new settler would need up to five thousand pounds of capital to make a venture viable. This sum underscores, if Hester's words are to be believed, the enormity of "Morgan's Folly", as his estate failed. The estate's legacy was a mere "five hundred pounds" after Gerald Morgan had invested his share of a substantially inadequate "eight hundred and fifty" towards the project (p. 53). It is likely that Rhys drew here on her own experience in portraying Morgan's decline. In her autobiography *Smile Please*, she recalls her father's fate soon after arriving in Dominica: "he was optimistic enough to buy two estates in the hills. . . . Optimistic because, being a doctor, he spent his life working in the town and the districts near it, and neither of his purchases was a paying proposition. The larger of the two, Bona Vista, was very beautiful, wild, lonely, remote."[7]

Hester's settler-colonial economy is new and exploratory. It is reliant merely on the economics of chance, rather than slow cultivation of property or manipulation of labour resources. Hester may sneer at the condition of the land in Dominica, but she is unprepared to concern herself with the thought of the time and effort involved in land improvement. It is clear that she elects to sell the remainder of her late husband's estate and return to England due to a lack of practical understanding of the time and effort required to develop a settlement: "I should think I did sell a place that lost money and always has done and always will do every penny of money that anyone is stupid enough to put into it and nothing but rocks and stones and heat and those awful doves cooing all the time" (p. 54).

Rhys at this point is indicating Hester's failure to understand the realities of colonial life and practice. Hester's distaste for the hot Dominican climate alone suffices to distance her profoundly from Rhys's and Anna's overtly expressed relish in the heat of the Caribbean sun. Rhys constructs Hester as a representative character demonstrating a particular kind of English ignorance that Anna

– and the novel – counters with a Dominican reality. This point is important to postcolonial readers of this late-colonial text, in that we see the depiction of a situation where the Dominican planter-settler class is internally fraught between factions: Anna's, which sees itself as West Indian, and Hester's, which sees itself as English and does not understand its colonial precedent in Dominica. Anna's faction, and indeed her young colonial generation, depends for its survival upon Hester's financial investment, which Hester withdraws upon returning to England. The decline of the Dominican plantocracy, and the suspension of the younger generation's colonial legacy and certitude of social status, is a concern that Rhys conveys with such skill that it constructs a model which postcolonial readers can recognize as a feature of the thematic canon of postcolonial literatures, comparable across plantation narratives from other former British territories.

Historically, Hester's viewpoint echoes contemporary paranoia concerning the fear of "going native" among colonists exposed to the climate and peoples of a colonized terrain. Hester repeats an imperialist, often racist, metropolitan view of England as superior to the heavily African-populated Dominica that she perceives. Contextually, Hester's viewpoint that colonials in the West Indies in time lose their characteristic incentive towards industry and end up falling into bad habits more befitting the Afro-Caribbean population coincides with ideas expounded in James Anthony Froude's *The English in the West Indies*, published in 1888.[8] Froude argued that Dominica is an island English only by name, where supposed administrators idle away their time, contaminated by a prevalent torpor and aversion to civilizing industry. In Froude's Dominica, "the island goes on in a state of torpid content", where nothing gets done and administrators drift indolently alongside their Afro-Dominican peers.[9]

Hester, in a Froudean vein, maintains a perspective at times decidedly antithetical to the settler viewpoint of the long-established Costerus family of Anna's childhood Constance Estate. Hester remains English. For Hester, Ramsey Costerus's illegitimate children are an index of his moral *degeneration* (p. 53). The concept of degeneration stems from an influential 1892 work by Hungarian social critic Max Nordau; Nordau critiqued what he saw as the dangerously decadent predilection for exotic art, cultures and peoples among the fashionable societies of the *fin de siècle* period.[10] Hester imposes an English ideology of racial and social norms upon her view of a "slack" colonial class that has been corrupted and rendered degenerate by spending too much time in the tropical colonies.

European cultural superiority may well have been assumed from the very outset of colonial adventure and encounter in the tropics, but it gained scientific credence with the cultural evolutionist theory of Edward Burnett Tylor's *Anthropology* in 1881 and the index on nigrescence in ethnologist John Beddoe's contemporary publications. Beddoe sought to subdivide even Caucasians across the Atlantic isles. He saw a distinction between the Anglo-Saxon, or neo-Aryan, tendency towards orthognathous or receding jaws, and the Irish or Welsh propensity towards prognathous or projecting jaws. The Irish and Welsh scored higher on the nigrescent index since their large jaws were purportedly craniologically similar to Africanoid or even Cro-Magnon skull formation.[11] Hester's description of Ramsay not only as having "exactly the laugh of a Negro" but also having "unfortunate propensities" (p. 56) – a phrenological term common in pre-Freudian psychology and prevalent throughout *Jane Eyre* to refer to inferior cranial development predisposing a person to fits of rage or disproportionate emotion – is rooted in contemporary discourses of degeneration and atavism.[12] Hester, like the craniologist, is keen to insinuate some hierarchy within whiteness and at the expense of "boozy", dissipated Bo Costerus, with whom Anna to an extent shares sympathy and even identification.

The warmth of the whisky that Anna drinks with her lover Walter facilitates her remembrances of her Dominican past. Yet while she cites her colonial forebears such as Uncle Bo as a precedent for her taste for strong alcohol, she also attributes her "rum" character to some desire for blackness. In conversation with Walter, Anna admits, "When I was a kid I wanted to be black, and they used to say, 'Your poor grandfather would turn in his grave if he heard you talking like that'" (p. 45). Anna's statement that she is the fifth generation of planter-settlers on her mother's side takes on a racial significance in this context. It is this mix that constructs the identity of the "real West Indian" that she boasts to be (p. 47), somewhat defiantly in the face of more reductive and racially binaristic notions of the difference between the white planter-settler ruler and the black ruled in the West Indies. Warmth again is the physical sensation that Anna explores and exploits to express a sense of selfhood beyond the language of race, gender and class.

The warmth of human feeling, sometimes triggered by a bedsit fire, huddled blankets or whisky, is not just a means by which Anna can express her sense of remembered West Indian self outside of language. Fire is also a trope of violent self-assertion. When Walter, Vincent and Maudie discuss Anna in such a way as to mock her as some untalented, end-of-the-pier child squeeze of the whimsically romantic Walter, Anna takes fire to exact her retribution against them: she brings her cigarette down hard on the back of Walter's hand. Considering that Anna identifies with the servant Maillotte Boyd, one asks whether the act of violence via fire could suggest some connection with other forms of revolt against oppression portrayed in the novel. Evidence to support this hypothesis comes compellingly at the climactic end of part four of *Voyage in the Dark*.

Anna, alone and pregnant in England and succumbing to a swirling, anaesthetized state of befuddlement during an induced backstreet abortion, recollects a childhood memory of hungrily viewing a threatening, fire-illuminated masquerade enacted by the local Afro-Dominican community, engaging in subversive carnival outside the Costerus Estate. We can read radically subversive and incendiary symbolism behind the revellers' choice of instrument, as they are depicted "*banging the kerosene-tins*" (p. 157). These tins, struck in an implicitly menacing carnival that in masked dance mimics and mocks the white colonists, are indexes of the explosive material they conventionally contain; as the drums are struck, they are figuratively ignited around the parameters of the Costerus Estate.

The symbolic potentiality of this ritual becomes clearer when one also notes Bridget Brereton's observation about Caribbean carnival and the street procession known as *Canboulay* (a Creolization of the term *cannes brulées*, translating as "burnt cane").[13] Crown authorities in Trinidad, for instance, were so nervous about the parade of lighted torches held aloft throughout the streets of Port of Spain, and its implications for inflammatory revolution and the torching of colonial properties, that the practice was banned ("not without a riot"[14]). The banging of kerosene-tins by Afro-Dominicans, wearing white masks to taunt their oppressors, inevitably reflects Rhys's own family history – and by extension historical experiences of anti-colonial resistance in Dominica – of the two attacks upon her maternal antecedents' Geneva Estate in Grand Bay in 1844 and 1930.

Throughout her writing career, Rhys continued to explore this key issue of the constant threat, and effect, of the destruction of the planter-settler order in Dominica, albeit in geographically displaced form. Her 1966 novel *Wide Sargasso Sea* substitutes Jamaica for Dominica and masterfully constructs an intertextual, even deconstructive dialogue with Charlotte Brontë's 1847 novel *Jane Eyre*.[15] Yet, in *Wide Sargasso Sea*, the local people riot against the landed elite just as they had done in Rhys's Dominica. The post-emancipation locals who stand around in groups to jeer at protagonist Antoinette Cosway's ailing, widowed mother at the start of the novel exhibit the *Schadenfreude* of a marginalized society for too long neglected and contained by plantocratic power. Their vengeful eyes, fixed on the Cosways' doomed Coulibri Estate, are similar to the watchful, mocking masks of the revellers outside the Costerus plantation in *Voyage in the Dark*. When Antoinette's mother remarries, to the prosperous Englishman Richard Mason, the latter in his arrogance and naivety refutes suggestions as to the locals' seething loathing of his control. The locals' torching of Coulibri is Rhys's ultimate expression of anti-colonial violence realized in the literal rather than figurative narrative of her Caribbean fiction – a violence alluded to and anticipated in the climax of *Voyage in the Dark*.

Wide Sargasso Sea was published in 1966, after Rhys's long absence from the literary spotlight. At this point, there was a critical rediscovery of the author's previous oeuvre, inclusive of *Voyage in the Dark*. Rhys's depiction of late-colonial Dominican society in *Voyage in the Dark*, similarly to her fictive rendering of Jamaica in *Wide Sargasso Sea*, came to be read over time as a particular kind of postcolonial novel emphasizing the extent of anxiety inherent in the family unit of the plantation.[16] Typically, in Rhys's plantation novels, colonial or imperial identity and authenticity are issues that polarize members of the same homestead. The younger protagonist, at the dwindling of colonial power, is alienated from her elder relatives and struggles to relate to a sense of future purpose or place in a society in which her role is no longer assured. This protagonist is ordinarily female; at this historical moment in plantocratic societies, she is less financially or ideologically bound to the success of ailing planter estates than the speculating male property owners who have to make the farm work. She is thus free to migrate or explore potential alternative paths towards individual and socioeconomic self-determination beyond the constraints of the plantation demesnes. Hester constitutes an example of a late-colonial archetype insisting on her difference from other colonials in asserting her identity and authority; Anna, as a young girl at the end of colonial rule, reacts against this typification and squirms at being pinpointed as somehow deviant from the preferred colonial model. Postcolonial critics have come to regard Rhys's work as *the* Caribbean example of novels depicting generational conflict within a declining colonial power structure. Readers of Irish fiction such as *The Last September* will see similarities in the portrayal of anxiety within the planter-settler caste with *Voyage in the Dark*, and conclude that *The Last September* can be read extensively through a postcolonial lens.

Lois Farquar, the Anglo-Irish protagonist of *The Last September*, is, like Anna Morgan in *Voyage in the Dark*, eighteen years old when she is first introduced.[17] Just as Anna Morgan is informed by the reality of her author Jean Rhys's life, so Lois Farquar is cast from the materials of Elizabeth Bowen's background. Elizabeth Dorothea Cole Bowen, the last descendant to a Cromwellian colonial dynasty, was born in Dublin, Ireland, on 7 June 1899. Hermione Lee, in her 1983 introduction to *Bowen's Court and Seven Winters*, explains that Bowen's Court was an archetypal North East Cork "Big House" flourishing in the pre-Union eighteenth century and maintaining, until the Troubles, a dominance over rural peasant tenants. Its history reads as metonymical of the aspirant, established and then declining fortunes of the Ascendancy as a whole:

> To an extent, the history of the Bowens is the history of the Anglo-Irish family, and of a class which came to flower in the late eighteenth century, went into decline thereafter and was, by the 1920s, an isolated minority cut off from the country it had once dominated. . . . The Big House builders' obsession with self-aggrandisement and self-perpetuation, the orgies of hunting and drinking, the lawsuits and deeds of sale, the notorious eccentrics . . . : many of these clichés are facts of the Bowen family history.[18]

Lois Farquar is a fictive construct of a young woman of Bowen's age, living at the end of British rule over what would by 1922 become partitioned Ireland. By the September of 1920, at the apex of the Anglo-Irish War, many Anglo-Irish landed estates were effectively garrisons under the threat of Republican attack and paramilitary land-grabs. Lois, like Bowen, is a young woman whose coming of age arrives at the most perilous point in colonial Anglo-Irish fortunes: her social identity, status and destiny are in immediate dispute. Bowen herself confirmed the self-reflexivity of the character of Lois Farquar when she stated, "I *was* the child of the house from which [the fictive Anglo-Irish estate of] Danielstown derives."[19]

Similarly to Rhys's Anna, Bowen's Lois is an orphan: she is the daughter of Ulster Protestant Walter Farquar and his wife Laura (sister to Sir Richard Naylor, landlord of the Anglo-Irish landed estate of Danielstown, County Cork). Lois, like Anna, has lived both on her island of colonial birth and in England. In her childhood, Lois was raised in Leamington, where she also boarded as a scholar. Just as Anna in *Voyage in the Dark* entered into the care of her stepmother Hester, Lois now resides at the Danielstown estate in Cork with her uncle, Sir Richard Naylor, and his wife, Myra. When visitors to the estate, Hugo and Francie Montmorency, discuss Lois and her unfortunate past with Myra Naylor, they acknowledge the fate of Lois's father as being one of predictable failure. Although the precise nature of the "terribly sad" fate of Lois's father Walter is never revealed, there is a consensus that his was an expected decline (p. 17). Myra's observation regarding Lois's similarity to her parents is thus rather ominous: there is an implication that she is destined for the same sad end. Lois's and Anna's colonial fathers resemble one another in failing in life, dying comparatively young and leaving daughters in the care of extended family at a point of the decline of the old plantocracy. Bowen and Rhys construct these men as representatives of the end of a colonial dynasty: they symbolize the failure at the heart of patriarchal colonialism, dying an early death without a son and heir or a strong financial legacy. Their female dependents are left in their wake to fend for themselves.

Orphanhood and fractured sites of growing up are aspects of late-colonial reality that both Bowen and Rhys construct in their novels as matters of crucial relation to the early development of their similarly fraught, female protagonists. Given that Rhys, unlike her semi-autobiographical protagonist Anna, was not yet totally orphaned on arriving in England at the age of sixteen, and Bowen was not totally orphaned at the same age as her fictive counterpart Lois, it is unlikely that Rhys and Bowen make their heroines orphans purely by coincidence or based exactly on their personal experience. There must rather be something significantly and comparably symbolic in their decisions as writers to render their female protagonists without parents, dislocated, anchorless, drifting and without a determined sense of origin or destination. Anna and Lois are characters in limbo, with no definite connection with a past. They are, of course, of planter-settler stock and ostensibly unlike, say, the historical slaves of Africa whose middle-passage journey across the Atlantic, and the limbo mindset that it produced, has been explored in postcolonial terms by eminent theorists such as Wilson Harris.[20] Yet, as late-colonials without a clear link to their immediate forebears, Anna and Lois can be read in postcolonial terms as ironically stranded at the end of an empire, at least psychologically, in a form of limbo. Unlike those trickster figures who learn to negotiate the space between origin and destination, however, Anna and Lois seem caught unaware by their plight: they are orphans cast out into the broader world and set apart from the rest of the plantocratic caste from which they derive.

Lois does not feel a visceral connection to the land of her planter-settler birth. Indeed, the third-person narrator of *The Last September* has enough access into Lois's focalized consciousness to be able to remark of Lois, "She could not conceive of her country emotionally" (p. 34). However, the particular Ireland that fails to stir Lois's feelings is the West British construct of Anglo-Ireland, "moored at the north but with an air of being detached and washed out west from the British coast". The other Ireland, beyond Danielstown's perimeter, incites Lois's emotional interest. Lois and Anna share a desire to connect and be one with the realm of the ruled, of the everyday people beyond their colonial demesnes. Lois is drawn to the shadowy trench-coated figure immediately beyond the perimeter of the Danielstown estate – a representative of a domain beyond the enclosed view of the ruler:

> First, she did not hear footsteps coming, and as she began to notice the displaced darkness thought what she dreaded was coming, was there within her – she was indeed clairvoyant, exposed to horror and going to see a ghost. Then steps, hard on the smooth earth; branches slipping against a trench-coat. The trench-coat rustled across the path ahead, to the swing of a steady walker. She stood by the holly immovable, blotted out in her black, and there passed within reach of her hand, with the rise and fall of a stride, a resolute profile, powerful as a thought. In gratitude for its fleshliness, she felt prompted to make some contact: not to be known seemed like a doom: extinction. "It's a fine night," she would have liked to observe; or, to engage his sympathies: "Up Dublin!" or even – since it was in her uncle's demesne she was straining under a holly – boldly – "What do you want?" (pp. 33–34)

In Lois's case, the figure in the dark foliage represents an anti-colonial, Republican threat to her caste with which she must somehow engage or risk extinction. Lois seems to associate saving herself by somehow joining in fellowship with this figure and ensuring the end of her colonial caste, as shown when she becomes aware of her desire to call to him, "It's a fine night", or even more blatantly, "Up Dublin!" The idea to challenge the threat to her uncle's estate is almost an afterthought: Lois's first instinct is to reach out into the tenebrous shadows and become one with a mysterious, psychic dark double who might reveal to her a way of conceiving herself and her place in Ireland on an emotional level. Anna Morgan is vitally aware of her place in Dominica through memories of the local people; Lois is remote from Republican Ireland but strives nonetheless to make that vital connection in pursuit of self-knowledge, even if it means the end of her plantocratic class.

Lois resembles Anna in resisting people's attempts to control her by identifying her via set national or supposed caste characteristics. Just as the terminology of caste difference, even between colonial strata, has a profound significance in *Voyage in the Dark*, so is this the case in the Anglo-Irish society of *The Last September*. Such stratification provides the means by which ideological boundaries of identity and community are established between the settler Anglo-Irish castes and the English from whom they originate. In Anglo-Irish society, such typification of cultural separateness is rife: Sir Richard Naylor wishes to characterize his fearlessness in the face of danger as an Irish trait by attributing to Englishness the negative qualities of hysterical fear. The first section of *The Last September*, "The Arrival of Mr and Mrs Montmorency", details a visit to Danielstown from a married couple of old friends who have heard rumours of Irish Republican insurrection against the landed gentry and the threat of imminent attack waiting in the near distance. Francie Montmorency is thought to be in ill health, where in fact her state of agitation is justified by a fear of attack by paramilitaries that the Naylors themselves ridicule. Francie believes Danielstown and its inhabitants to be prime targets for gunmen, while the Naylors think this sort of notion unbecoming of the proud and calm Anglo-Irish. For instance, when Francie Montmorency worries that the Danielstown party might be shot if they sat outside the house on its steps too late into the dark evening, Sir Richard Naylor replies, "You're getting very English, Francie! Isn't Francie getting very English? Do you think maybe we ought to put sandbags behind the shutters when we shut up at nights?" (p. 23).

Such blitheness and naivety – the fatal error of a colonial class turning a blind eye to the inevitability of anti-colonial violence – is typical of a sort of plantocratic landlord that both Bowen and Rhys choose to identify, perhaps suggesting a kind of colonial degeneracy in which the patriarchs of the later generations are simply unable to see the forces of history that are about to sweep them into oblivion. It is the younger women who see more clearly, but of course nobody will pay any attention to them. Richard Naylor is very similar here to the arrogant Richard Mason of *Wide Sargasso Sea*, who foolishly downplays the threat to the Coulibri Estate from the local, ruled population. The colonial patriarch claims to know better than his guests the true extent of the danger to his estate. The colonial is a class apart: supposedly wiser and more aloof than others. As it turns out, in overstating his separateness from other castes and classes and appearing to dismiss any anti-colonial threat, Richard Naylor – like Rhys's Richard Mason – is hubristically oblivious of outside forebodings of his own demise.

Lady Naylor is another colonial who constructs a sense of Anglo-Irishness that she insists is vastly different from the Englishness of the imperial motherland. This difference is an assurance of the perpetuation of her caste since it is founded on agreeable attributes of character. She ascribes to Englishness first a bland anonymity ("Practically nobody who lives in Surrey ever seems to have been heard of", p. 58), and second, an annoying "disposition . . . to be socially visible before midday" (p. 193). Even the "Honourable" Mrs Carey, who attends a Danielstown tennis party fortified by representatives of the local garrison and their English wives, adds her view of polite disgust at the English when, in reply to military wife Betty Vermont's exclamation that "Your scrumptious Irish teas make a perfect piggy-wig of me", she replies with a sublimely stilted, "Does it really?" At the same time, Mrs Carey muses internally on "a tendency, common to most English people, to talk about her inside" (p. 46).

Lois is acutely sensitive to the damning effect that Anglo-Irish colonialism has on constructing discourses of difference between the Ascendancy and the English officer classes, or of typifying and labelling identity in general. It is perhaps for this reason that Lois cannot bear to overhear Francie Montmorency and her aunt Myra Naylor talking about her and describing her in terms that will deprive her of her individual means to self-expression or self-realization, or that will keep her forever confined to the terms of the traditional language of the Anglo-Irish. Lois awkwardly stands in her bedroom overhearing Francie and Myra discussing her in the anteroom. Lois feels the urgency to stop them by making her audience known, strategically at the point when Francie is about to typify her once and for all with a telling adjective. Lois thus disrupts and silences Francie's speech in mid-sentence, at the crux of "Lois is very –". She does this by kicking over a pail and rattling furniture in her room. Lois balks at being confined to a neat linguistic formula: "She didn't want to know what she was, she couldn't bear to: knowledge of this would stop, seal, finish one" (p. 60).

The Anglo-Irish Ascendancy might necessarily seek to define itself, and its constituent population, in terms of its difference from Englishness. Yet the more bohemian Lois, whose art-school inclinations draw her to expand beyond the constrictions of the Big House and even to consider marriage with the English soldier Gerald Lesworth, counters all attempts to limit her within the linguistic constraints of any concept of caste identity. Lois will not be "clapped down under an adjective, to crawl around lifelong inside some quality like a fly in a tumbler" (p. 60).

Phyllis Lassner remarks that the result of Lois overhearing herself being talked about rather than spoken to "is to diminish the sense of a living self". Lois's act of rebellion challenges her transformation "into someone else's fictional creation", namely that of an "Anglo-Irish character . . . modelled on one's ancestors[, where] the individual becomes submerged in a rigid pattern".[21] Lassner's argument can be taken further (and with postcolonial dimensions) when one explores how Lois, like Anna, resists types of colonial or imperial language that limit the possibility for her to develop an individual identity that might cross physical or cultural boundaries. Lois will not allow her peers to label her in such a way that she is represented solely in the language of Anglo-Irish society. Very soon after the episode with the kicking of the pail, Lois accompanies Hugo Montmorency on a tour of the local small farms – in particular the farm of a Michael Connor, whose son Peter is on the run from the British authorities for alleged Republican activities. Lois's conversation with Michael on the topic of his wife is framed in language betraying exceptional intimacy across social or sectarian divides, between the landlord and the tenant classes. Lois does not just show the kind of beneficent regard for the Connors as might be expected from the more genteel and conscientious landlord classes: she demonstrates an uncommon depth of feeling. She asks Michael to send his wife her love: a strong and arguably inappropriate admission of affection, given the political power structures in play between the rulers and the ruled in Ireland, separated by the fortifications of a Big House demesne boundary.

Lois code-switches between the class systems of the Anglo-Irish gentry and the indigenous peasantry on the level of feeling and sympathy. When Francie tries to sum Lois up in language that inevitably will express the idioms and prejudices of the Anglo-Irish ruling-class mindset, Lois ventures out beyond the realm of Danielstown and makes a vital connection with the local people. Similarly to Anna Morgan remembering Dominica as a land of the ruled going about their everyday business in the thriving marketplace, Lois constructs Ireland emotionally, and even her own sense of Irishness, in the landscape of the people over whom her caste has governed for centuries. When Lois can prevent people from castigating her via choice epithets, she is free to explore and define her own complex selfhood as a young woman, born into a dying planter-settler caste but seeking to transcend its physical, psychic and linguistic constraints.

What Lois desires is achieved in the fire that ultimately destroys the Big House. Indeed, the first point of prolepsis of Danielstown's destruction, by fire, is via focalization from Lois's perspective. In chapter 12 of the novel, Lois visits Marda Norton's guest room on the pretext of showing her a book of drawings. Here, Lois's complex, sexually ambiguous and passionate response to Marda's apparent lack of interest in her precipitates an example of violently inflammatory focalization in which Lois unconsciously wills the destruction of her caste. Since Marda Norton is due to leave Ireland to marry Leslie Hawe in Kent, she represents for Lois simultaneously a symbol of escape from the parameters of the Anglo-Irish landed estate and a continued imprisonment within the patriarchal confines of provincial middle England – a place to which colonial women seem inexorably drawn to return, diasporically, in pursuit of economic and gender definition. Marda Norton is one of these emigrants who, in *The Last September*, chooses marriage in England as her prerogative. At this point, Lois begins to harbour incendiary fantasies of the immolation of the Anglo-Irish Big House. Fire in the Anglo-Irish imagination is a symbol of the destruction by Irish Republican forces of the Anglo-Irish Big House – a widespread act of paramilitary vandalism intended to dispossess the Ascendancy in a nationalist land-grab, or symbolic gesture of anti-colonial triumphalism – during and following the War of Independence. Lois is desperate to transcend colonial activity and mentality ("She wanted to go wherever the War hadn't"; "She liked unmarried sorts of places"; "Could one travel alone?", p. 99). Lois's focalized perspective reveals her most subversive desires. Lois fixates upon the bedroom carpet in Marda's Danielstown guest room, with its "strange pink fronds", and meditates upon fire's emancipatory potentiality:

Lois thought how in Marda's bedroom, when she was married, there might be a dark blue carpet with a bloom on it like a grape, and how this room, this hour would be forgotten. Already the room seemed full of the dusk of oblivion. And she hoped that instead of fading to dust in summers of empty sunshine, the carpet would burn with the house in a scarlet night to make one flaming call upon Marda's memory. Lois again realized that no one had come for her, after all. She thought, "I must marry Gerald." (p. 98)

From staring at Marda's bedroom carpet in Danielstown, Lois starts to fantasize that a fire in time will engulf Marda in her marital bedroom in Kent. Such flames would emancipate Marda from the patriarchal-imperial demesnes within which her class and gender's destiny has been planned for generations. Since Lois's fantasy originates with staring at a fixture of a Danielstown interior, it becomes fused with Marda's Kent homestead to the degree that Lois's desire is implicitly as much for Danielstown's destruction as for the end to all patriarchal confines.

This is an important point to consider, since the origin of Lois's desire is predicated upon her physical presence seated in a marital guest bedroom in Danielstown. The room in which she sits symbolizes confinement within patriarchal, imperial parameters. Lois displaces her wish to destroy the threat of her own incarceration within Danielstown, and the social imperatives of a dynastic ascendancy, by metamorphosing the decor of her room into the imagined topography of Marda's future Kent bedroom. Fire is a way to freedom from being "made" by the stone walls of the male-run, patrilineal homesteads of the landed gentry. Thus, Lois's dream is as much an expression of desire to escape Danielstown and the colonial gentry as it is a wish for Marda to escape marriage in Kent. Elizabeth Bowen once noted how, while "[a] Bowen, in the first place, made Bowen's Court . . . , Bowen's Court has made all the succeeding Bowens".[22] Lois desires freedom from the sterilizing influence of Anglo-Irish tradition. She refuses to be "made" by Danielstown.

Lois's daydream runs counter to the interests, security and perpetuation of her caste, so she cannot overtly articulate her dangerous wish to see the Big House burn to the ground, or admit to identification on any significant level with Irish Republican sentiment. Phyllis Lassner, who argues for considerable correspondence between Elizabeth Bowen's biography and the fictive Lois in *The Last September*, acknowledges that Bowen wrote of the repressive effect of

Big House living on her own emotional development. She discusses Bowen's remark in *Bowen's Court* about how the lives of generations of her family were "submerged" in conventional adherence to the dictates of Big House living. Lassner observes, "Describing a stay in Bowen's Court, Bowen reflects how the emotional and political legacy of past inhabitants is felt to be part of its walls and atmosphere." Lassner goes on to propose that "Bowen's conception of her family home is reconstituted in the relationship between Danielstown and its residents".[23] She maintains that, although the female characters of Danielstown, particularly Lois, are not incapable of fantasizing (whether on a sexual or emotional level) for some sense of selfhood and escape, free from the constrictions of Big House familial society, it is part of Bowen's design to show that they ultimately reject "anarchic" self-expression in favour of impotence and survival within the sterile environs of Danielstown. Lassner's view might be supported to an extent if one observes how, in Bowen's novel, the Oxford-educated Laurence informs Hugo Montmorency that "I should like to be here when this house burns. . . . And we shall all be so careful not to notice" (p. 44). Laurence's comments are dismissed as merely a posture. They are indicative of "the undergraduate of today", or, at least, the undergraduate shipped to an Oxford relatively autonomous from the Ascendancy. In real terms, such beliefs would be unspeakable within the context of the Ascendancy itself, home in Ireland. It becomes clear that Lois, who remains based in Danielstown until the conclusion of the novel, is therefore unable to express in clear, realist prose her incendiary, anti-colonial desires to escape the ideological and physical confines of the Big House.

There are nuances between the textual parallels of *Voyage in the Dark* and *The Last September*, which are determined by positioned historical and geographical factors particular to Dominica and Ireland. For instance, Lois's aunt, Myra Naylor, and Anna's stepmother, Hester Morgan, demonstrate viewpoints that are determined by the specificities of, respectively, Anglo-Irish and Anglo-Dominican colonialism. Myra is a descendant from generations of a Protestant Irish community perceiving itself as separate from – and superior in refinement, manners and intellect to – the imperial centre in England. In contrast, Hester is a first-generation English settler in Dominica. Hester, unlike Myra, is not familiar with the historical character of settler-colonial life. Hester repeats an imperialist, often racist, metropolitan view of England as superior to the heavily African-populated Dominica that she perceives, while Myra always sees the Anglo-Irish as superior to the English.

Hermione Lee argues that Bowen "knows her subject" in constructing Myra Naylor as a particular type of "Anglo-Irish upper-class" snob who can be distinguished greatly from her English counterparts. Thus, Myra Naylor is distinct from Rhys's character Hester Morgan, who is more in line with Bowen's English characters in the Anglo-Ireland of *The Last September* such as the "[v]ulgar, patronising Mrs Vermont".[24] Myra's repeated attempts to define a national or cultural quality of Irishness, as opposed to Englishness, hail from a long-established and recognized tendency of her caste dating from pre-Union, Grattan-era Ascendancy, Protestant Irish nationalism. Myra espouses a dated, pro-Ascendancy, counter-English construction of self-identity that contradicts what the historical contextualization of the first section of this chapter shows to be the modern reality of her class's increasing tendency to migrate to England in the Ascendancy's decline. Additionally, the increasing involvement of the Anglo-Irish with the officer classes of the British Empire over the late nineteenth and early twentieth centuries renders Myra's snobbery decrepit, if not quite yet defunct. In chapter 3, Myra is clearly promoting Anglo-Irishness over Englishness. She relates the story of an Anglo-Irish friend, Anna Partridge, who has left Ireland for the provincial environs of a Bedfordshire village. Anna now reportedly has to tolerate "village women sitting round in hats and so obviously despising her". Myra concludes from this information that stupidity is an incurable trait of provincial English village females, which an Anglo-Irish woman can sadly do nothing to remedy. Myra decides, "really what can you do with people with so little brain" (p. 27).

Myra's viewpoint adheres to the attitude of many a landed Protestant of her time, or at least to the views of those late-Ascendancy folk studied by historian Michael McConville.[25] In spite of the Land Purchase Act of 1891, and while faced with the inevitability either of "some sort of compromise with Irish Nationalism" or the alternative option of migrating to England, McConville comments that many chose to remain in Ireland. They saw themselves as part of a class that maintained their historical sense of Ascendancy while determined "to dig their heels in stolidly, resist all attempts at change, and give way grudgingly and progressively only when forced to do so by decisions taken at Westminster by British politicians".[26]

Myra defends her decision to uphold her status as a bastion of Protestant

Irish privilege. She even regards the English as bestial, in an inversion of a Saidian Orientalist scenario where the settler-colonial perceives herself to be superior to her provincial English peer. Explaining her defiance at the thought of emigration to England, she proclaims, "and I said [to Anna Partridge] that I wouldn't live among people who weren't human" (p. 7).

The Naylors host a tennis party at Danielstown for Ascendancy families and soldiers from the First Rutlands, stationed at nearby Clonmore. The event serves as a reminder of the caste's precarious privilege in an Ireland on the verge of independence. Myra seems anxious to establish the lineage – and by implication, the continuing dynastic future – of the landed Protestant classes, pointing out that one guest at the party, the wife of Colonel Boatley, "was a Vere Scott, a Fermanagh Vere Scott" (pp. 36–37). Her inference is that, although by her married name Mrs Boatley might *seem* to belong to the British military class, she retains her distinctive Protestant Irishness through a distinguished heritage.

However, the relics in Danielstown's upstairs anteroom signify the Naylor family's previous connections with imperial adventurism. There are "animals drawn from skins on the floor by the glare of the morning" and "a troop of ebony elephants brought back from India" (p. 10). These artefacts reveal that Myra Naylor's attempts to affect an unbroken linear inheritance of an exclusively Protestant Irish imagined community, insular and unimpeded by British militarism or politics, deny historical reality.

Myra's own nephew Laurence studies rather than joins the British army, and thus appears on the surface to accord to a continuing Ascendancy tradition. Yet Laurence perplexes Myra by being part of a new trend among a younger late-colonial society: a trend towards moving to England and studying in Oxford with its modern, "wrong" and "inconvenient" ideas (p. 39), rather than staying in Ireland at the conventional institution for Anglo-Irish Protestants, Trinity College Dublin. Laurence's departure indicates, in spite of Myra's denial of events, the inevitable forging of stronger links between Protestant Ireland and the British establishment, and the consequent erosion of a separate Protestant sense of a sovereign, imagined national community where the elite is educated at home in a purpose-built Dublin university. In chapter 5 of *The Last September*, we discover through focalization that Laurence, in sharp contrast to Myra, "did not consider that he had anything to do with the race" of the Ascendancy (p. 44).

Myra's sense of the unsuitability of the doomed subaltern, Gerald Lesworth, to be Lois's husband remains ideologically situated in an anachronistic, eighteenth-century sense of exclusive and dynastic Anglo-Irish community, when a class elected to intermarry within its own settler-colonial parameters rather than in congress with England. Lois's marriage is hampered through the machinations of Myra, precisely due to the latter's denial of the increasing symbiosis of Protestant Ireland and England in the face of land-grabs and political gains by the Catholic Irish majority. Myra Naylor is a consummate literary construction by Bowen. Myra serves to depict an exemplar of the last, self-defeating generation of Anglo-Irish society, which is caught in a supremely ironic double-bind. Myra's caste needs to perpetuate its own dynasty in order to survive. Yet it is so immersed in an insular colonial class system, admitting no dilution by external cultural elements, that it represses its young by forbidding them the only means by which they can continue (by marrying outside of Anglo-Irish society). Myra Naylor would never have allowed a Hester Morgan into her network.

A postcolonial reader of *The Last September* will compare the portrayal of Myra Naylor with Hester Morgan and acknowledge that the two women characters relate specifically to their own historico-geographical and sociocultural contexts. However, such a reader will also observe what should be stressed as the *consequences* of why Elizabeth Bowen and Jean Rhys create these elder female characters as representatives of a particular generation of colonial women. A postcolonial comparative reading of the novels shows that Myra Naylor and Hester Morgan embody the notion that women of an earlier generation in colonial society were still bound by certain social limitations and operated to maximize their status within a limited set of conditions. For instance, Myra Naylor tries to free Lois from the socioeconomic risk of marriage to an English soldier, Gerald Lesworth, who has neither land nor a title. Myra may be assisting Lois in finding a future without dependence on men, or more pointedly, she may also be trying to preserve the future of her colonial caste by making sure her young ward Lois does not marry below the salt. Bowen then constructs Lois as a figure who is younger and no longer inhibited by the necessity to maintain the plantocratic dynasty to which Myra belongs. Bowen is indicating that at the heart of Irish colonial society is a growing rift between female generations that might well contribute to the death of the Ascendancy. In *Voyage in the Dark*, likewise, Hester and Anna

Morgan are constructed to show a conflict between colonial female generations. According to a letter sent to Hester from Uncle Bo in Dominica – and read out to Anna by Hester – Anna was due to inherit her father's ailing estate, Morgan's Rest, if it were not for Hester's decision to sell the property, ingest Anna's share and move to England, devouring the farm's liquidated assets for herself (p. 52). Hester brazenly denies Bo's accusations to the pointedly silent Anna's face, yet it is clear by Hester's over-elaborate self-defence that she is guilty as charged. Hester Morgan does admittedly withdraw from the colonial estate in Dominica and help herself to Anna's rightful inheritance, but her fortunes are still bound to the length of time that her dead husband's Dominican money – and Anna's money, such as it is – can last. Anna is poorer, disenfranchised, desperate and rootless, but in many ways as a migrant drifter in London she is also freer than Hester from dependence on her father's and ancestors' legacies. Similarly to Bowen in her construction of Lois, Rhys shows that Anna encapsulates a new generation of women of planter-settler backgrounds whose destinies, however uncertain, are potentially "post" any colonial moment in that they can no longer be controlled by many of the conditions that determined the lives of their forebears.

In sum, the publication of *Wide Sargasso Sea* in the 1960s was met by such a critical response that Rhys's West Indian novels came to be written about in exhaustive detail. The concerns of critics reading Rhys's plantation novels complemented the evolution of what by the 1990s was known as postcolonial studies. Rhys's novels such as *Wide Sargasso Sea* and the much earlier *Voyage in the Dark* received so many dedicated readings as depictions of colonial society in crisis that they came to be established by Caribbeanists and postcolonialists as the template for other novels of their ilk. In writing *Voyage in the Dark* in particular, Jean Rhys very carefully crafted a novelistic investigation of how a young girl of planter-settler heritage would struggle to cope and define identity in the loss of a colonial estate to which she never quite felt she belonged. She shows her colonial class as on the verge of extinction and its descendants scrambling for selfhood, trying to come to terms with the loss of a dubious inheritance.

This chapter has drawn out a number of attributes of Elizabeth Bowen's *The Last September* that should situate it as a prime novel of postcolonial Irish literature, as it so closely fits with the critics' template of *Voyage in the Dark* as an exploration of the angst-ridden consciousness of the female youth of late-colonial planter-settler society in the declining decades of the British Empire. Rhys and Bowen exploit the possibilities of the novel form in the late 1920s and early 1930s as a mode of presenting their social studies in fictive form. *The Last September* is significantly similar to *Voyage in the Dark* in that its author critiques a ruling society in its last throes, and uses the benefit of her own experience and her literary skill to hold a microscope to – and construct, in prose narrative, the youthful experiences of – the last generations of women to try to negotiate a new sense of self amid the anxieties of colonial decline.

3.

Matriarchal Economies

C.L.R. James's *Minty Alley* and Patrick Kavanagh's *Tarry Flynn*

THIS CHAPTER FIRST EXPLORES RADICAL POSTCOLONIAL DIMENSIONS of matriarchal society and domestic economy in Trinidad, as portrayed in C.L.R. James's canonical Trinidadian novel *Minty Alley*, published in 1936. *Minty Alley* details the social education and enlightenment of a comparatively privileged, middle-class, young Afro-Trinidadian male who, over time, becomes immersed in, learns about and develops sympathy with the lives of ordinary people – particularly women – in the barrack yards of the island.

While Trinidadian society is, ostensibly, both colonial and patriarchal at the core of its early twentieth-century power structure, women in work and in the family are shown in this novel to significantly influence the societal order. Second, tthe chapter seeks, via comparison, to draw out a fresh understanding of Ireland in the 1930s, as portrayed by Patrick Kavanagh in his 1948 novel *Tarry Flynn*. *Tarry Flynn* depicts its young male protagonist in relation to a rural Irish society that, though being patriarchal at its root, is at the local level strongly founded upon the radical industry and influence of women. A standard *Bildungsroman* might conventionally portray and champion the development of a male hero. However, a comparative reading of *Minty Alley* and *Tarry Flynn* reveals that it is part of the two novels' purpose and design to illuminate that the women with whom each protagonist comes into contact are the true heroines of the novels and the societies in which they are depicted, as they modify and challenge the old patriarchal imperial order. This chapter thus seeks to re-evaluate *Tarry Flynn* alongside the canonical *Minty Alley* as a novel by a male author that sets out to reappraise the radical role of women who challenge the normative constructions of putatively male-led societies shaped by patriarchal colonial histories.

In chapter 1, I discussed the critical context within which the writers of the *Beacon* era – inclusive of C.L.R. James and Alfred Mendes – came to be seen as seminal authors of a body of Caribbean writing since the 1920s that strove to give representative autonomy to the interior world and voice of marginal West Indian men and women. Without straying into excessive repetition, it is important to recall that from the late 1960s through to the 1980s and beyond, works such as Mendes's *Black Fauns* and James's *Minty Alley* were reappraised by academics such as Rhonda Cobham and Kenneth Ramchand respectively. These novels' republications by New Beacon Books constituted the origin of their situation within a canon of West Indian literatures in English. Ramchand's 1970 book *The West Indian Novel and Its Background* was instrumental in proposing a Caribbean novelistic canon, in which the *Beacon* writers were decisively represented. *Minty Alley* was published very early in New Beacon's effort to distribute key Caribbean fiction to a new academic audience and readership engaged in the growth of Commonwealth studies and what eventually mutated into postcolonial studies. It was published in 1971 with an impressive introduction by Ramchand that offered illuminating biographical, historical and cultural backgrounds to James's early literary career in Trinidad and the foundations of the *Beacon* movement.

Minty Alley is a realist rather than modishly modernist novel, set in the 1920s and told in stylistically uncomplicated third-person narration by what appears to be a male, omniscient voice. This narrator, in the main, treats the young male hero – Haynes, a middle-class, twenty-year-old Afro-Trinidadian – as the chief focalizer of the text. However, the narrator, and indeed the author, do not construct *Minty Alley* as a straightforward, unproblematic narrative of a young man's path to social and moral individuation that harks back to older, Victorian literary precedents. Rather, the narrator and James want to show that Haynes has, up until the crisis of his mother's death, been somewhat sheltered as a child by middle-class privilege. Haynes's path to wisdom opens his eyes to the extent to which his comfort has been assisted by the sweat and toil of working women. Haynes's status at the start of the novel has already been enabled in the main by his single-parent, school headmistress mother's hard work and his having been aided by a female servant, Ella. Therefore, James allows the reader to see that the very basis of the hero's status is due to female ingenuity and endeavour. Haynes proceeds in time to adjust to the blow of his mother's death and the reality of an inherited mortgage via the self-imposition of austerity measures. Under Ella's advice, he rents out his property and continues working for a small wage in a bookshop by day. He also elects to save money by moving out of his house completely and renting cut-price local accommodation with people – mostly hard-working women in service or catering occupations – who live ordinary lives previously obscured from his view. Haynes's social education in *Minty Alley* is not simply an eye-opener to the lives of the poorer classes but also to the resilience of women who make the best of their conditions. Haynes realizes his dependence on women across all classes throughout the novel, in the mud of a backyard slum and on the Trinidadian barrack yard.

Minty Alley depicts in novelistic form the extent to which women, whether (self-)educated or working in a variety of occupations, shape and inform Trinidadian economy, family life and society. James casts the protagonist's deceased mother as a former school headmistress who in life, and in her persistent legacy of influence after death, exerts a steady and informed concern for her son's educational advancement and material security. Mrs Haynes has a shrewd understanding of economic opportunities. Through Haynes's focalized reflection, she is heard to advise Haynes to study medicine, since "Law wouldn't suit you, my child. You are your father's son."[1] Mrs Haynes lectures her son that "in these islands for a black man to be independent means that he must have money or a profession" (p. 22). Mrs Haynes's pronouncement has historical evidential support. Rhoda E. Reddock, for example, analyses census data from the early decades of the twentieth century. Reddock observes that women undertook many Trinidadian working-class occupations in a period in which there was a dearth of job opportunities for unskilled males: "[A]t this time the real ruling class was restricted to the white, landed bourgeoisie, commercial bourgeoisie and colonial bureaucracy. For blacks, coloured and Indians the only possibility for social mobility was to become part of the middle strata of professionals (doctors, lawyers), civil servants or teachers."[2]

Mrs Haynes's own rare occupation as a school headmistress points to her radical achievement in the historical contexts of women and labour in Trinidad, particularly in a period before widespread female entry into higher education and training into higher-earning professions such as law and medicine. Mrs Haynes is a groundbreaking, educated, decolonizing force who uses her intellect to aid her son in resisting the limitations of class and colour barriers to success in the colonial island. Tellingly, Mrs Haynes's ambition for her son is not only realistic, pertinent and instructive as to the pressures facing Afro-Trinidadian males as they attempt to secure a profession. It is also a vicarious expression of a wish for employment opportunities for herself, restricted in her historical period due to her sex. Matriarchal influence in *Minty Alley* is a way of asserting decolonizing female power by proxy: the sons of strong Trinidadian women will attain middle-class occupations and supplant the British colonial masters.

Mrs Haynes, in spite of her remarkable achievements and efforts, was constrained in her lifetime by a patriarchal economic system and so sought to escape her plight via her son's success. This proposition can be supported by analysing the limited wages and social flexibility of women within what was supposedly the most fluid social strata for Afro-Trinidadians in the early decades of the twentieth century. In the novel, Mrs Haynes's departed husband is said to have "suffered" by not securing a solvent occupation, while at least Mrs Haynes's position had afforded her the ability to purchase "the house on a stiff mortgage" (p. 22). It is likely that Mr Haynes was not a member of the middle strata of occupations and that the Haynes household appeared at least on the surface to invert a nucleated patriarchal familial form in favour of a matriarchal economic breadwinning model. However, Mrs Haynes's own wages were not substantial. For, while Rhoda E. Reddock claims that "[t]he teaching profession was by far the most important means of social mobility for the blacks and coloureds", she adds that teachers – particularly females in the profession – nonetheless "worked for low wages and under difficult conditions".[3] Women – even head teachers – earned somewhat less than their male counterparts: whereas in 1918, a first-class, certified Trinidadian male head teacher might earn £85–£200 per annum, his female equivalent would only earn £75–£160.[4] Mrs Haynes, therefore, had no real chance to train for another middle-strata occupation and earn more money since, as Reddock indicates, "Women doctors and lawyers did not emerge until the 1930s. For example, not until January 1932 was the first barrister, Gladys Ramsaran, admitted to practice law in the country. . . . Predictably, most girls lost in the competition for higher education against their brothers, and the first girls' university scholarship was not awarded until 1947."[5]

After the Education Code of 1935, while married and widowed Afro-Caribbean women such as Mrs Haynes would have been able to continue working in the teaching profession, many unmarried women found themselves out of employment due to governmental attempts to enforce greater, patriarchalist sexual divisions of labour through a programme of "housewifization" that restricted work for single women. Reddock notes that ironically, although this move made employment of women far more selective, it also "had the advantage of greatly raising the social status of those involved".[6] If the novel had been set after 1935 and seen a rise in his mother's status and salary, one might conclude from the corroborating context of Reddock's information that – if the circumstances in the novel were indeed historically accurate – the fictive Haynes's finances would not have been so precarious and his move to Minty Alley might not have been necessary. Therefore, *Minty Alley* contains an important historical context regarding the setting of Mrs Haynes's socio-economic status as a schoolmistress, prior to improvements in pay for married members of the teaching profession in late-colonial Trinidad. Mrs Haynes achieves much in her time, yet she is of her time, and thus she hopes instead for her son to carry the torch of her ambition.

Although Haynes's point of view is the main perspective narrated in the novel, there is evidence, in one crucial passage at the start, of Mrs Haynes competing to take control of the narrative voice. This can be observed in the dialogic nature of the passage where Haynes is recollecting how his mother would have planned his future for him, had she lived (p. 22). One can perceive consonance between three identifiable narrative levels leading clearly to Mrs Haynes's authoritative voice.

First, one notes the omniscient narrator's reportage: what one might call the outermost, most immediately identifiable layer of narrative discourse "telling" actions and happenings in the story. Second, reading more closely, one can observe Haynes's free indirect thought remembering his mother's words. This is the next, inner layer of discourse, which is free in that that it recounts remembered action without the diegetic "He thought" to indicate it as reportage, and indirect in that the thought is not presented directly as monologue but via a mediating narrative voice. In the narratological terminology of Dorrit Cohn explained in chapter 1, this type of focalization is called consonant psycho-narration in that it reproduces the speech patterns of the focalizer's thought patterns while also rewording them in the overall narrating context of telling about a past event.

Thirdly, we encounter Mrs Haynes's voice. Although Haynes is the focalizer in this passage, he is actually remembering Mrs Haynes's spoken dialogue, which itself is recollected in free indirect speech. So, the narrative discourse takes on a Russian-doll effect with omniscient narration, opening up to focalization, finally arriving at Mrs Haynes's free indirect speech. The question of which voice has authority is always going to be problematic due to the very fact that the passage's language is so internally dialogic. However, this matter is decided by Mrs Haynes's choice of grammar and her application of double verb constructions, which suggest her intended coercion or control over Haynes's destiny or narrative path. For example, Haynes is recollecting his mother's stipulations regarding the course of his adult life (had Mrs Haynes lived long enough to dictate her son's career): "Haynes was to work in the island for a year or two and then, when the mortgage had been paid off, she would send him abroad and keep him there. Medicine it was to be" (pp. 22–23). One should note the double verb constructions in this passage. When spoken in their original spatio-temporal context as direct speech, Mrs Haynes's statement to her son, "You are to work in the island", is a verb + verb formulation. The combination of the second-person present-tense form of the verb "to be", with the infinitive of another verb "to work", implies an imperative or the determination of a pronouncement: "You must/shall work." The narrative discourse reframes this statement as indirect speech via the substitution of the past-tense third-person of the verb "to be". Then follows the phrase "Medicine it was to be", a doubling of two forms of the verb "to be" (the latter being the infinitive). This was likely originally spoken in Mrs Haynes's direct speech as "Medicine it is to be" (suggesting the future-tense, imperative "Medicine it shall be"). Mrs Haynes's voice seizes the narrative flow of the text at this moment.

It is not just the fictive corollary of James's own mother whom the author seeks to champion in *Minty Alley* as one of the truly heroic female actants changing late-colonial society. A living, active working-class woman who plays a key role in Haynes's life makes an appearance in the opening chapter of *Minty Alley*. This woman is Ella, former servant to Haynes's dead mother and now servant to Haynes. Servant she may be, yet – while "[w]herever she was, whatever she was doing, she seemed to have one ear open in case Haynes called" – Ella soon makes it clear in the course of the novel that she does not adhere exclusively to patriarchal command, but rather honours the wishes of a dead matriarch (p. 19). She defers not to Haynes but to "the influence of his dead mother" when she refuses his invitation to sit down for a long talk over his plan to save money by letting half his house and living in the remainder. Through focalization, even Haynes's free indirect thought is represented as evaluating that "[t]he influence of his dead mother still dominated the house. She was a perfect mistress, but never would she have asked Ella to sit down. And Ella remained standing" (p. 19).

Haynes is thus under no developed illusions as to his total patriarchal usurpation of the home's historic gynocracy. Even when Haynes attempts to assert command over his inherited house's economy by suggesting that he could save money if he should "live in half the house and let the other half", Ella quickly checks his speculations. Ella proves to be another character in *Minty Alley* who reveals that women in colonial Trinidad use their wit to survive and even to maintain some surprising extent of control in an ostensibly male middle-class world. She indexes her doubt over, and even dismissal of, Haynes's economizing scheme through the slight but decisively authoritative, wordless gestural index of turning "her head sideways" (p. 19). She also displays business acumen in coordinating, with executive skill, an alternative plan to find Haynes lodgings that might benefit local urban businesses, from boarding houses to auctioneers and their repair employees. Where Haynes believes he has given his financial situation some thought, Ella demonstrates in her dialogue that she has thought far harder, more intensively and practically. Ella reveals her own quasi-matriarchal intention to benefit other businesses in her community, while acting *in loco parentis* for Haynes by remaining his cook:

> "If you don't want to board and lodge and you want me to go on seeing after things, sir, get a room, sir, a large room. It will cost you about four or five dollars. All I will want is a place to cook. You can take in your own things from here, sir. We can sell the piano and the furniture and use the money to repair the kitchen and the fence and help to pay some of the mortgage. I was talking to the man from Price & Co., sir. They will auction the things, sir, and take on the repairs and give you the balance. You can leave that to me, sir. They wouldn't cheat me, sir."
>
> "God, I wish I were rid of all this bother." He put his elbows on the table and

rested his face on his hands.
"Don't let it trouble you, sir. You need a change, sir. You should move from this place." (p. 20)

Ella demonstrates the true extent of her attempt as a Trinidadian woman in a service occupation to transcend the limitations of her socioeconomic status, and to influence middle-class male society to her own benefit, when she expresses consternation over the fact that her plans for Haynes begin to go awry. Provisionally, Ella suggests that Haynes take a vacant room "in a house in Charles Street, [with] Mr. Newstead, the solicitor, and his wife" (p. 21). Interestingly, while Ella is keen to orchestrate Haynes's move to benefit herself and local businesses in the bargain, she wishes for him to remain socially within his middle-class milieu. Her plans, however, are problematized when Haynes prefers her second, more reserved suggestion to try Mrs Rouse's lodgings at Minty Alley, which she tries to distract Haynes from considering by adding a litany of caveats such as, "It's not nice, sir", or "They are ordinary people, sir" and "Not your class of people" (p. 21). Ella's concerns might not be the expression of regard for Haynes's well-being and social standing that they seem. They can also infer unspoken fears and even narrative prolepsis regarding Minty Alley's landlady Mrs Rouse's later attempts to usurp Ella's position as Haynes's cook. (These are suspicions that one of Minty Alley's lodgers, Miss Atwell, corroborates to Haynes in chapter 6 of the novel, when she advises him how Ma Rouse and Nurse Jackson plan to charm and then rob him.) Ella is looking after Haynes's interests, but of course she also wishes to safeguard her own welfare in a competitive market where Mrs Rouse, a veteran matriarchal petty-trader, is also skilled at the arts of persuading customers to patronize her services.

Ella signifies a responsible, informed, erudite and skilful female personal-services employee who operates to serve the lower-middle-strata, Afro-Caribbean female Mrs Haynes – and, on her death, her son. Ella would be classed as a "general servant" since she would be performing many tasks ordinarily designated to a range of between five and seven servants occupied in a more affluent middle- or upper-middle-strata household. She would be expected to perform tasks such as waiting tables, cooking and attending to laundry, though not to the specialized degree of domestic servants in a large house.[7] Her position also provides an index to the novel's historical context: she must be astute in fending off competition from petty-traders and boarding-house keepers such as Mrs Rouse, since the wages of domestic workers, both male and female, were comparatively small and decidedly precarious. As Rhoda E. Reddock observes,

> In spite of their recognized presence, domestic servants were not accepted as "real workers" for the purposes of legislation. Throughout the period [1891–1931], a gradual reduction in the recognition of domestic service as a legitimate occupation can be discerned. The 1920 Wages Committee Report made no mention of domestic servants and neither did the 1935 Wages Advisory Board consider them in their calculation of a minimum wage. After 1931 the number of women domestics decreased steadily, possibly as some of the services . . . were taken over by commercial establishments.[8]

When Ella's sickness and absence from town tempts Haynes to reconsider boarding with Mrs Rouse, at twenty dollars a month (so as to supply his financially struggling landlady with some "'mateeral' assistance", p. 155), Ella makes a fast recovery. Ella once again demonstrates her tenacious networking skills across the urban working classes regarding work opportunities or competition, and she promptly returns to town, making a last-ditch attempt to secure Haynes's patronage by warning him of his new landlady's deceit: "Goodbye, sir. I sorry the day I ever take you to No. 2, sir. I know from the first that they was goin' to try and get you away from me, sir. That Mrs. Rouse! She don't look it, but she is as deep a trickster as the rest, sir. Beware o' them people, sir" (p. 157).

"Ma" Rouse constitutes a prime signifier of an urban, barrack-alley matriarchal businesswoman who manages a petty-trading business in urban Trinidad in the early twentieth century. In *Minty Alley*, it is around Ma Rouse's female-headed petty-trading business (where cakes are produced in the home kitchen and then sold to small, local vendors, such as the nearby Gomes) that, together with lodging money, much of the economy of the novel's barrack yard is made.

Mrs Rouse employs casual labour such as Aucher in between his stints at His Majesty's Pleasure: Haynes's first focalized evaluation of Aucher is that "He seemed rather dirty to be making cakes" (p. 29). Yet *Minty Alley* also provides a discourse illustrating how such businesses, while marginal, still show a matriarchal centre and motivated female-run locus of discipline (however much they might be statistically "unrecorded" or how casual their labour might be). For example, while this cake-selling enterprise might seem to dispense with formalities such as employee code of dress, Mrs Rouse plays very much an executive role in overseeing Aucher's work that, in its intensive attention to productivity and detail, points to her strict authority over her staff:

> First there was Mrs. Rouse, who gave [Haynes] a fine good morning, but had no time for anything else. She concentrated on the contents of two or three pots on the fire, but at intervals turned to a table. . . . She called frequently to one Aucher, a tall, heavily-built, quiet-looking youth of about twenty – dressed in a patched and dirty pair of blue trousers and an old jacket without shirt or merino. He seemed rather dirty to be making cakes. He put large sheets of tin covered with cakes into the stove and took them out for Mrs. Rouse to see if they were baked enough, usually at the dictation of Mrs. Rouse, who from her frequent admonitions and exhortations to those around her was clearly the officer commanding. (p. 29)

Mrs Rouse's influence over Aucher seems to transcend professional superiority, for the latter, though "by fits and starts a well-known thief, of bicycles, goats, clothes, cigarettes, [or] anything he could put his hand on", respects his semi-regular employer sincerely enough never to steal from her or any of the other employees at No. 2 Minty Alley (pp. 67–68). Within Aucher's personal life, Ma Rouse therefore exerts a matriarch's stabilizing, nurturing command over his more wayward impulses and shows social power beyond the remit of her business skills and discipline.

In chapter 18, Mrs Rouse reveals in conversation with Haynes – who is progressively taken into her confidence – that her cake-selling career began following the collapse of her first marriage. While she had cooked in her family home – notably also female-headed – prior to her wedding, she had never considered selling cakes until necessity precipitated her new endeavour:

> I grew up as a young lady in my mother's house, Mr. Haynes. . . . I didn't used to work. I used to make cakes and I was a good hand at it. But that was for my home, Mr. Haynes, and for my friends. It was not to sell.
>
> After I was married eighteen months, my husband start to be unfaithful to me. . . . I leave him and went home. I didn't ask him for no support, Mr. Haynes, and he and the woman leave and go to America. I stay at home for two or three years and then I started to make cakes and bread and send out. (p. 123)

However, what might seem here to be Mrs Rouse's radical potentiality as a matriarchal businesswoman finding self-sufficiency in starting her own cake-selling business is tragically compromised by her trade's origin from her liaison with a second, ill-chosen male. Historically, Mrs Rouse represents a stage in urban Trinidadian women's self-sufficient labour – prior to the emergence of more independent, educated young women such as her niece Maisie – which constitutes part of the hardest-working section of the population but is still to an extent constrained by dealings with the whims of less industrious men.

Mrs Rouse's realization of strength as a female petty-trader and lodging-house keeper is ultimately deprived by her emotional dependence upon the parasitical and philandering Benoit, with whom she had maintained a relationship for nearly two decades ("Seventeen years we been together, he never went to look for work", p. 85) until he left her for their tenant, Nurse Jackson. Doubtless through his manipulative guile and amorous charm, Benoit had convinced Mrs Rouse to become both his romantic and professional partner. He consolidated his control over time on the strength of her inheritance of family property that enabled the founding of the business at an unfortunate moment in the housing market, on the outbreak of the Great War, when "[p]rices went up" (p. 124). Benoit's borrowing, in the early days of their association, from the hard-working Mrs Rouse had contributed to the collapse of their first "restaurant-parlour" and the resultant opening of a smaller "cake-business" (p. 125). Financial difficulties did not encourage Benoit to adopt a frugal lifestyle but rather, "He eat the best drink the best, and whenever he was going out, five, ten, fifteen dollars in his pocket" (p. 125).

When contrasted with her niece Maisie, Mrs Rouse can be seen historically as a comparatively uneducated Trinidadian urban female in the early twentieth century. In spite of her potential as a matriarchal businesswoman surviving in the barrack-alley slums of a Trinidadian town, she is still thwarted to a degree by being financially tied to a man who, in spite of his indolence and lack of moral right to the business, owns the house jointly in name.

The house at Minty Alley had been mortgaged "for six hundred dollars at twelve per cent", and Mrs Rouse and Benoit were expected, irrespective of the difficulty of terms, to "pay forty-three dollars a quarter – eighteen dollars interest and twenty-five dollars on the principal" (p. 118). While Mrs Rouse had been working to pay off this mortgage, Benoit saw to "spend nearly every cent"

(p. 119). Crown Colony law regarding women's property rights was roughly concordant with the Married Women's Property Acts of 1882 and 1893, which granted women freedoms regarding autonomy of ownership of inherited wealth. Mrs Rouse thus had no legal need to submit partial ownership of her property to her absent husband or to Benoit and was legally placed to protect her interests without deference to a male partner.

Ma Rouse was without the necessary education or existing women's support framework to understand or maintain strength of female independence from older, patriarchal practices in family law. Ma, meeting Benoit as a young woman in the 1910s, did not inhabit a historical period where the full legal benefits of being a sole female homeowner, protected from the predatory machinations of males such as Benoit, would be a common factor of an organized, emancipatory working-class women's discourse of rights. Even when the women's movement known as the Coterie of Social Workers was founded in 1921, it involved and catered mainly to women from the middle strata rather than working-class women. By the 1930s it preoccupied itself with representing middle-class, educated and married Afro-Trinidadian women who, because of "housewifization" programmes and attempts to legislate greater sexual division of labour, found themselves unable to find work in teaching and the civil service and forced into occupations such as domestic service. The prerogative of the Coterie was to prevent downward socioeconomic mobility among the female bourgeoisie rather than focus on representing or advising the rights of the long-term female working classes.

A reader of *Minty Alley* will take this social and historical contextual information into account and regard James's depiction of Ma Rouse as a highly accurate and astute representation of older Trinidadian women in the 1920s and 1930s. It is somewhat unusual that a male author such as C.L.R. James should have such a prescient and sensitive insight into questions of women's labour, domestic freedoms and proprietary rights, years before such topics were documented by a feminist social scientist such as Reddock. Yet one should take into account the committed will of *Beacon*-era writers such as Alfred Mendes and C.L.R. James to provide such a socio-realist novelistic depiction of Trinidadian life that presents a previously unrepresented society. It is likely that James, similar to Mendes, has a socially prescriptive intention to enlighten his audience as to just how much society depends on the toil of people in menial occupations. James, like Mendes in his careful examination of this hidden world of the barrack yard, finds that the most resourceful and hard-working of the barrack-yard people are women. Women are thus accordingly the cornerstone of the fictive society of *Minty Alley*.

A reader will also examine the construction of the character of Maisie in relation to James's portrayal of her as a relatively educated younger woman who refuses to limit her potentiality to the socioeconomic confines of the island. James conveys in *Minty Alley* the proposition that, up until the time of the presented action of his story, it sufficed for a previous generation of women – embodied in the novel by Ma Rouse – to stay in Trinidad and forge a living by working in urban domestic or service occupations. Now, James shows, a younger generation of women has been buoyed by the benefits of schooling. These women experience the necessary immersion in the possibilities of another life abroad, and they express the will to migrate where their socioeconomic circumstances might be significantly ameliorated. For example, Maisie differs from her aunt in that she has had experience of a private school education. Maisie confides in Haynes, during a late-night conversation in chapter 8, that due to the encouragement of Nurse Jackson she was able to attend a fee-paying school at the sum of "five shillings a month", regardless of Benoit's chauvinistic assertion that "what women want to get on in the world, they born with it" (p. 60). Reddock states, "By the beginning of the 20th century, only one girls' secondary school existed, the St. Joseph's Convent started in 1836"; yet by 1920, "49 girls were enrolled" at a new, fee-paying establishment aimed at "a 'higher class' for girls": the Tranquillity Government Practising School.[9] During the 1920s, more girls' schools opened, all of them fee-paying. Given that prior to 1947, according to Reddock, "no scholarships were available for girls" and, thus, "virtually no working-class or peasant girl had any opportunity to obtain secondary education", Maisie's access to education is uncommon.[10] Still, Maisie's education speaks of a clear ambition towards social mobility in the forgotten, barrack-yard slums of the towns. Nurse Jackson well understands this (herself elevated in status, through education, from alleged prostitute to nurse).

C.L.R. James here again shows an astuteness that precedes the feminist social science of Reddock by decades, as he observes not only the influence of Maisie's schooling on her upbringing but also Maisie's utilization of her education to radical effect. In *Minty Alley*, the education that Maisie has briefly received is colonial. Maisie would have been instructed in some of the ideological precepts of British education, which prior to the growth of girls' schools on the island of Trinidad operated to create a largely male administrative and professional sector in mimicry of the colonial model – and which, even for girls' schools, still abided by its colonial civilizing aims. Maisie has had a taste of bourgeois middle-class life, if not its luxuries, and can no longer accept her marginalization in a male-orientated Trinidadian island society. Maisie has not become brainwashed by British colonial bourgeois values. Instead, she uses her education to self-decolonizing and emancipatory effect; she is aware of a hope of better opportunities outside of the barrack yard.

In the novel, James depicts Benoit's chauvinistic assertion that women's education "is a waste of money" as a personification of typical male resistance to younger female attempts at self-improvement: James thus portrays the barrack yard as a grounds of ideological, gender and generational contention. Maisie's will towards self-advancement is so unprecedented that Benoit scoffs at it. Benoit's viewpoint regarding female education is not merely the reductive opinion of an uneducated, disenfranchised and defensive male. Rather, James depicts Benoit with such observational precision that, contextually, one can see that Benoit's androcentric opinions are similar to those of the (male) leaders of the educational profession in the early twentieth century. The Teachers' Association, in Trinidad, published a periodical called the *Teachers' Journal* in which the efficiency and viability of high-fee-charging girls' schools were debated. The necessity for secondary-level education for women was considered by the writer of one unsigned journal article ("The High School") to be negligible, since "[women] will be matrons and housekeepers and will need no Latin, French or Mathematics" come the end of their studies.[11] Whether or not James was specifically acquainted with the more misogynistic musings of the *Teachers' Journal*, James certainly caught the mood of a more unreconstructed, early twentieth-century Trinidadian male society in the character of Benoit. James employs Maisie as an agent of profound change in women's self-perception and self-determination in the Caribbean of the 1920s and 1930s, working against the dominant mindset of the Benoits of her world.

Under patriarchalist, Crown Colony rule there were no university scholarships available to women; in spite of Maisie's education and tantalizing glimpse at social mobility within a more bourgeois, fee-paying school system, she seems destined to work for Mrs Rouse. Maisie asserts her superiority to her seemingly inevitable class position by insulting the hard-working Philomel, a young

Indo-Trinidadian girl who embodies the industriousness of an indentured tradition of labour, though now transplanted in the early twentieth century from a rural to an urban sphere of general domestic service. Maisie steals Mrs Rouse's beef and tries to blame the unfortunate Philomel. Maisie then expresses dismay that Mrs Rouse would believe in Philomel's innocence rather than hers, in such a way that not only expresses a notion of racial, hierarchical superiority over "the coolie" but also, tellingly, a belief in social superiority over "the servant" merely on account of her familial ties with Mrs Rouse ("I am Mrs. Rouse's niece. Why is she always taking up for the coolie?", p. 104). In a matriarchal business where Ma Rouse oversees and nurtures the well-being and trust, and even trustworthiness, of employees such as the small-time criminal Aucher, Maisie clearly disregards the transactional nature of "family" ties, whether biological or professional, in the domestic economy of No. 2 Minty Alley. From a feministic perspective (and James shows feminist traits in his conscientious aptitude for convincingly rendering the lives of Trinidadian women in *Minty Alley*), Maisie's education facilitates her independent, feministic disapproval of Mrs Rouse's dependence on the predatory Benoit and allows her to distance herself critically from the reliance on unreliable men – romanticized as love – that is typical in her barrack yard. James is, in sum, arguing that, for all its complexities and faults, a bourgeois colonial education is ultimately of some significant social good for Trinidadian women as it at least allows women such as Maisie to make choices regarding their own destiny. With an education, young Trinidadian women are empowered in being able to understand opportunities beyond the slum, which were not available to uneducated women of previous eras. Maisie can see the limitations placed upon her aunt. Mrs Rouse may indeed be a matriarch in that she runs her business like a family with herself at the head. Mrs Rouse even blurs sexual divisions in labour in being the ostensible breadwinner of a female-headed business. However, what Maisie knows is that Mrs Rouse's wealth is dissipated by Benoit, who has philandered and absconded, leaving Mrs Rouse heartbroken and still codependent on Benoit. Maisie refuses to be subservient to a man, and she derides the thought of being as dependent on a male as her aunt is on Benoit ("I tell you if I was living with a man and he wanted to go he could go . . . I would have sent Benoit packing long ago", p. 92).

Although Miss Atwell dismisses Maisie's spirited independence as the mark of impetuous youth ("You is young, child . . . and love, a woman's true love, have not touch your heart", p. 92), Maisie admonishes her for not knowing the full story behind the break-up of Mrs Rouse and Benoit. Maisie demonstrates a full understanding of the vicissitudes of social interaction and turmoil in her barrack-yard environment. Not only is Maisie fully involved in its comings and goings (as opposed to Miss Atwell, who is in self-maintained quarantine against bailiffs much of the time), but also, and more importantly, Maisie's education – and her immersion in the more socially fluid class of educated, fee-paying girls – has allowed her the necessary distance to perceive her barrack-yard world objectively for its limitations and its possible exit routes.

Due to the indulgence of Nurse Jackson, Maisie has savoured the consumerist glamour of "a dress . . . and a pair of shoes and so on" (p. 60); these niceties are a world away from Aucher's makeshift, shabby work outfit of "a patched and dirty pair of blue trousers and an old jacket without shirt or merino" (p. 29). It is important to note Maisie's dismissive, distancing use of the definite article, rather than the demonstrative adjective "this", when she says "I feel to run away from the place" (p. 60). Psychologically, Maisie imagines herself detached from the confined space and the social world of the barrack yard, as if she is not really there but considering it as an abstract proposition.

Haynes might ostensibly be the main character of a *Bildungsroman* where a middle-class male awakens to a greater sense of social consciousness in discovering the role that working-class women play in keeping him comfortable. Yet, in some respects, Maisie can be seen as the true, anti-colonial, feminist protagonist of James's novel. Irrespective of her class snobbery, her Anansi-type trickstering, quickness to slander all opposition and mischievous mendacity, it is Maisie who, with a mix of street smartness, education and guile, most significantly escapes the barrack yard at the end of the novel (although the middle-class Haynes had been groomed by his mother for emigration to England). Maisie represents what can be seen through reference to Reddock as a historical context of evidence for a further stage of decolonizing women's experience beyond the generation of her aunt Mrs Rouse, in that she transcends the parameters of female-headed economy and kinship structures in colonial Trinidad by embracing the chance of economic migration from the island.

Minty Alley is significant for gendered readings of postcolonial fiction, as it is a late-colonial fictive representation of the role of women in countering the prevalent structures of patriarchal colonial society. White and middle-class

Afro-Trinidadian males may constitute the visible governing order on the island, but women in domestic occupations, hidden in the barrack yards and inner urban areas, produce much of the work and maintain much of the (matriarchal) social fabric of society upon which the comforts of privileged males often depend. C.L.R. James's novel, admittedly, has much of the naturalism of a late-nineteenth-century novel such as Zola's *Germinal*, in that it experiments with taking a male protagonist of a certain background and with recognizable traits and dropping him into a volatile social environment to see what will come about as a result. Yet James also manages to suggest that his protagonist Haynes is often more a passive observer of a social world that is slowly revealed to him than he is an active agent in his own destiny. It is women, in the hidden world of the Trinidadian slum, who are most active in making the most of, and even seeking to transcend, the degrading and impoverished conditions that male-led British colonial power structures have over centuries put upon them. These women destabilize conventional nuclear familial structures and adapt the parameters of colonial economy in key decades of decolonization.

Now I turn my attention to Kavanagh's *Tarry Flynn*, considering the postcolonial dimensions of its thematic confluences with *Minty Alley*'s representations of women. Patrick Kavanagh resembles C.L.R. James with regard to his personal biography and the influence of strong female figures in his life. Both writers were born in a turn-of-century period when their native islands were under British rule. Unlike James's mother, Kavanagh's mother, Bridget, was not very literate and did not place stock in advancement through education. She was a product of a small, rural Monaghan farming community in which reading and writing were considered time-wasting activities that had no evident benefit to the family farm. Bridget's farming classes sought largely to improve upon the legacy of post-Famine poverty through hard family farming labour and careful farming economics. According to Antoinette Quinn, Kavanagh's principal biographer and scholar, Kavanagh's mother was an astute farming businesswoman of "shrewd, calculating intelligence".[12] The Kavanagh family's improving finances demonstrated how Bridget Kavanagh's industry aided the household in acquiring land as well as shoemaking equipment. In an ostensibly patriarchal society, and even within a patriarchal and familistic farming economy created largely under British economic colonialism, Bridget in Ireland – like C.L.R. James's mother, Ida James, in Trinidad – created a real-life model of a woman making the most of the restrictions on her economic and gender definition and playing an active role in ameliorating her familial life. James's and Kavanagh's novels thus owe a great deal to their own family backgrounds in late-colonial islands; they were in deeply informed positions to adapt the sociocultural lessons of their lives into the fictive material that they present in their novels.

Tarry Flynn tells the story of a matriarchal family in the fictive village of Dargan in County Cavan. The ostensible protagonist is a twenty-seven-year-old widow farmer's son and would-be poet who dreams of beautiful, unapproachable young women of the district while attending to the day-to-day chores of life on the fields. The novel on the surface seems to follow Tarry's rite of artistic passage towards some form of creative transcendence or independence from the mundanity of his life. However, the novel subtly provides a social critique on gender norms in rural Ireland and shows how his mother and sisters are much more engaged, canny and practical than Tarry in their dealings with rural patriarchy, parochialism and agricultural market practices. *Tarry Flynn*'s first chapter is particularly illustrative of the gender politics and the gendered socioeconomics of a country that still, post-independence, works according to a late-colonial British agricultural model. It also encapsulates how matriarchal farming operated in early twentieth-century Ireland and how it will be presented by Kavanagh throughout the course of the novel. It establishes Mrs Flynn as a fictive exemplar of a business-minded, actively controlling elderly widow matriarch. Mrs Flynn is deferential neither to political or religious patriarchy in parochial Ireland. If patriarchy is the legacy of two empires, founded in London and Rome, then Mrs Flynn challenges these imperial norms. The main character is the titular hero, but the true protagonist of the action in the first chapter is Mrs Flynn. Kavanagh devises her in much the same way as James does Ma Rouse. In a late-colonial or residual-colonial economy, one might expect a young adult male to capitalize on the advantages of his gender and relative social freedoms in a colonial man's world. Instead, according to Kavanagh's and James's novels, it is women who radically determine the lives of young men around them and successfully manipulate the domestic and economic structures of their local society.

Mrs Flynn's matriarchal role as head of a small labour unit, and her influence in the life of the novel's male protagonist, show a number of clear similarities with those of Ella, Mrs Haynes and Ma Rouse in *Minty Alley*. These likenesses point to confluences between the texts' representations of the effect of colonial economic arrangements upon female-headed families and women's labour. Although a subaltern in gender and colonial terms, the farming widow Mrs Flynn administrates for her son Tarry – similarly to Ella administrating Haynes's personal effects, lodgings and the finer points of the sale of his chattels, or the urban boss Ma Rouse dictating the standards of work in her cake-making kitchen, in *Minty Alley*. Moreover, Mrs Flynn speaks with authority over the text's male protagonist, seizing the narrative of *Tarry Flynn*'s opening chapter to the point that she almost usurps Tarry's supposed protagonistic role for herself, centralizing her lived experience and interior world as the focalized and spoken voice of much of the chapter. The close reading of *Tarry Flynn* that follows bears in mind these parallels with *Minty Alley*.

For the purposes of providing a detailed and substantial close reading of gender politics at play in the novel, I shall concentrate specifically on the opening chapter of *Tarry Flynn* with some reference to later chapters. It is in the first pages of *Tarry Flynn* that the reader can see immediately how Kavanagh fictionalizes matriarchal society in what is still a residue of late-colonial economy, in parallel with *Minty Alley*. The first chapter positions the text spatio-temporally and historically in the Flynn farmhouse on the early morning of the Christian feast of Corpus Christi, 6 June 1935. It is worthwhile noting that, contextually, little has changed since independence in the familistic farming economy of Ireland. Pre-independence promises of economic reconstruction and industrialization have not been kept, and Ireland's economy has remained agricultural.[13] In many respects, then, the lived ideology of Ireland in the 1930s is as it was in the colonial era. Therefore, the economics of post-independence Ireland are comparable with late-colonial Ireland and thus, by extension, with late-colonial Trinidad in being a society where women make the best in an economy devised under British rule.

Although Tarry Flynn is the novel's putative protagonist, the novel's opening exchanges of dialogue and aspects of diegesis – including examples of focalization not into Tarry but rather his mother's consciousness – emphasize the agency and dominance of the matriarch in the construction of any social realist discourse representing the composition of domestic Irish rural life. Tarry exclaims, "Where the devil did I put me cap? Did any of you see me cap?"[14] His epistrophic, rhetorical repetition of the noun "cap" clangs at the climax of both questions in his opening speech. It suggests that he is overreaching in appearing anxious to locate his headwear prior to his supposedly imminent departure for first Sunday service. He immediately characterizes himself through his dialogue as a potentially poetic lover of words and orchestrations of sound, rather than wordless, masculine action in searching busily for the cap. Tarry is easily distracted in his ostensible quest by the discovery of "an old school book that lay in the dust" atop a dresser, turning him away from single-minded and responsible commitment to finding his cap and departing with alacrity to first mass at Dargan as male representative of the Flynn family (p. 5). Tarry here mirrors the bookish Haynes in *Minty Alley*, whose knowledge of housekeeping and the organizational particularities of maintaining domestic economy is vastly less practised than that of his astute servant Ella. Tarry, like Haynes, for all his posturing, is quite helpless without a woman to organize him.

Flynn's mother assumes the role of strict disciplinarian, chastising Tarry for his wayward daydreaming and lack of attention to his immediate responsibilities. In the opening pages of the novel, Mrs Flynn demonstrates that she inverts and assumes the senior-male role of figurehead within the archetypal peasant-agrarian family unit. She shows full charge of maintaining the running of the farm, right down to micromanaging her son's prioritization of tasks to perform in the course of the day, in a manner that corresponds with *Minty Alley* and Ella's skilled ability to oversee the minutiae of Haynes's plan to let his house and rent at Ma Rouse's boarding house.

Mrs Flynn dictates how her son is to be perceived in the social sphere of Sunday mass as the Flynn's representative at first service. (She remarks critically that even his sister Aggie has left for mass before him, implying to Tarry his lack of manhood in allowing his perceived role in the patriarchal social realm of the parish to be usurped by a female.) Mrs Flynn is concerned at how Tarry, and by extension the Flynn family, is seen by the parish priest and their peers. In her view, Tarry must maintain status by being seen to be early and present at church, rather than incongruously late in view of fellow parishioners – even if, with marked irony, his presence is only ensured by matriarchal domestic force. This parallels Mrs Haynes's insistence to her son that he must "have money or a profession" in order to maintain (and implicitly therefore be seen to have) status in his community (p. 22).

Mrs Flynn's rejoinder to her son is a paragraph-long demonstration of spoken monologue. Her speech here characterizes her by revealing not only her psychological domination over Tarry but also her peripheral vision and hyperawareness of the exigencies of running a farmhouse through fear of the repercussions of any demonstration of negligence. She cajoles Tarry for leaving his search for the cap until so soon prior to departure for mass and at "such an hour of the morning" (p. 5). She implies in her exasperated plea ("Are you going to go to mass at all or do you mean to be home with them atself?", p. 5) that Tarry is so trapped by the damning vice of procrastination that he would bring shame upon the family by being publicly conspicuous to "them", the parish (colloquially "atself", or themselves demonstrably present at mass). Mrs Flynn's fear of the destructive effects of Tarry's negligence mirrors Mrs Haynes's fear that her son will fail to distinguish himself in a society where few opportunities present themselves to males without formal education or the will towards hard work.

Mrs Flynn's juxtaposition of an image of Tarry at home while the rest of the parish is itself at mass (and thus capable of forming negative impressions regarding Tarry's conspicuous absence) implies her opinion that being late for mass gives the appearance of failing to be able to adhere to one imperative of a small farming economy – that is, being an early riser. Even if Mrs Flynn is in reality the matriarch of the farming business, her son must be seen to be, at least in the patriarchal social sphere of the village church, its responsible male figurehead. Mrs Flynn's matriarchal concern for her son, and her fears that his indolence might prove his undoing, parallel the late Mrs Haynes's fears for her own boy (cf. *Minty Alley*, p. 22).

Mrs Flynn reinforces her dismay at Tarry's absent-mindedness in a manner reversing androcentric stereotypes of the rational male adult condemning a female child's irrational, vague Otherness. She admonishes her son's dreamy preoccupation with irrelevant concerns atop the dresser, his unmanly lack of dexterity and lumbering awkwardness, and his lack of awareness of the chickens running around the farmhouse interior ("Looking on top of the dresser! Mind you don't put the big awkward hooves on one of them chickens that's under you", p. 5).

When Tarry vainly attempts to reassert his power role and question his mother's judgement in allowing the fowl to run free in the homestead ("A bloody fine place to have them", p. 5), Mrs Flynn counters her son to devastating effect. She reminds him of his economic impotence as a financially dependent, socially gender-defined widow farmer's son who for as long as Mrs Flynn lives has no property in a rural economy where the privilege of proprietorship rests with the matriarch: of the chickens, Mrs Flynn indicates to her son, "They'll make more money than you anyway" (p. 5).

Tarry's mother cautions her son by illustrating his likeness to his errant uncle Petey. Petey, to Mrs Flynn, displays a characteristic tardiness. He never allows himself "more than five minutes to walk to Mass". He displays narcissism in "looking at himself and looking at himself in the looking glass till, honest to God, it 'id make a body throw off their guts to see him" (p. 5). These characteristics suggest conventionally negative feminine traits of sloth and solipsism rather than traditionally positive masculine characteristics of industry, social awareness and responsibility.

There is a suggestion in the extremity of her language here that Mrs Flynn is living vicariously through her son by using negative psychological reinforcement to will him to achieve the status in an ostensibly patriarchal community that she cannot officially be recognized to have attained herself. This resembles Mrs Haynes's intense, implied wish for her son to attain the socioeconomic success denied to herself (and, by extension, female schoolteachers in early twentieth-century Trinidad). James and Kavanagh are thus demonstrably comparable in wanting to show the extents or limitations of women's socioeconomic power in late-colonial societies. What these women cannot achieve for themselves, they wish for their sons, the patriarchal instrument in society of their matriarchal will. The older women characters whom James and Kavanagh create have realized that they can determine their destinies to some degree, but only via proxy and via the young male representatives of their family units.

Tarry defends his lack of urgency in leaving for church by protesting, "Amn't I taking the bike, I tell you." Mrs Flynn nonetheless counters that the most unsatisfactory aspect of Tarry's lateness is his failure to attend to any of the early morning chores of farm life, bike or no bike. As matriarch of the rural family business and homestead, Mrs Flynn can list a persuasive litany of Tarry's unchecked tasks and practical errors. They are, in her mind, failures concerning the implicit responsibility of an active male farmer ("Hens not fed, the pot not on for the pigs – and you washed your face in the well water, about as much as we'll have what 'ill make the breakfast", p. 6). Similarly, although Ella in *Minty Alley* operates in a technically subservient capacity to Haynes, she implicitly interrogates Haynes's assumption of masculine authority by instructing him on a list of tasks which she – in a female-headed socioeconomic milieu – understands would require the attention of a financially responsible adult.

Ella's knowledge of the duties and responsibilities necessary to survive in a scant economy allows her to usurp her employer's position. Both Ella and Mrs Flynn teach the young men in their lives the reality that men's comforts depend upon female-headed domestic and labour units. If Haynes's and the Flynns' homesteads can be read as microcosmic of larger units of gender power relations in late-colonial and residual-colonial economic structures, then James and Kavanagh are here implying a serious critique of patriarchal colonial society. They are showing that patriarchal colonial society is really far less potent than it assumes: it is a facade that depends necessarily upon the foundations of the day-to-day labour, social and intellectual powers, and acumen of women.

On hearing from one of her daughters, Mary, that "The white cow has a tear on her teat that's a total dread" (p. 8), Tarry's mother attributes this disaster to his characteristic negligence. She overtly questions Tarry's fundamental inability, as a deficient adult male, to demonstrate conventional masculine qualities of industry or attention to necessary detail. She is exasperated by his failure to pre-empt flaws in the farm's exterior fencing, paling and barbed-wire ringing – signs that she considers would be, to the passer-by, indexes of male labour and order on the farm: "'Oh, that's more of this man's doing!' cried the mother. 'How many times did I tell him to fix that paling and not to have the buck wire trailing half way across the field. *To look at this place a person would think we hadn't a man about it*'" (p. 8, emphasis added).

It should be noted that, although Tarry Flynn is the ostensible protagonist of Kavanagh's novel, it is Mrs Flynn into whose focalized consciousness the heterodiegetic narrator first plunges in the novel's opening chapter. The significance of privileging Mrs Flynn's free indirect thought as the first interior world presented in the spatio-temporal frame of the novel points to her empowered centrality (rather than peripherality) as a female character in the novel. It challenges patriarchal narrative expectations that the male protagonist would be, by virtue of relevance and precedence in the text, the first and pre-eminent figure into whose interior thoughts the reader would have access:

> The mother's imagination followed her son as he cycled down the lane towards the main road. She loved that son more than any mother ever loved a son. She hardly knew why. There was something so natural about him, so real and so innocent

and which looked like badness. . . . It was a risk to let him out alone in a horse and cart. The heart was often out of her mouth that he'd turn the cart upside down in a gripe while he was dreaming or looking at the flowers. (pp. 9–10)

The most striking feature of the passage as it continues conveying Mrs Flynn's focalized thought is that, although it reveals, contrarily to Tarry, her deference towards and fear of the power of "the priests" in Dargan ("And then the shocking things that he sometimes said about the priests. She was very worried about all that", p. 10), it still allows her to voice an expression of matriarchal protectiveness over her son that indicates overt defiance against the broad, patriarchal influence of the Holy Roman Catholic and Apostolic Church.

The church's will operates remotely from Rome, via the agency of local priests such as Dargan's Father Daly. It wields great power in conditioning the social, parochial order of rural, post-independence Irish Catholic society at an administrative and religious-ideological level. However, while Mrs Flynn wishes not to invoke the priests' "ill-will", she would still ultimately assert her matriarchal law, a love answerable not to Rome but to her instinct. The narrative relates that she is a "true mother" in that she would defend her son even if it meant cutting the Pope's throat (p. 10).

When Tarry Flynn is in favour with his mother, it is often at the expense of his three sisters. Mrs Flynn uses Tarry to assert dominance over her daughters whenever they might question her matriarchal dominance over the homestead, or her business skill as head of the agricultural family unit. For example, Mrs Flynn's prime weapon of attack against her unmarried daughter Bridie is to emphasize not merely the latter's superannuated singlehood, but more directly her comparative lack of marriageability in a rural farming economy where a woman ensures her economic security and destiny through finding a husband ("I could be twice married when I was your age", p. 25). In a rural society where young women marry elderly men and inherit their farms on the latter's death, Mrs Flynn reminds her daughters of her own superior erstwhile marketability within familistic economy. When Bridie retorts, in an interrogation of Mrs Flynn's self-belief, that if she were so shrewd at playing the game of marrying into rural economy, "A wonder ye didn't make a better bargain" (p. 25), her mother censures her with a reminder of Bridie's junior place in the Flynn order of power in relation to her brother Tarry. Mrs Flynn might often use reverse psychology to cajole her eldest son into action. Yet, faced with challenges from a would-be upstart matriarch-in-waiting, she is quick to demolish her daughters' opposition by reminding them of their brother's industrious endeavours and, implicitly, superiority as a male in the family pecking order, irrespective of their protests that "we're doing more than him" (p. 25).

Mrs Flynn equates daughters with unprofitable self-absorption, indolence and sickness ("Oh a family of daughters is the last of the last. Half the time painting and powdering and it would take a doctor's shop to keep them in medicine", p. 25); she implicitly insults her daughters further, manipulating their sense of frustrated powerlessness in the family, by advising Tarry not to work too hard or "try to do a bull-dragging day" (p. 25). Mrs Flynn divides and rules over her family, forever retaining the capacity to damn and praise any one family member at the expense of another in her ultimate self-interest.

The close of *Tarry Flynn*'s first chapter conveys a humorous illustration of rivalry between neighbourly matriarchs who exploit each other's farming resources to their individual ends in a competitive dairy-farming market. Mrs Callan enters the Flynn farm to survey its terrain for her ducks, which she suspects have been enticed by Mrs Flynn to lay eggs on her property. Mrs Flynn resents "the suggestion that she was exploiting Callan's ducks", although the matter of whether in truth she has been making gains from where the ducks choose to lay their eggs is never explicated. She seeks to outwit her business adversary, implying that Mrs Callan is negligent in feeding her ducks and thus a poor farming wife, by pointing out how the ducks can always be seen "about our street . . . when we're feeding the hens. They are the boys for aiting me hens' feeding, Mrs. Callan" (p. 26).

Mrs Flynn asserts her superior knowledge of duck habits in that it is unlikely that they would opt for laying eggs "about a stranger's place" (p. 26). Mrs Callan almost bests Mrs Flynn in this battle, countering, "It's a wonder they'd be coming, then, to ait your hens' feeding seeing that they have the run of the fields and the bog – the two bogs at that." Yet Mrs Flynn checkmates her opponent: she gets Tarry to corroborate that the ducks were last seen "making for Cassidy's field of oats" (p. 26). In one move, Mrs Flynn not only manages to send Mrs Callan on her way looking in another farm for those "terrible travellers", but she transfers Mrs Callan's suspicions regarding the exploitation of her ducks to another rival farm. As Mrs Flynn divides and rules her family, she similarly manipulates her opposition in her broader Drumnay community. Her competitiveness in local economy echoes Ella's own machinations to preserve her status against Ma Rouse in *Minty Alley*. Here, James and Kavanagh again demonstrate a wish to fictionalize – with surprisingly careful observational skills for male writers – the business enterprise and street-smart shrewdness of women who have to haggle and barter in order to survive with pride in, and even capitalize on, a small and fiercely competitive local economy.

In later chapters of *Tarry Flynn*, we see how Tarry unwittingly becomes a business substitute for his dead father, to his mother's delight. Tarry converses with the aged neighbouring farmer Petey Meegan and accidentally cultivates the latter's interest in making a marriage match with his sister Mary. However, Mary already has a "fella about town" and alternates between fleeing Meegan at every opportunity or staying and insulting him mercilessly (pp. 70–73). Mrs Flynn sees potential for marrying off all her daughters similarly ("If this Mary goes they may all go", p. 70). In time, a dispute between Tarry and neighbour Joe Finnegan over land that Mrs Flynn has recently purchased, and Meegan's surreptitious decision to side with the Finnegans, effectively severs any connection between the Flynns and local superannuated marriage suitors, to Mrs Flynn's (but not Mary's) dissatisfaction.

Meegan makes a last, half-hearted and vain attempt to convince Mary of the value of marrying him, when she and her sisters elect to finally break away from the soul-destroying limitations of familism and set up an "eating house" in the nearby town of Shercock. In Mary's response to Meegan, she demonstrates that she is not to be exploited just to maintain a farming economy with a much older male. She has the option of economic migration and decolonizing emancipation from the legacy of the Famine, and a right to determine her own sexual and economic destinies (not one and the same, through her commodified labour as farmer's wife and mother to successive farming generations, but separate and motivated by her individual will). She points out, with mocking cruelty and distinct clarity, the preposterousness of any concept that a young woman should for reasons other than love marry a man "not trusting on sixty" (p. 147) and about whom there are circulating rumours of "unnatural" behaviour, or even bestiality ("I wouldn't like to eat the eggs his hens lay", p. 148).

Mary's salacious remarks conceal a suggestion that the entire culture of familism and enforced celibacy encourage unnatural behaviour in aged bachelors and deprivation in younger women destined to be their wives. Rather than being a divinely sanctioned model for nuclear-familistic, peasant agrarian society that ensures procreation within wedlock in the interests of economy in a post-independence, agriculturally self-sufficient Ireland, in Mary Flynn's implied view it licenses behaviour that runs counter to the spiritual imperatives of men and women who constitute the creative but stifled future of the Irish Free State. Mary's words, in their view of the unnaturalness of unions between older men and younger women, mirror Maisie's in *Minty Alley*: Maisie consistently rejects the dominance of patriarchal influence in a female-centred economy. Following the departure of Benoit, Maisie deliberately sabotages the date between Ma Rouse and the superannuated Mr Parkes on the grounds that "I don't want any old man with whiskers in this house" (p. 178).

Due to the sheer geographical distance separating Maisie from her desired migrant destination, America, the way in which the novel deals with her departure is very differently handled from the migration of the Flynn daughters from their mother's homestead to a nearby town. Following her final physical confrontation with Mrs Rouse in the muddy wrestling ground of Minty Alley's yard, Maisie leaves Trinidad altogether to realize her glamorous dream of a new life, and work as a stewardess in order to travel and stay with an uncle in America. Reddock cites the *Labour Leader* from 1923 as reporting that "a review of passenger lists for the last six months" for people leaving the island for the States "showed that 90 per cent were women".[15] Maisie is part of this migrant trend. Of course, true to character, Maisie is not entering the United States as a legal immigrant but is aiming to flee her boat crew at the first opportunity. There is no mention in *Minty Alley* about the possible fate, social obstacles or racial politics awaiting Trinidadian migrants to America: Maisie's migrant optimism has a historical context in documentary records of the time, which show the numbers of women willing to chance emigration as a route to better life than that on the island. Judging from evidence presented by Reddock, it would seem that if any reports of America's poor race relations had filtered through by the 1930s to Trinidadian female emigrants, they were clearly not deterring young women from leaving Trinidad for the United States on passenger boats. Maisie simply disappears from the narrative, into the unknown. So, any lacunae in the text regarding what might befall migrants on their arrival in America complements documentary sources suggesting either innocence or disregard of this issue by economic female migrants. Young women were hardly deterred in their priority to escape the colonial island economy, which was failing to ensure "adequate means to earn a living".[16]

In *Tarry Flynn*, the sense of a gamble for young women to escape the confines of a matriarchal family economy is far less than for long-distance migrants in the Caribbean. Mary Flynn's inclination to migrate to Shercock takes her only a matter of miles, and if her venture should fail, which it does, she can always return home. Her wish to leave is a significant demonstration of the collapse of familism as a dominant ideology and the growing sense among young Irish women that migrancy and its promises of self-sufficiency were a greater personal priority than supporting a redundant and unrewarding socio-economic system that continued to render them dependent. Mary's migration to a small Irish town somewhat reflects the evidence from demographic study of low-level, rural-urban internal migration within County Laois (if Laois as a mid-Irish county in the province of Leinster can be considered in its representation of general migratory trends to be comparable with the Ulster counties of Cavan, or Kavanagh's native Monaghan).[17]

The sense of peril in the adventure for Mary and her sisters is thus far less profound than in the case of Maisie, in that it does not have the same suggestion of finality as Maisie's exodus from Trinidad.

Minty Alley is a canonical postcolonial novel that has been celebrated as a pre-eminent example of Caribbean literatures in English since the early 1970s, following that period's reappraisal of the *Beacon*-era writers from the 1920s and 1930s. One can see on close reading of the novel that it offers a microscopic socio-realist focus on the lives of working women that is revelatory, particularly given the novel's male author and male focalizing narrator, Haynes. In *Minty Alley*, C.L.R. James is committed to investigating the gender politics of Trinidadian society. James critiques the assumption that late-colonial Trinidad is patriarchal, as he traces a young, male, middle-class narrator's discovery that his comforts depend on the hard work of the women in occupations around him, including his mother, Ella and Mrs Rouse. He also shows that through the benefits of educational opportunities on the island, young women such as Maisie can determine their own socioeconomic fate and use their ingenuity to leave the island and find work elsewhere, transcending the ambitions and potentiality not only of women but many men on the island.

If *Tarry Flynn* is read in a comparative postcolonial context, it provides not only a useful corollary alongside which to read *Minty Alley* but also a deeper understanding of how Patrick Kavanagh, like James, was an author set on showing the crucial importance of women in what had traditionally been understood as a patriarchal colonial society. Although the Ireland of *Tarry Flynn* is that of 1935, after independence, and while Kavanagh's novel was published in 1948, the agricultural economy demonstrated in the text is essentially similar to that created under the British. *Tarry Flynn*, like *Minty Alley*, shows women working to improve their conditions under a late-colonial, supposedly patriarchal economic structure. Patrick Kavanagh, if not indeed his protagonist Tarry Flynn, realizes that the luxuries and dreams of men are often facilitated by the industry of the women in their environment. Kavanagh, like James, cleverly and not without humour shows that it is women in marginal occupations who are the bedrock of an economy instituted by the British. An older generation of shrewd and forceful women, represented by Mrs Flynn, still attempts to make the most of this economy, as it did under British rule. Yet now a younger generation of females, represented by Mary, Aggie and Bridie Flynn, shows the development of a new decolonizing stage in women's reactions to the economic strictures of the time, and seeks escape via economic migration. These younger females make for a striking corollary with James's Maisie in displaying the new extents to which women are finding ways to transcend the limits of their path to socioeconomic autonomy. The two novels are written by men and have male protagonists, yet it is the older matriarchs and the young women of the texts who define decolonizing economics away from the patriarchal colonial standard. It is the women of *Tarry Flynn* and *Minty Alley* whom their authors create as fictive representatives of a gendered, decolonizing economics in Ireland and Trinidad in the early decades of the twentieth century.

4.

"A Missile without Provenance or Target"

Sam Selvon's *The Lonely Londoners* and Samuel Beckett's *Murphy*

SAMUEL BECKETT'S *MURPHY* (1938) HAS NOT HERETOFORE received substantial critical consideration as a novel of Irish migratory experience in 1930s London. This places it in contrast with Sam Selvon's *The Lonely Londoners* (1956), which has, since its first publication, been reviewed and discussed as a novel principally concerning Caribbean migrant arrivals and attempts at settlement in the London of the 1950s.

Selvon's short novel consists of a sequence of calypso-like, balladic episodes concerning Trinidadian Moses Aloetta and his diasporic peers, who negotiate the shock of long-distance boat travel to the cold, alienating, unreal imperial metropolis. They hustle temporary and transitory accommodation and female companionship, dodge debts, experience hunger and seek fellowship amid the loneliness of the migratory predicament in London.

The migrant novel constitutes a substantial part of what critics have come to establish as a postcolonial canon. It continues to be central to postcolonial studies in terms of its portrayal of themes such as displacement, rupture from origins, geographical and psychological transit and limbo, nationhood and identity, and the enigmas of arrival and settlement in a new and not always welcoming country. This is not surprising, as the issue of migrancy is hugely relevant to the lived experiences of so many subjects and former subjects of the British Empire and Commonwealth. As such, migration is a theme that is central or at least incidental to a wide range of notable postcolonial texts. Alfred Mendes, Jean Rhys, Elizabeth Bowen, C.L.R. James, Patrick Kavanagh, Samuel Beckett, Sam Selvon and George Lamming all migrated to Britain at least for a short period at some time in their literary careers: all wrote about migration at some point in their careers, some significantly via the novel form. Selvon's novel is thus certainly not without precedent. Jean Rhys's *Voyage in the Dark* (1934), discussed at length in chapter 2 of this book, tells of a Dominican chorus-girl's descent into the world of a nocturnal London *demi-monde* in the years running up to the outbreak of the First World War. Later, the BBC Empire Service/Overseas Service programmes *Calling the West Indies* (1939) and *Caribbean Voices* (1943–58) were instrumental in broadcasting, for the first time, migrant Caribbean writers in Britain (including Selvon) voicing reflections upon issues of diasporic experience.

George Lamming, a fellow contributor to *Caribbean Voices*, followed the publication of his novel *In the Castle of My Skin* a year later with *The Emigrants* (1954), which traces a migrant journey to Britain and the consequences of dislocation and settlement, prior to Selvon's own novel on this theme. Nonetheless, given its critical reception, *The Lonely Londoners* is very arguably to date *the* canonical epitome of the innovative migrant Caribbean-British novel of the 1950s and 1960s. The novel's reception as a prime text of anglophone Caribbean migrant-themed significance is evident from observation of discussions, since the start of this century, by Susheila Nasta, Roydon Salick and Alison Donnell. Nasta regards *The Lonely Londoners* as a seminal and canonical text of "black British" and "migrant writing", going on to describe the novel as groundbreaking and important "both in terms of its strategic reinvention of London as a black city of words and for its innovative experimentations with language and literary form".[1] Donnell and Salick argue separately that *The Lonely Londoners* is now so established in Caribbean studies that the novel obscures Selvon's lesser-known works. Salick in particular complains that much of Selvon's novelistic work has been neglected by critics at the expense of his novels *A Brighter Sun* and *The Lonely Londoners*.[2] Although Donnell contends that Selvon's 1955 novel *An Island Is a World* demonstrates a superior identification with the vernacular and experiences of Anglo-Creole Caribbean migrants, she still accepts that *The Lonely Londoners* is a classic migrant text that has also come to epitomize Selvon's writing.[3] The fact that *The Lonely Londoners* should have its central canonicity in Selvon's and in broader

Caribbean literatures questioned in relation to his other writings is testament enough to the novel's established position in anglophone Caribbean literary studies.

By contrast, the critical reception of Samuel Beckett's *Murphy* is far less concerned with its migrant-themed or even broadly postcolonial implications than with foregrounding the novel's philosophical or comedic content. Chris Ackerley argues that *Murphy* was largely forgotten by critics until it was reissued by Grove Press in 1957; even then, it was mainly scrutinized in the United States by writers such as "Hugh Kenner (1961) and Ruby Cohn (1962) who accentuated the Cartesian and comic elements".[4] Indeed, Kenner's book-length study of Beckett describes *Murphy* as "his first comic book" with a characteristically "daft freedom" of form and content.[5] He considers Murphy in Cartesian terms, to the extent of discussing Murphy's near-architectural construction of a "bodytight" mind closed to the world without, in terms of the philosophy of the "second-generation Cartesian" Arnold Geulincx (1624–69). However, the economic migrant contexts and significance of Murphy's passage to London are not explored. Kenner does at least provide the occasional aside regarding Beckett's views on post-independence Ireland (one remark being that Beckett preferred France at war to Ireland at peace).[6] Cohn's study of Beckett, however, steadfastly avoids any biographical or historical contexts in her close textual reading of the comic elements of *Murphy*, or, for that matter, any work of Beckett's canon.

Ackerley remarks that critical attempts to reread Beckett's work in terms of Irish studies, from John P. Harrington's *The Irish Beckett* in 1991, to Anthony Cronin's biography *Samuel Beckett: The Last Modernist* in 1996, have proved "unconvincing".[7] Although Ackerley's comments in this regard are scant, they are generally instructive in at least directing the reader to realize the dearth of Irish (and certainly postcolonial Irish) *Murphy* criticism. Aidan Arrowsmith, whom Ackerley overlooks, does at least offer a two-paragraph reading of *Murphy* – presented in the context of a broader essay on representations of marginal Irish migrants in Britain, which constitutes something of a postcolonial Irish reading of the novel. He reads *Murphy's* "central imagery of constriction and escape [as an echo of] the protagonist's departure from Ireland and Irishness into the freedom of exile". Patrick Bixby's more recent *Samuel Beckett and the Postcolonial Novel* (2009) offers an illuminating reading of Murphy as considering the relationship between private consciousness and public life in the unhomely space between Dublin and London.[8] Yet these aforementioned discussions of *Murphy* are all that precedes this chapter by way of a postcolonial evaluation of the novel.

There are some neglected similarities in migrant trends from Ireland and the Caribbean to England, involving the mass of a diasporic population consisting of skilled and unskilled workers. Cumann na nGaedheal's failed post-independence agricultural policy between 1923 and 1932 precipitated mass economic migration from Ireland to Britain's industrial towns and cities.[9] This corresponded with Britain's early 1930s construction work initiative and creation of an industrial reserve army to offset the Great Depression. Britain proved more attractive than America to many Irish migrants, as it was nearer to home. If the economic migrant venture failed in Britain, a return passage was possible and affordable. London was a prime migrant destination, due to London Underground tunnelling and the constant construction work in the British capital city and heart of the Empire. Likewise, Caribbeanist Clive Harris proposes that the Caribbean economy after the Second World War was still "argely agricultural. Former Caribbean Royal Air Force soldiers had returned home to find few employment opportunities. British prime minister Clement Atlee (1945–50) pursued a prerogative of "full employment", recruiting cheap overseas labour. Jamaican governor John Huggins sought incorporation of a migrant Caribbean workforce within the European Volunteer Worker scheme.

The Lonely Londoners and *Murphy* are remarkably similar in that they represent the experiences of migrants, from territories with a British colonial history, in London. These characters are not part of the unskilled or skilled working population making up the bulk of the surplus migrant manual labour force. Consequently, they find work, money and permanent accommodation to be comforts persistently beyond reach. After desultory job hunts (motivated externally by insistent girlfriends rather than internal impetus), they find work in marginal, nocturnal occupations keeping them trapped on the fringes of the society in which they live. Few migrant characters in either novel stay in one lodging-house for long.

At the start of Selvon's novel, its Trinidadian protagonist Moses Aloetta, a veteran migrant of some years, meets Henry Oliver – Galahad – at Waterloo Station. Moses has found himself delegated by islanders at home as a one-man support network for new migrant arrivals in the city: it is an onerous, exhausting task for one man alone. ("He don't know how he always getting in position like this, helping people out. He sigh."[10]) Moses, on meeting Galahad at Waterloo, finds that Galahad is dressed entirely inappropriately for the British winter weather. The evening has been "getting colder and colder and Moses stamping he foot as he stand up there". Moses marvels, in this harsh climate, at Galahad in his "old grey tropical suit and a pair of watchekong and no overcoat or muffler or gloves or anything for the cold": Moses feels the need to double-check whether this is not "some test who living in London a long, long time and accustom to the beast winter" (p. 32). One cannot help but feel that Galahad is far from the type of economic migrant who himself has made efforts at reconnaissance to learn the climate, customs and expectations of arrival and settlement in England. In fact, one wonders as to Galahad's motivations for coming to England at all, given his utter absence of preparation.

Their first meeting sets these two fellow islanders in a curious binary opposition with regard to the semiotics of their dress, particularly as Moses is wearing "long wool underwear and a heavy fireman coat that he pick up in Portobello Road". Galahad's claims that "In fact I feeling a little warm" provokes Moses's exclamation, "Jesus Christ! . . . What happen to you, you sick or something?" Galahad's bravado and evident unpreparedness for London right down to his choice of clothing on arriving from the boat-train renders him extremely vulnerable to sudden, unavoidable culture shock. Moses is flabbergasted at a migrant arriving from Trinidad so ill-prepared for or lacking expectations of his destination that he would not even carry luggage, duty-free cigarettes or rum with him on arriving at the station. He is also suspicious of Galahad's nonchalant guffawing at his incredulity: Moses advises Galahad to "take it easy" (pp. 33–34).

Moses realizes that Galahad's cavalier attitude will eventually precipitate a crisis when he sees how different London is from Trinidad, and adjusts his conversation to prepare him accordingly. ("Moses make up his mind to treat Galahad in a special way because he behaving as if he think he back home in Port of Spain or something" [p. 35]). Moses begins to warn Galahad of the poor weather, scarcity of work and social isolation of migrant life in London. However, it appears that the more Moses advises Galahad that there is no island fellowship to be found between migrants in London – "it ain't have no s--- here like 'both we is Trinidadians and we must help out one another'"

(p. 37) – the more his dialogue betrays his unconscious need as an isolated Trinidadian to reach out to a fellow islander and reclaim some sense of place or origin, a sense of home, in words. The two men speak of commonly shared memories of place and local character:

> "Where you used to live?"
> "Down south, San Fernando, in Mucurapo Street."
> "Eh-heh! You know Mahal?"
> Mahal was a mad Indian fellar who used to go around town playing as if he driving car, putting in gear and stepping on the x and making hand signals and blowing horn.
> "But how you mean? Everybody know Mahal!"
> "He must be catching arse with the new type of gear it have on them cars now!" Moses laugh.
> Galahad laugh. "He still driving old-model." (p. 37)

And so, Moses "start to get nostalgic now that he have a friend who just arrive from Trinidad" (p. 37). Moses constructs Trinidad mentally and in his nostalgic dialogue with other migrants as a counter-metropolitan ideal, and as a psychological retreat representing a solace of familiarity from the alien environment of a fog-laden, day-to-day and pervasively strange London.

It is the depiction of Galahad's shock in London, which Moses has predicted, that constitutes a moment of the reversal of migrant hopes by the hostile reality of London life. Galahad has been on the boat-train from Southampton to Waterloo and heard fellow Caribbean migrants talking "about how you could go on the dole if you ain't working, and how they intend to find out about it before they start to hustle" (p. 40). He is hesitant when Moses presses him to assert that this is not his plan: he suggests a vague plan for his economic future, claiming, "If I can't get electrician work I will take something else for the time being." He offers some quick bravado, maintaining, "Me, I am a born hustler." Yet as soon as Moses leaves him at the tube station in the morning, at Queensway, he finds himself for the first time alone in London and struck with terror:

> Galahad make for the tube station when he left Moses, and he stand up there on Queensway watching everybody going about their business, and a feeling of loneliness and fright come on him all of a sudden. He forget all the brave words he

was talking to Moses, and he realize that here he is, in London, and he ain't have no money or work or place to sleep or any friend or anything, and he standing up here by the tube station watching people, and everybody look so busy he frighten to ask questions from any of them. You think any of them bothering with what going on in his mind? Or in anybody else mind but their own? (p. 42)

Without the comfort of Moses's nostalgic conversation to supply him with a mental image of home, Galahad is appalled by the pale, uncanny appearance of the sign of an English sun presenting unfamiliarity where familiarity is expected ("like a force-ripe orange"). He is further terrified by the bleakness of a city sky without its expected colour ("When he look up, the colour of the sky so desolate it make him more frighten" [p. 42]). This moment of psychic fragmentation culminates in a torpid daze:

> He ain't even remember the name of the street where Moses living. In the panic he start to pat pocket to make sure he have money on him, and he begin to search for passport and some other papers he had. A feeling come over him as if he lost everything he have – clothes, shoes, hat – and he start to touch himself here and there as if he in a daze. (p. 42)

Galahad seems not to make a good recovery from this break, even though Moses quickly finds him and steers him to the employment exchange.

Galahad nonetheless continues to show some great enthusiasm for "Brit'n" after this point, and this often places him, particularly midway through the novel, in opposition to Moses Aloetta, whom Kenneth Ramchand claims loses "something vital" the longer he faces the trials of living in London.[11] However, towards the close of the novel, Galahad is hardly more acquainted with London life after nearly four years in England than in his first days in the country. He psychologically retreats to a Trinidad of the mind – in lone thought, just as he had achieved on his first night with Moses, in nostalgic talk of home – to remind himself of a point of origin and to make sense of England's strangeness and lack of material comforts or necessities.

Towards the novel's conclusion, and during "one bitter season, when . . . nobody can't get no work, [and] fellars who had work losing it", the jobless Galahad finds himself starving. He drifts through Kensington Gardens, the ubiquitous and never-ending "fog never clear enough for him to see down to High Street Ken" (pp. 122–23). In his starvation, not being able to see hope in his external locale, he retreats to a San Fernando of the mind and maps a solution to his hunger. Galahad recalls, "When he was a little fellar his father had a work in High Street in San Fernando, a town about forty miles from Port of Spain. It used to have pigeons like stupidness all about the street – nobody know where they come from, and Galahad father used to snatch them and send them home to cook." As with Galahad, avian migrants, whether pigeons or seagulls, seem to have a mysterious origin: "Which part these seagulls come from? He wonder, for he always think that seagulls belong to the sea" (p. 123) His memory of eating migrant birds as part of a staple diet in Trinidad leads him to attempt to smuggle a pigeon into his coat, with a view to cooking and eating it there and then in London. However, the incompatibility between his remembered lifestyle in Trinidad, where snatching and cooking such birds is commonplace, and his present situation in England – where a dog-walking, animal-loving English woman can spy him surreptitiously grabbing a pigeon and scream at him, "You cruel monster! You killer!" – is not easily hybridized.

By secreting the pigeon in his coat rather than killing it in the open, Galahad is clearly not ignorant that his practice contravenes social norms in an England where high-street pigeons are not usually preyed upon for food. He simply lets his remembered cultural values, unadulterated as a positive solution in memory to the dreary hopelessness of his migrant circumstances, light his path out of the fog of hunger and want in a London that has failed to become a new setting for prosperity.

Where Galahad has not found a real sense of economic migrant destination, he chooses to rely instead on a mental construct of origin for survival and custom. He tries to reimagine the physical space of Kensington Gardens in the mental image of his remembered San Fernando. However, his ploy to hybridize and synthesize his current surroundings with his remembered environment is problematic. He does not take into account the vast disparities in value systems between the inhabitants of the two localities.

The divide between Galahad's mental image of home and his present plight in London is amplified when he flees the English woman, first to his own lodgings, but then to Moses's with the pigeon for cooking. ("'Moses in this country long,' he say to himself, 'and if he could eat it I don't see why I must feel so guilty'.") At first, on seeing Galahad at his door with the bird, Moses warns Galahad about relative cultural values between Trinidad and England ("'Boy, you take a big chance. . . . You think this is Trinidad? Them pigeons there to beautify the park, not to eat. The people here will kill you if you touch a fly'" [p. 125]). Nonetheless, Moses is content to help cut up the bird and prepare it, home-style, with rice (with the token caveat that Galahad should not repeat his feat of bird theft). This culinary slice of Trinidad life is a stimulus for more nostalgic dialogue, as the men briefly forget their migrant surroundings and try to resituate themselves mentally back in their island of origin:

> The pigeon and rice have Moses feeling good and he in the mood for a old talk.
> "Aye Galahad," he say, "you used to know a fellar name Brackley in Charlotte Street?"
> "Brackley? Charlotte Street? But how you mean? You think I would be living in Port of Spain and don't know Brackley! Ain't he the fellar who ain't have no nose, and he always riding about town on a ladies bicycle, peddling with his heels, and his fingers sticking out on the handle bars? And if you tell him anything he curse you like hell?" (p. 127)

The illusion of oldtalk cannot be maintained, however. The strategy of retreat via dialogue to the past only serves to propel Moses crashing into the present: "Galahad laugh until tears come, and Moses suddenly sober up, as if it not right that in these hard times he and Galahad could sit there, belly full of pigeon, smoking cigarette, and talking about them characters back home. As if Moses get a guilty feeling, and he watch Galahad with sorrow, thinking that he ain't have no work and the winter upon the city" (p. 127). For the migrant, memory and mental play is no hiding place from Britain and its daily ills. Moses confides in a characteristically mocking Galahad that "sometimes when we oldtalking so I does wonder about the boys, how all of we come up to the old Brit'n to make a living, and how years go by and we still here in this country. Things like that does bother me" (pp. 128–29).

A second migrant drifter figure conforms to a similar narrative pattern: arrival, moment of psychic fragmentation caused by London's hostility and alienation, and withdrawal into dissipation and a transitory, hand-to-mouth existence. Selvon's novel uses flashback techniques to relate its principal character Moses's earliest days on arrival in London and his meeting with Captain or "Cap", a Nigerian who has been sent by his father "to study law" but who "went stupid when he arrive in the big city . . . [and] start to spend money wild on woman and cigarette" (p. 47). Moses and Cap meet while at a hostel, an incubatory location where migrant newcomers with good intentions for a new life in Britain lodge, prior to being able to "branch off on their own and begin to live in London". While the hostel "had some genuine fellars who really studying profession", more often than not "it also had fellars who was only marking time and seeing what tomorrow would bring". Cap is precisely this type of migrant. His reason for being in London is at the instruction of his father, rather than his own compulsion to seek a new economic future in Britain. He does find "plenty work, but he only stay a few days at any of them" (p. 49). Settlement and the security of permanent accommodation become improbable.

As Cap resides in a hostel with anglophone Caribbeans, he is homogenized with other colonized migrants largely on the basis of colour. Harris remarks that colour prejudice and landlords' refusal to offer rooms to migrants of perceived colour was one cause of an accommodation shortage that led to overcrowding in hostels.[12] Effectively, Cap's marginalized hostel life becomes that of his English-speaking Caribbean counterparts: by this point Selvon's novel has already satirized the tendency of the mainstream British media in the 1950s to see all black migrants as "Jamaican" (pp. 27–28), and in this vein Cap becomes homogenized with his Caribbean peers. What he does share with his peers is the consideration of having travelled far on a potentially one-way journey from the colonies, with no guarantee of stable settlement in England.

At a key moment in Cap's migrant experience, he undergoes a peculiar form of psychic breakdown. Hiding in Moses's hostel room to escape paying rent to the landlord, he excitedly claims to behold the apparition of "a white pigeon flying over his bed". The pigeon is a motif; apart from signifying migrancy, flight and escape, it symbolizes the persistence of a remembered world left behind that still pervades but cannot fuse with the everyday reality of living in London. It is a spectre of foreboding that reminds the migrant of his inability to settle in London, and of his still being in migrant flight or transit, without a clear destination in spite of a hope for arrival:

> "It ain't have no pigeon in here," Moses say.
>
> "But I tell you I saw it!" Cap drawing back the blankets. "It must be the spirit of my father from Nigeria."
>
> Another night Cap wake Moses up. "Believe me, I saw an angel with a harp playing over your bed," he tell Moses.
>
> "Listen," Moses say. "The next time you see that angel playing a ——ing harp

over my bed, you don't say or do anything. I like harp music, and he come to inspire me." (p. 50)

This point of psychic turmoil complements Galahad's moment of daze, highlighted above. Like Galahad, from this stage onwards, Cap's level of dissipation and aimless, transitory movement around London increases. It is even interesting that the spectre of the pigeon, a commonplace migrant bird that never settles but is seen everywhere, is a means by which both characters imagine themselves in relation to a London in which they cannot make a permanent home, and the remembered familiar sights of a place of origin to which they might never return.

Cap, sliding into a life of pointlessness, enters the used car "racket, and make a hundred pound, but it went through his hands so quick that the morning he wake up broke he was surprise" (p. 50). The narrator's mode of storytelling might be comically ironical at Cap's expense, yet it contains a grain of sapient observation that Cap is by this point not quite in command of his faculties. Cap soft-talks the other residents of his hostel so as to sponge off them for meals; he affects a hale appearance and bonhomie, even though he is unable or unwilling to stay in employment for more than a few days at a time. And when Cap is inevitably evicted from the hostel, he enters into the mode of trickster-figure to attain fleeting accommodation at the best hotels. ("Brazen as ever, he went to a hotel and put on the soft tone, explaining he was a student and expected his allowance any day", p. 50.) When his allowance fails to arrive, Cap moves on. He soon exhausts places in Bayswater to implement this repeated ruse, and "[h]e had to widen the area after a time". Cap might map out a sense of migrant terrain in London but it is hardly a sense of permanent fixture or place; Cap's London is always drifting, always transitory:

> One day you would hear he living Caledonia, another time he move to Clapham Common, next time you see him he living in Shepherd's Bush. Week after week, as landlord and landlady catch up with him, the Captain moving, the wandering Nigerian, man of mystery. Nobody could contact Cap, is only by chance you bouncing him up here and there about London.
> "Where you living now Cap?"
> A kind of baby smile, and "Victoria." (p. 51)

With no fixed location for settlement in London, Cap drifts in and out of the lives of the other characters and the narrative of *The Lonely Londoners*. The ballad of Cap offers no hint of forthcoming resolution to his predicament.

Readers of *Murphy* might be perplexed at this point as to how its main character matches this migrant formula. However, one should acknowledge that *Murphy* is a novel that begins *in media res* and requires some rearranging before one can trace the chronological trajectory of its *fabula*. Once this is done, one can see that the story of Murphy's arrival from Ireland to London around February 1935, and the sequence of events that follow until his death the following October, correspond in significant ways with the tales of Galahad and Cap. For instance, Murphy and Cap both receive a stipend from a relative. While Cap lives for a time on handouts from his unsuspecting father in Nigeria, who believes him to be hard at study, Dublin-born Murphy, though "he belonged to no profession or trade", receives "[s]mall charitable sums" from "one uncle, a Mr. Quigley, a well-to-do ne'er-do-well, resident in Holland".[13]

In fact, just as Moses Aloetta in *The Lonely Londoners* is in ways a fictive refraction of Sam Selvon in his first years in England, Murphy resembles his author, Samuel Beckett, in many of the respects just mentioned. Beckett had been an academic at Trinity College Dublin from 1930 to 1931, lecturing in French and assisting the professor of Romance languages. However, he had given up the post after only four terms. After some time in France (which he first visited in 1928), he spent the years 1933 to 1935 miserably in London. His father had died and left him a stipend on which he eked out a rather paltry existence, jobless and progressively withdrawn in a West London attic garret resembling Murphy's.

Murphy's early migrant experiences can be explained as similar in points of narrative to *The Lonely Londoners*. For instance, in the novel's fourth section, set on 19 September 1935, Murphy's former mentor at the Pythagorean academy in Cork – an esoteric eccentric by the name of Neary – resides in Dublin while seeking information regarding his former student. It transpires that since leaving Neary's "gymnasium" and last being seen in Ireland in February of 1935, word of Murphy has been scarce. In fact, "the only news of [Murphy] was that he had been seen in London on Maundy Thursday late afternoon, supine on the grass in the Cockpit in Hyde Park, alone and plunged in a torpor from which all efforts to rouse him had proved unsuccessful" (pp. 33–34).

It appears that in the weeks in which Murphy's whereabouts and life had been unaccounted for, he was merely continuing in England a meditative practice begun in Ireland. The torpor in which Murphy is found is similar to a Galahad-esque daze of shock at London's alienating and inhospitable environment, and a dismay at not finding "home" in migration. It can even be argued that Murphy's Cartesian retreat into his mind, described in section one of the novel but taking place in mid-September 1935, at least six months after his arrival in London, is a *result* of a disillusion with London. Murphy now seeks to migrate corporeally back away from London, but by way of self-hypnosis. Prior to leaving Ireland, Murphy had supplied a rejoinder to Neary's declaration that "all life is figure and ground", stating that it is rather "a wandering to find home" (p. 4).

Why Murphy might have seen London as home invites speculative commentary regarding how Dublin in 1935, with its Georgian Ascendancy architecture and still-standing Nelson's Pillar, could have resembled, for the author Beckett, a post-imperial quasi-metropolis. Dublin in 1935 was, for Beckett and for many inhabiting its space, inevitably (at least architecturally) a dead, vacated body of the Empire. It is possible that the author created a migratory route for Murphy, only for Murphy to become – like Beckett, who left London in 1935 – disillusioned with the city. What is significant, for the purposes of comparison between *Murphy* and *The Lonely Londoners,* is that, by mid-September, Murphy retreats from his view of London, framed by the window in his West Brompton garret. That spectacle of a mew "of medium-sized cages of south-eastern aspect" (p. 3) condemned to imminent demolition suggests the impermanence not only of London's physical topography but even of the very imperial ideology in which its doomed metropolitan structures are housed: such a vision alienates the migrant spectator seeking a sense of permanence and fixture in the city.

The mundane, mercantile modernity of a clockwork, mechanical life is embodied in the early paragraphs of *Murphy*, as the fusion between the sounds in the protagonist's ears of a nearby cuckoo-clock and the half-imagined "echo of a street-cry", which, "now entering the mew gave *Quid pro quo! Quid pro quo!* directly". All physical congress here is commodified within a doomed landscape: Murphy feels despondent and alienated by these "sights and sounds that he did not like" (p. 3): these are signifiers of a London reduced to a crumbling marketplace far from any absolute imperial ideal. His response of a decisive withdrawal of interest in his environment resembles that of Moses in *The*

Lonely Londoners, who, in discussion with Galahad, confesses that he has lost his belief in fortuitous arrival and settlement in a large, romantic and vital city:

> "What do you think, Moses?" [Galahad] ask Moses.
> "Ah, in you I see myself when I was new in London. All them places is like nothing to me now. Is like when you go back home and you hear fellars talk about Times Square and Fifth Avenue, and Charing Cross and gay Paree. You say to yourself, 'Lord, them places must be sharp.' Then you get a chance and you see them for yourself, and is like nothing." (p. 85)

Most tellingly, the narrator supplies a sentence from Murphy's focalized perspective dealing with Murphy's disappointment with London and his feeling like a lonely migrant outsider. The text claims that the sights and sounds of London "detained [Murphy] in the world to which they belonged, but not he, as he fondly hoped" (p. 3). On one level, this sentence might be saying that Murphy foolishly or sentimentally hopes that he does not belong to part of an external world from which he, a Cartesian exponent of divorcing mind from body, seeks liberation by way of retreating into his freest fluxes of thought. However, on another, it might also be saying that the sights and sounds of London trap him in a London to which he had lovingly hoped, but has failed, to belong. It is this suggested sense of alienation that, on arriving in London in early 1935, might be seen to have precipitated Murphy's torpor and retreat into himself. The migrant emotion on arrival is one of hope. It is soon followed by disillusionment.

A similar alienation affects Galahad in Selvon's novel, on his first morning in Queensway. He has been full of hopeful "big talk" on first arrival. Now, he feels an outsider and part of the landscape in a city where everyone else seems to be going about their business. Bumping into "a woman coming out of the station but she pass him like a full trolley before he could say sorry", Galahad feels that "[e]verybody doing something or going somewhere, is only he who walking stupid". It is this moment of exclusion that leads to his confusion staring up at the cold sun "in the sky like a force-ripe orange" (p. 42). Yet while Galahad at least for a time attempts to maintain some enthusiasm for London – a matter to which I shall return – Murphy gives up on his environment and rocks his chair in the shadows of his room, seeking to silence his body and all physical sensations completely as he migrates into the darkest corners of his mind.

Cap's status as a migrant drifter can be seen to be matched in a number of important respects by Beckett's Murphy. These two diasporic figures of vaguely academic background, who receive stipends from relatives and move from temporary lodging to temporary lodging, do not conform to an economic migrant labour force in Britain, and have to be berated by their girlfriends into searching (half-heartedly) for any available work in London. In Cap's case, following his apparent breakdown in Moses's room, he starts to demonstrate a profligacy with his scarce finances squandered in entertaining casual acquaintances with "women that he pick up here and there about the place", after the allowance from his father is severed. He finds himself in a progressively fragile material state of affairs. Nonetheless, he meets "an Austrian girl who was a sharp dresser" – she is also a sharp thinker who is soon "trying she best to make Cap look for work":

"Why don't you get a job", she tell Cap, "there are many jobs around, and all your friends are working."
"Jobs are hard to get," Cap say cagey, "it is not as easy as you think. I have tried many times." (p. 51)

Still, Cap seems to "evade work so much that the Austrian start to get vex with him". The Austrian cajoles Cap to find night-work with Moses to the extent that he lies to her, pretending that "yes, he get a night-work same as Moses, and he would be starting right away". Such work would consign Cap to the nocturnal margins of working society, yet, ironically, Cap is already living a peripheral lifestyle in his indolence: "So what he doing is sleep in the day, and go out in the night to look for cat and sponge a meal whenever he could" (p. 50). On Cap's first apparent night of work, the Austrian girl "come to the tube station with Moses and Cap, and she buy the platform ticket and went down the platform with them, and she kiss Cap and wish him luck, and Cap and Moses get on the train and went". Yet, "[w]hen the train reach Notting Hill Gate Cap get off and went to hustle woman as usual". After a couple of weeks of pretending to work and producing no pay to the Austrian girl, Cap claims that he has quit this job also, "because it too hard" (p. 53).

Similarly to Cap, Murphy dwells in a transitory bedsit environment. Murphy's first noted place of abode is his flat in a condemned West Brompton mew (p. 3). Like Cap, he has aborted his academic career (Cap's schooling, in London, has been in law, while Murphy's, in Ireland, has been in theology).

Murphy resembles Cap in shambling about London in a mouldy-greenish-hued, timeworn suit connoting a poverty-stricken migrant's effort to reflect a half-forgotten status of respectability. Whereas Cap's is green-striped, Murphy's is "not green, but aeruginous . . . , in some places . . . as black as the day it was bought" (p. 47).

Although Murphy's narrator obtrudes to mock the near-destitute, self-preoccupied protagonist as a "seedy solipsist", Murphy, like Cap, has one point of corporeal connection with his London environment that is not severed by his economic disenfranchisement: his involvement with women. Murphy's main, current interest in London is Celia Kelly, who, like the Austrian of Selvon's novel, is not an English native but a migrant: Celia herself is a childhood arrival from Ireland. In Selvon's text, Cap's Austrian girlfriend is physically self-aware of her own power over men as "a sharp dresser, all kind of fur coat in the winter, and in the summer some kind of dress that making fellars whistle and turn around" (p. 51). She proves herself to be more than an object of Cap's lust by asserting her strong will and coaxing him – albeit unsuccessfully – to find permanent and lucrative work.

Celia Kelly in *Murphy* similarly shows that migrant women at least can assert the will to survive in their new environment, even if men present no such faculties. They are the motivating force lambasting their drifting lovers for not making at least some effort to find a job. Celia demonstrates a physically self-aware "swagger that could not be disguised" as she walks around London in echoes of her former "beat" as a street-prostitute (p. 94). However, she is not an unambiguously exploited and objectified victim of transient male desires. Instead, Celia exemplifies virtues of pecuniary ambition and socioeconomic intelligence in pestering Murphy, from the start of their relationship, to find a job:

> "But we cannot go on without any money," said Celia.
> "Providence will provide," said Murphy.
> The imperturbable negligence of Providence to provide goaded them to such transports as West Brompton had not known since the Earl's Court Exhibition. (p. 16)

Celia, it appears here, is even more persistent with Murphy than the Austrian girl with Cap. She resumes her life making money on the street "[w]hen there was no money left and no bill to be cooked for another week". She announces that "either Murphy got work or she left him and went back to hers. Murphy said work would be the end of them both" (p. 16).

When no employment is immediately forthcoming to suit his theological and philosophical diversions, Murphy – like Cap, who cannot even find storekeeping work on a railway to remotely reflect his aborted legal background – gives up serious pursuit of an occupation and ventures instead, at Celia's ultimatum, "on the jobpath" (p. 46). This search, for want of many better and even antonymical words, is conducted in the least proactive of fashions, largely due to self-realization of his own unemployability. Just as Cap bids *au revoir* to his hopeful girlfriend at the train platform only to spend the night hours he pretends to be working by chasing other women, so Murphy affects to be out seeking work while in reality wandering about London's streets until precisely the time he is due to return. ("The punctuality with which Murphy returned was astonishing. Literally he did not vary in this by more than a few seconds from day to day", p. 46.)

By the point in the chronology of the novel on which he embarks on his jobpath, Murphy has left his West Brompton mew and is now, Cap-like, drifting across London's transitory bedsitter land, the realm of migrants with no work or roots. He resides with Celia in Brewery Road and his trudge ends daily at their door after a repetitive plod of self-aware futility, demonstrated in the following example of focalization: "The truth was that Murphy began to return in such good time that he arrived in Brewery Road with hours to spare. From the practical point of view he could see no difference between hanging about in Brewery Road and hanging about say in Lombard Street. His prospects of employment were the same in both places, in all places" (p. 46).

By pure accident, one lunchtime in a seedy cafeteria, Murphy is accosted by Austin Ticklepenny, a poetaster, dry dipsomaniac and unwilling employee at a nearby psychiatric institution called the Magdalen Mental Mercyseat (or MMM). Ticklepenny begs Murphy to relieve him of his charge of "male nurse in a hospital for the better-class mentally deranged" (p. 57).

Murphy thus deviates from Cap in securing employment, albeit only for the last week of his life, until a gas-pipe explosion from the lavatory to his latest temporary abode, a workplace attic garret, awards his body the final quiet his mind had wished in life to bestow upon it (p. 158). In taking employment that culminates in a night shift (in which he passes the time playing an anti-logical chess game with a "schizophrenic of the most amiable variety", Mr Endon),

Murphy in the end slots into a labour reserve. Yet he must still be read as a migrant figure in that he joins the significantly nocturnal migrant workforce, in very similar fashion to Selvon's Moses Aloetta (p. 116). Murphy's work experience, like Moses's, belongs to that range of Irish London Underground construction and maintenance tunnellers, Caribbean London Underground railway staff, Irish and Caribbean factory workers, and Irish and Caribbean nurses in the National Health Service in Britain in the middle decades of the twentieth century. Murphy's ultimately chosen way of working in London is in the manner of many migrants on the margins of day-lit, nine-to-five society.[14]

As a migrant whose academic training situates him outside of the surplus labour reserve, Murphy fashions himself as an artist of sorts. In picturing a complex topography of his mind, he expresses in metaphor the extent of his migrant isolation from the city in which he now dwells. The heterodiegetic narrator of the sixth section of *Murphy* has exclusive access to the design of Murphy's mental composition, which "pictured itself as a large hollow sphere, hermetically closed to the universe without. . . . The mental experience was cut off from the physical experience" (p. 69). It is in the innermost compartment of this imagined mind that Murphy considers himself most "sovereign". The choice of this adjective is interesting in a postcolonial context, as it implies that Murphy's art is a form of figurative strategy for decolonization, and for breaking free from the enslaving chains of his everyday diasporic life in the first city of the British Empire. Moses in many respects resembles Murphy in that he begins to formulate an artistic response to the city, in pursuit of imaginative freedom from the "great aimlessness" of being a lonely migrant Londoner. He recalls his friend Daniel "telling him how over in France all kinds of fellars writing books what turning out to be best-sellers. Taxi-driver, porter, road-sweeper – it didn't matter" (p. 142). Poised on the banks of the Thames, Moses meditates on the sight of a tugboat in mid-journey across the river, neither at its point of origin or destination. The tugboat is, at least seen in an instant captured out of time, isolated from a point of departure or arrival. It offers a figurative device for imagining the migrant artistic spirit for once as free and sovereign. The tales of Murphy and Moses are to a degree portraits of postcolonial artists seeking a sovereignty of the migrant imagination.

Thus far, this study has observed the extent to which the positioned histories of anglophone Irish and Caribbean migration to London have converged in the parallel representations of migrant drifters in Selvon's and Beckett's novels. What remains is to test the extent of these parallels in the light of further consideration of historical nuances between the texts. The employment of narrative discourse is a textual aspect of the novels that presents their nuances of difference. In Bakhtinian terms, *The Lonely Londoners* is a more evidently dialogic novel than *Murphy*. Selvon's text is multi-perspectival, whereas a very interjectory and opinionated authorial voice presents the third-person narrative of Beckett's novel. This point is of significance to a postcolonial reader in understanding how Selvon and Beckett respectively wish to approach variant African and Caribbean, or Irish, experiences of migration in London. Selvon tries to show that there is some measure of commonality or community between the migrant characters on whom he bases his material and whom he presents in his novel. Such a sense of community is constructed in Selvon's discourse as a plural narrative voice of migrant experience. Beckett, on the other hand, depicts several Irish migrant characters in his novel, but he shows them as detached and alienated from one another. Their lack of communal cohesiveness as a migrant, non-labouring Irish population in the London of the 1930s is demonstrated by the relative absence of their agency in the narrative: the omniscient narrator instead does most of the talking for these lost characters.

A close comparative reading of the novels can show these variant enunciations of a migrant voice in operation. For example, *The Lonely Londoners* ostensibly operates via a slightly formalized, "writerly", Trinidadian Creole mode of authorial heterodiegesis. This voice is heard at the text's very beginning: "One grim winter evening, when it had a kind of unrealness about London, with a fog sleeping restlessly over the city" (p. 23). It should be pointed out that since Selvon's authorial voice in his previous novel, *A Brighter Sun,* was Standard English, one should not conflate the real Selvon with the writing effect of the Creole narrator. That being said, the level of consonance between the narrative voice of Moses Aloetta, focalized using free indirect discourse in the novel's second paragraph, points to a strong level of dialogism between the voices in the text. Note the dialogism in the line, "He had was to get up from a nice warm bed and dress and come out in this nasty weather to go and meet a fellar that he didn't even know" (p. 23). The authorial voice might not necessarily be Selvon's writing voice in his previous novels, yet it fuses with Moses's (right down to the idiomatic Creole "had was"); Moses's tale can be seen contextually to relate to Selvon's own biography.

For example, although Sam Selvon was of middle-class Scottish and Indo-Trinidadian background and Moses is working-class Afro-Trinidadian, the similarities between author and novelistic protagonist are tangible. Selvon's first months in London were spent at the Balmoral Hotel in Kensington, with many other immigrants. The setting provided the basis for the hostel recollected by Moses throughout *The Lonely Londoners*: it was at such a location that both author and protagonist came into contact with migrant drifters and their London plight. After several years in England, Selvon, like Moses, found himself becoming familiar with a largely male Caribbean community faced with the prejudicial ignorance of the British people. The main authorial voice is not that which Selvon had used prior to *The Lonely Londoners*. Still, there is enough of his personal experience, environment and home vernacular refracted through the novel's authorial narration and the focalized consciousness of the semi-autobiographical Moses to suggest a dialogism between the real chronotope of Selvon's lived experience and that voiced in the novel.

The heterodiegetic narrator of *Murphy*, on the other hand, while omniscient and able to plunge into the most recondite recesses of the protagonist's consciousness, frequently employs devices emphasizing distance rather than dialogic consonance between his stance and Murphy's. At the start of section six, the narrator apologizes directly to the reader for the task of explaining Murphy's mind as Murphy perceives it: "It is most unfortunate, but the point of this story has been reached where a justification of the expression 'Murphy's mind' has to be attempted. Happily we need not concern ourselves with this apparatus as it really was – that would be an extravagance and an impertinence – but solely with what it felt and pictured itself to be" (p. 69). The interjection "Happily we need not concern ourselves with this apparatus as it really was" is an obtrusive, implied remark illustrating that the authorial narrator has greater knowledge of Murphy than he has of himself. This comment indicates a level of perspectival and ideological distance between narrator and protagonist, which is certainly more pronounced than that between the narrator of *The Lonely Londoners* and Moses Aloetta. A postcolonial reader thus sees how Selvon and Beckett are both writers who seek to portray what it is to be a migrant without provenance or target in London in the middling decades of the twentieth century. Such a reader can also assess that while Selvon and Beckett each portray migrant drifters with little opportunity for setting down permanent roots in one place in the city, Selvon at least offers the hope that through a shared enunciation of a plural West Indian voice, the characters in his novel might in time forge a permanent Caribbean-British community. Beckett's novel depicts the Irish migrant characters of 1930s London as – so far, at the very least – unable to synthesize a collective, heterogeneous Irish-British migrant narrative.

It is reasonable to conjecture that a jobless Irish migrant might struggle but manage to secure passage home, but for a Caribbean migrant without a job, the enormous sum of money required might take years of saving. Since Galahad's stay in the country is likely to be one-way, he has financially and emotionally invested so much in his passage and arrival in Britain that he makes considerable efforts to avoid disillusionment, in spite of his initial terror at being stranded alone in Queensway. He attempts to invest in the place names of London a sense of mystique, befitting someone of his own romantic name, which is ultimately undermined by his true-life encounters with the city:

> He had a way, whenever he talking with the boys, he using the names of the places like they mean big romance, as if to say "I was in Oxford Street" have more prestige than if he just say "I was up the road". And once he had a date with a frauline, and he make a big point of saying he was meeting she by Charing Cross, because just to say "Charing Cross" have a lot of romance in it, he remember it had a song called "Roseann of Charing Cross." And this is how he getting on to Moses:
> "I meeting that piece of skin tonight, you know." And then, as if not very important, "She waiting for me by Charing Cross Station."
> Jesus Christ, when he say "Charing Cross," when he realize that is he, Sir Galahad, who going there, near that place that everybody in the world know about (it even have the name in the dictionary) he feel like a new man. It didn't matter about the woman he going to meet, just to say he was going there made him feel big and important, and even if he was just going to coast a lime, to stand up and watch the white people, still, it would have been something. (pp. 83–84)

At Charing Cross, Galahad's colour is noticed by a child, who cries when he seeks to calm her. Galahad notes that due to casual prejudice, while the child's mother might have been friendlier on this occasion if not in such a public place, she is in this instant reticent. Galahad apostrophizes the colour black and curses it for his misfortune. In time, Galahad tends to romanticize his remembered native San Fernando more than his day-to-day London, especially during the incident where he steals a pigeon to eat, again at Queensway.

However, Galahad's long-term efforts to settle in London and to romanticize it separate him decisively from some of the short-term migrant characters in Beckett's *Murphy*, such as Neary and Miss Counihan, who have no intention of staying in London but travel there to seize the novel's protagonist and coax him back to Ireland. If anything, it is the Irish Free State that these migrants hold in romantic esteem. Murphy's departure from Ireland is for his peers a worrying critique of a popular myth of the country's post-independence allure as a free, once-again Gaelic nation. In their view, why should Murphy abandon Ireland for Britain, the former oppressor? He should be returned to Ireland immediately.

For example, Neary is seen at Dublin's General Post Office, the historical location where Padraig Pearse read out the Proclamation of Irish Independence in April 1916. Neary is clinging on to the rump of a statue, fashioned in the prime of Irish Revivalism, of the Gaelic Ulster Cycle hero Cúchulainn. This image is sardonic and astute. The bronze statue in the General Post Office, sculpted by Oliver Sheppard (1865–1941), might well have appealed to an emergent romantic nationalism at the time of its production in 1911, yet it is of a figure who existed in remote myth rather than a more recent history. What is more, although this is a work of the Irish Revival and thus an attempt at reinvigorating a heroic Irish warrior heritage as an antidote to a British imperial hegemony, Cúchulainn is shown to be dying. The inference here is that one cannot truly revive a pre-colonial past that is dying in modern memory, especially if it never demonstrably happened, however much one clings to its buttocks in the hope of massaging it into life. Neary's desperation to grasp on to a pre-colonial Irish idyll and work it into a postcolonial Irish ideal is thus represented as folly. It is such an attempt to fashion post-independence Ireland into a Gaelic fantasy that Murphy may well have fled, over a short distance, to the former British colonizer.

It might be ambitious to characterize Murphy as a "West Briton" or Anglophile, yet he certainly betrays none of the nationalist, Revivalist tendencies of his Irish peers whom he leaves behind: they follow him to England to reclaim him, seemingly for the cause of Ireland. As the 1938 unsigned reviewer of *Murphy* in the *Times Literary Supplement* notes of the novel, Neary loves a woman who loves Murphy. This woman, left behind in Dublin, is a Miss Counihan. Her name suggests an intentional and clever conflation of the name Cathleen ní Houlihan – like Cúchulainn, another romantic nationalist Irish figure of art, performance and ballad, who became the title character of a Revivalist 1902 play by W.B. Yeats and Lady Gregory.

Cathleen ní Houlihan is intended to represent an independent Ireland, the prize for which Irish nationalists should fight, yet she harbours the unfortunate propensity to lure young men to their violent deaths in pursuit of her objectives. Beckett's Miss Counihan is, as a *femme fatale*, the embodiment of a post-independence Irish nationalist allure from whose clutches Murphy (and the superannuated Neary, for that matter, or his accomplice Wylie) cannot be allowed to escape. Murphy has, according to the romantic, flighty and unreliable Miss Counihan, left for England to "set up for his princess, in some less desolate quarter of the globe, a habitation meet for her. When he had done this he could come flying back to claim her" (p. 34). The comic hyperbole of this fairy-tale rendering of Murphy's migration to England is preposterous not least because it implies that Murphy is an economic migrant, building a nest for his love. It is also unlikely that Murphy would return to claim her, but given her physical proximity to England, she could always seek to reclaim him. So, she boards the Saturday B&I ferry from Dublin to Liverpool and takes the train to London. However, once in the capital, her bewitching Gaelic charms fail: Neary is "cured" of "Jezebel Counihan" on arrival in England, and Wylie, if not cured, is convalescent (p. 124). The implication here is that the post-independent Gaelic romantic ideal might function to seduce and constrain people in Ireland but its reaches cannot extend to its diaspora, particularly those headed to the former imperial metropolis of London.

This is very different from the attraction of home in *The Lonely Londoners*, which seems to become stronger in Galahad's mind over the course of years. Since, in Selvon's novel, home is something likely never to be seen again, it must be restored imaginatively in the location of arrival. So, wandering around Queensway hungry and seeing pigeons cooing plentifully, Galahad is transported to a San Fernando of the mind, a landscape where value systems are different and pigeons are food acceptable by society to kill and eat. The short distance of time and space from Ireland to England (and, implicitly, back again) in *Murphy*, however, seems to rob Miss Counihan of her potency to embody an Ireland of the mind to other Irish migrants: her long-term romantic appeal depends upon a more permanent migrancy and transatlantic destination, such as the Americas.

The matter of geography and finance thus situates these two otherwise similar narratives of migrancy to London in the mid-twentieth century as positioned Irish and Caribbean responses to a diasporic phenomenon. However, irrespective of such historical and geographical considerations and the resultant nuances in the ways similarities between migrant characters and narrative in Beckett's and Selvon's novels are played out, what characters such as Neary, Miss Counihan, Cap, Murphy and Galahad share at varying levels is an uncertainty over origin or destination. Neary clasps an uncertain pre-colonial Irish myth while searching for a sense of identity that he feels Murphy might be more successfully migrating towards. Miss Counihan tells a confused romantic tale reconstructing the reasons for Murphy's migration, while seeking to reclaim him for fear that he has lost his sense of origin in her arms. Cap imagines seeing spirits from Nigeria in the England in which he is stranded: this former student has been disowned by home and, without a permanent residence, is unlikely to arrive at any sense of a migrant destination in London, at least socioeconomically. Murphy apprehends, albeit not without the posture of some pleasure, "the sensation of being a missile without provenance or target, caught up in a tumult of non-Newtonian motion" (p. 72).

Yet it is Galahad in Selvon's novel who best forges an ability to hybridize a sense of provenance and target, even though financial constraints preclude him from finding a fixed address or occupation in London as a physical place for migrant destination. He focuses on the pigeons strutting around Kensington Gardens. These birds belong not to his remembered Trinidad, or to London, he opines, but "to the sea" (p. 123). The long-distance, transatlantic migrant Galahad realizes fleetingly here that much of his identity is, like the pigeons are, inextricably tied to his act of sea passage rather than to those places from which he came or still hopes romantically to reach, such as Charing Cross. This sense of migrant identity being decided in the journey is the key to negotiation of the problematics of finding a place and space for arrival among the migrants of Selvon's novel. Murphy, however, for all his pretence at having found a mental realm without a sense of origin or destination of physical forms and movements, is still seeking to target the innermost recesses of the mind as a migrant destination.

Murphy, like Galahad, would be best suited to consider the realm of physical objects – and the imaginative potentiality of the sea between those ferry ports he passed the previous February – as the space to inhabit as a means of negotiating provenance and target, so that his mind might be truly free of the psychic problems of migration. This conjecture depends for proof on whether Murphy's return journey from Liverpool to Dublin allows him enough time for epiphanies regarding his migration. Beckett never presents this proof. Selvon's Galahad, on the other hand, has a whole month drifting on a boat journey between Caribbean periphery and supposed imperial core. Whatever the case, comparison of the texts incites a provocative reading not only of instances where migration is an explicated theme of *Murphy* but how its lacunae or loose narrative ends suggest important migrant contexts and implications.

5.

Shadow Kings

George Lamming's *In the Castle of My Skin* and
Michael Farrell's *Thy Tears Might Cease*

GEORGE LAMMING'S FIRST NOVEL, *IN THE CASTLE OF MY SKIN* (1953), enjoys such a strong reputation that it remains in print sixty years after its first publication.

Castle is often read as a chief precursor for postcolonial texts that followed: Ngũgĩ wa Thiong'o claims that it "in many ways anticipated many of the themes in Fanon's *The Wretched of the Earth*; Albert Memmi's *The Colonizer and the Colonized* and numerous other anti-colonial texts".[1] Lamming criticism and scholarship continues strongly: Anthony Bogues's 2011 edition *Caribbean Reasonings: The George Lamming Reader* contains a variety of essays touching on *Castle*'s importance not only to Caribbean thought, but to postcolonial studies as a whole.[2] Thus, *Castle*, from its first publication, has played a vanguard role in what has come to be called decolonizing thought.

Michael Farrell's sole, posthumous novel, *Thy Tears Might Cease* (drafted in the 1930s but published in 1963), on the other hand, has had barely any reception or critical history, is out of print, and has certainly to date not been read in postcolonial terms.[3] Brendan Kennelly had offered some promise of the novel's future critical profile in regarding it as "the first Irish novel of epic stature since *Ulysses*".[4] However, with the novel's author dead and Irish bookshops favouring religious literature over the novel, *Tears* eventually fell into obscurity. There has never been an article on the novel in *Irish University Review* (since 1970 one of the foremost critical journals in Irish studies). Peter Costello's

1977 book *The Heart Grown Brutal* gives the most extensive reading of *Tears* to date, and even then, the reading only constitutes several pages. Costello appraises Farrell's ability to identify the ideological complexity of Ireland at the time in which the novel begins, the Redmond era of Home Rule party politics. He writes, "Farrell is honest enough to draw for us the complexity of feelings in Ireland then, where all that was good and dignified was Protestant, and all that was grubby and conniving seemed to be nationalist."[5] However, Costello's reading of *Tears* is set within the relatively narrow scope of reading revolutionary forces and themes in the Irish literature from the death of Parnell to the death of Yeats.

In this chapter, I shall reappraise *Tears* and show how greatly it accords with the thematic preoccupations of the archetypal postcolonial novel, *Castle*. I shall first look at *Castle* in order to identify its major concerns. For instance, I shall consider why Lamming's novel devises a wide-scale revision of the *Bildungsroman* model of the novel from a late-colonial Caribbean standpoint. I shall move to address the postcolonial significance of its narrative depiction of a moment of historical verisimilitude: a flashpoint of anti-colonial violence and its resulting impression on local communities. I shall then discuss the significance of Lamming's critique of the pitfalls of national consciousness through the portrayal of a would-be messianic, capitalistic local traitor of his trusting community. I shall then turn to a detailed comparative reading of Farrell's novel that demonstrates its close parallels with the preoccupations of Lamming's text. My aim is to reveal the extent to which *Tears* should be reread as a postcolonial novel, by showing how it so significantly parallels narrative modes and key themes of Lamming's canonical text.

Castle is a semi-autobiographical novel outlining the coming of age of a sensitive young Afro-Barbadian boy, G., the son of a single mother, in a plantation village immediately before, during and in the years following the Barbados labour riots of 1937. G. and the village in which he lives are forced into a confused but rude awakening as to the oppressive nature of the semi-feudal hierarchy at the bottom of which the people have lived for generations, and to which many have blithely and unconsciously deferred. Over the course of the novel, G. struggles into awareness of himself, his village identity and community, and the history of colonialism and slavery.

The German term *Bildungsroman* means a novel of education. It refers to a form of literary fiction in which a young, unusually astute protagonist undergoes a rite of difficult passage, from apparently impoverished or unpleasant childhood conditions into economically improved or psychically enlightened adulthood and individuation. Goethe's *William Meister's Apprenticeship* (1795–96) is arguably the provenance of the novel form of the *Bildungsroman,* and the term to describe it was first used in 1819 by the German philologist Johann Karl Simon Morgenstern.[6] Throughout Europe and America over the course of the nineteenth and twentieth centuries, the novel of education or self-cultivation became increasingly popular. In Britain, Charles Dickens heavily popularized the *Bildungsroman* in such works as his semi-autobiographical *David Copperfield* (1849–50) and *Great Expectations* (1860–61).

Lamming offers a variation of the English-speaking fictive *Bildungsroman*, in that *Castle* has historical roots in the horrors of the Atlantic slave trade. In *Castle*, the protagonist belongs to a Barbadian community marginalized and exploited by British colonialism. Effectively, what Lamming achieves here is a seminal example of what has in time become a postcolonial cliché of writing back incisively to the centre of the English literary canon. Lamming gives G. a clear voice to operate in, and interrogate, the high literary medium of the novel in English.

In the opening chapter of *Castle*, G. introduces himself to the reader as a first-person narrator recalling his ninth birthday. Lamming startles novelistic convention by setting his heroic tale in the impoverished plantations of Barbados. Creighton village is based on Lamming's native, plantocratic Carrington village in St Michael, near Bridgetown, south-west Barbados: in this respect, it is hardly surprising that Lamming would choose it as his source setting. However, that he would use the conventional childhood narrative of coming-into-awareness and turn it on its head to represent life under semi-feudal economy and rule is its most striking attribute in postcolonial terms.

G. is the son of a single mother – not the product of an orthodox nuclear family. G.'s semi-parentlessness is of course not a matter for postcolonial reading in itself: many *Bildungsromane* feature protagonists without one or either parent, such as Jane Eyre.[7] G. is a typical *Bildungsroman* hero when he notes, "My birth began with an almost total absence of family relations."[8] G. has no recollection of forebears through which to formulate selfhood. He must instead fashion a narrative in order to create a sense of an "I" in relation to family, community and locality. His sense of lineage has been ruptured by colonial history, by slavery and transplantation, and by economic migration. When G. learns of his ancestors, they are shown to be absent characters notable for leaving the homeland behind for reasons with clear colonial implications. They flee the weak economic opportunities of British Barbados and seek work in the construction of the Panama Canal or in America. G. is a boy characterized by a lack of self-knowledge precipitated by the vicissitudes of colonial history in Barbados:

> And for memory I had substituted inquiry.
> "Where did you say my grandmother went?"
> "To Panama," my mother answered. "It was the opening of the canal. She is now in Canal Zone. It's time you wrote her a letter."
> "And my grandfather who was your father?" I went on.
> "Oh, he died, my child; he died before I was born."
> "And my uncle who was your brother?"
> "My brother went to America," my mother said. "It's years now." (p. 4)

G. acquires a narrative of memory from his mother, who cannot remember her relations either, since they left Barbados when she was two years old. G. and G.'s mother each seek to recreate a sense of origins from a past marked by the rupturing social influence of historical forces upon families. Lamming clearly frames his narrative around the effects of colonial history upon his characters' lives in Barbados.

A typical *Bildungsroman* will chart its protagonist's path through and beyond the harsh conditions in schools: *Jane Eyre*, for example, depicts its heroine surviving the hardships and pestilences of Lowood Institute. Yet *Castle* deliberately sets out to show something different and precisely of import to what postcolonialists would see as significant in the context of late-colonial Barbadian society to G.'s growing up. The novel dramatizes the impact of the power structure on the lives and roles of teachers and their treatment of children. Lamming demonstrates G.'s early school environment in the 1930s, prior to the labour riots that altered the class-consciousness of Bajan society. In Creighton village, G.'s teachers are not part of the colonizing caste or class but are still inevitably part of an education system that causes division and self-loathing among the local people. To a degree, G.'s teachers are as manipulated and exploited by the power structure as the boys they teach. The teachers' frustration turns to anger and loathing of their caste. They are brutalized and they treat their pupils brutally in turn. G. witnesses the injustices of the social unit of the local school as an agent of repressive power. These harsh experiences of village school life under colonial rule are in time counterbalanced, ironically, by pleasant experiences of "true" colonial education. They thus complicate his allegiances to colonizing or colonized castes. The village schoolteachers of G.'s first boys' school are of the same Afro-Barbadian community as their pupils, while answering to an English school inspector. The teachers inflict harsh punishment on the children that implies a measure of their own frustrated social status under the Crown.

For example, in the novel, Lamming chooses to illustrate the vulnerability and volatility of the local men in charge of the village youth via a representation not of an ordinary school day but of perhaps the most important day in the school calendar, Empire Day, 1937. Empire Day, a celebration of imperial power, is the day when white British administrators and inspectors come to the school and visibly assert their authority and critical eye over the Afro-Barbadian teachers. The British in charge remind the teachers, by their very presence, of the precariousness and meagreness of the latter's position in the hierarchy of imperial power. Under this huge pressure, the anger of the head teacher explodes into rage in an incident in which he reacts against a perceived threat to his personal and professional status and power.

On this day, the head teacher's own sense of superiority and respect within the school has already been undermined by rival would-be usurpers within his staff. He has just discovered, to his horror, compromising photographs involving his wife, which have until recently been in the possession of fellow teacher Mr Slime. Then, when a boy – Boy Blue – asks the head teacher "if the queen's bloomers was red, white, and blue", another unnamed boy, presumably Trumper, is mistaken for the culprit and the head teacher attacks him in a way that the boys later discuss as unnatural. It could be the allusion to female undress that reminds the head teacher of his lack of status in his own bedroom, or it could be the thought of a child's shocking, public disrespect for Queen Mary in front of his British superiors that triggers the head teacher's violence. It is likely a combination of both factors that precipitate his attack on the boy. In any case, Lamming dramatizes the head teacher's outburst in order to show the impotence and frustration of Afro-Barbadian provincial male professionals. They cannot rally against their superiors or immediate usurpers, and can only repeat their repression by their masters upon the backs of the most vulnerable of their society, their schoolchildren. The local boys sense the perversity of this cycle of abuse:

> *First Boy*: I never see him beat anybody like that. Never ever.
> *Second Boy*: Nor me as far as my memory can remember has I seen him take off his jacket in that sort of fashion to fix up a fellow. I didn't do it, but I nearly did dirty myself, when I see him bring that belt down on yuh bambam.
> *Third Boy*: Seems as though he sort of had it waiting for you and you only. 'Twustn't what you would call a nat'ral beating.
> *Fourth Boy*: That's as much as I says to myself. 'Twustn't nat'ral the way he went 'bout it. (p. 36)

The teachers' anger is born of their own subjugation. Mary Chamberlain writes that the racist organizational structure of Barbados amounted to a form of apartheid. Opportunities for socioeconomic improvement for black people were very few, and the education system seemed set up to enforce divisions between rich and poor. There were very few secondary schools on the island and only a small number of Afro-Barbadians had enough education to pass the examination.[9] Anthony Layne also remarks that Barbadian colonial education was overtly elitist, and geared towards maintaining the dominance of the planter-settler order over the rest of the population.[10]

G. in *Castle* explains that the teachers at the village school – the head teacher included – answer directly to a supervising minister, and an "inspector who gave orders" (p. 210). The school is merely an instrument of British rule. The village schoolteachers are interested mainly in silencing and repressing the children via violence, for fear of censure by the British authorities. As G. narrates in *Castle*, "the village school served the needs of the villagers, who were poor, simple and without a very marked sense of social prestige" (pp. 210–11). In time, G. himself is shown to become, in the true manner of a protagonist of the *Bildungsroman* narrative, astutely sensitive and reflective, even generous, with understanding the reasons for the follies of his cruel elders. He pinpoints fear as the motivating force behind the violence of the teachers in the village school: "The head teacher and all the assistants carried their canes as though they were in danger of attack from the boys, and they used them on all occasions and for all sorts of reasons" (p. 208). Yet this fear is different from that generated in the scenario of the repressive school in English school fiction: it is born of a colonial power structure in a Caribbean island.

Over the course of the novel Lamming shows the effects of a more genteel imperialist education system upon the development, and complication, of the protagonist's identity and social sensibilities, as he matures into adolescence and beyond. When G. proves a successful scholar and wins a place at the island's prestigious High School, he encounters a very different educational environment from that which he has known previously. If this event in *Castle* is reflexive of George Lamming's schooling, then the institution is based upon Combermere, a school situated not far from Carrington village in Waterford, St Michael. Keith A.P. Sandiford writes that colonial Barbadian elite schools such as Combermere, the Lodge and Harrison were set up to emulate Victorian English public schools, with an emphasis on promoting the "three Cs" (or core, "civilizing" values). These schools prized Christianity, classical education and scholarship, and cricket (a "civilizing" force for strengthening an elite colonial mind and body, in line with the social Darwinian ethos of *mens sana in corpore sano*).[11] As G. comes to prefer the superior facilities of the High School's cricket pitch to those provided in the village, he increasingly becomes part of the High School's implied class separation from the rest of the village. It is no longer "safe" for G. to be seen by his school peers playing at the old crossroads (p. 212). He is, to all intents and purposes, required to be indoctrinated into Englishness. He is expected to shun his village community and accept the English education system as his own, right down to reading the Norman invasion as "his" history. G. struggles to find a place between contrary worlds. In Fanonian terms, he is a young black man expected to wear a white mask.

This establishment does not wallow angrily in a sense of its own limited educational and social reach, as was the case with Creighton village school. Rather, it mimics and aspires to an English prototype in all areas including its topographic design, with its quintessentially English tall orchards, broad playing fields and that signifier of British colonial culture, the cricket pitch. The High School is a Little England simulacrum. It constructs for its pupils an England of the mind in order to produce potential Cambridge candidates who might one day return to the island and mimic their British masters in manners and bureaucratic efficiency. Only a late-colonial *Bildungsroman* would depict and interrogate the theme of the inculcation of Englishness via the educational system of the colonized island. Here, *Castle* paves the way for future

Caribbean *Bildungsromane* such as V.S. Naipaul's *The Mimic Men* (1967) and Merle Hodge's *Crick Crack, Monkey* (1970). The novel thus creates a staple theme of the canonical postcolonial novel, namely a protagonist's ambiguous sense of identity and loyalty to his or her community, complicated largely by the workings of a colonial education system.

Castle shows how the British education system works as a socially divisive and hierarchical construction separating bright children from their village community because of their recognized usefulness to the state. Trumper, Bob and Boy Blue, G.'s old friends, are left behind at the village school and destined for a trade while G.'s future is in a profession. However, Lamming challenges the dictated way of Barbados's social world by showing that G. cannot so easily forget his old friends, or become a simulacrum of an educated English pen-pusher. Rather, G. is shown to harbour a continuing urge to socialize with the Creighton villagers even though he is meant to feel somewhat apart from them. G. is not yet at the stage in his development where he will be prompted to perceive a sense of a race consciousness, a race history or a sense of his people.

Lamming cleverly depicts G. as a psychological and social embodiment of conflicting cultural identity constructions at this stage in his life and career. G. is a fictive example of the ruled, encouraged to mimic the ruler, while struggling to negotiate loyalties between communities. Frantz Fanon once argued that this is a crucial stage in decolonizing intellectual and psychological development:

> In order to ensure his salvation and to escape the supremacy of the white man's culture the native [intellectual] feels the need to turn backwards towards his unknown roots and to lose himself in his own barbarous people. Because he feels he is becoming estranged, that is to say because he feels that he is the living haunt of contradictions which run the risk of becoming insurmountable, the native tears himself away from the swamp that may suck him down and accepts everything. . . .
>
> This tearing away, painful and difficult though it may be, is, however, necessary. If it is not accomplished there will be serious psycho-affective injuries and the result will be individuals without an anchor, without a horizon, colourless, stateless, rootless – a race of angels.[12]

Lamming portrays G. as a young man subjugated by a colonial education system and battling to reconcile his loyalty to his native village community with his wearing of the white mask of a British education. A schism in G.'s sense of identity is clearly apparent, for, although over time the village is claimed to have "receded" from his consciousness, he nonetheless cannot forget it (p. 211). Lamming represents G. at this point in his youth as on the cusp of the two possible futures suggested by Fanon: tearing away from the psychologically damaging tendency to imagine himself as both Afro-Barbadian and as a replica of the British colonial model, or retreating from the bourgeois model once again towards his own people.

However, Lamming might also see a way beyond Fanon's argument in allowing for G. to try to reconcile these contrary impulses, as long as G. eschews the worst propensities of a colonial education to adopt a false self over his formative sense of identity and community. In ways, Lamming anticipates Homi Bhabha's concept of the decolonizing power of *distanced* mimicry here, or repetition with a difference.[13] G. receives an education in which he is encouraged to mimic his British superiors. The discourse of British superiority implicitly accepts no alternatives, as it is the emblem of civilization: it is singular, monologic and universal. G. adheres to this model well as a schoolboy learning the curriculum of British education, but he is inherently different from the standard and even the geographical locale of the archetypal British schoolboy. He is from Creighton village. He is of the Afro-Barbadian population, a population historically transplanted, enslaved and oppressed. He cannot be a carbon copy of a singular notion of British identity. He adulterates that standard, inevitably, with the markings of his own inheritance, of which he is slowly coming into consciousness. Over time, G. questions his always uncomfortable idea of identity, worries at it and deconstructs it. G. might receive a colonial education but he does not attain the Western European ideal of selfhood or independence as a result of this. Slavery, semi-feudal plantation life, the disruptive influence of the necessity for economic migration on families, and the divisive role of colonial education – all challenge G.'s route to individuation according to the parameters of the novel of education. Yet they inform the integral structure of the postcolonial *Bildungsroman*, exemplified by Lamming's novel.

Castle is, as a semi-autobiographical *Bildungsroman*, historical. It furthermore provides an event that, as a narrative centrepiece, is of considerable postcolonial significance in that it relates a key moment of anti-colonial violence, the

Barbados riots of 1937. These riots were the largely spontaneous reaction to news of the secret deportation from Barbados of Trinidadian-born trade union pioneer Clement Payne (1904–41). Payne had arrived earlier in the year to organize worker resistance, against attempts by the Barbados Produce Exporters Association to enforce austerity measures in the sugar industry and shipping trade by way of cutting pay and denying trade union powers. Payne had educated Barbadian workers about suppression of collective bargaining across the British Caribbean; he was regarded as such a threat to the Barbados Produce Exporters Association that he was arrested by Barbadian authorities on a (false) charge of having entered the country on a claim of Barbadian birth. Although Payne was cleared of this charge in a trial on 22 July, he was expelled in clandestine fashion: consequently, on 26 July, riots flared in Bridgetown.[14]

Lamming devises a way of detailing the events of the Bridgetown riots indexically, so that they are shown to encroach confusedly and rapidly from without upon the everyday lives of the Creighton villagers. The significance of this type of narrative is to show that anti-colonial violence is inflicted by a comparative few, while the lives of ordinary people continue as usual until the shock of the event irreversibly permeates their lives and initiates a process of disengagement from colonial power. The first word regarding events in the city arrives via snippets of rumour: "The parents couldn't understand what was happening, but one of the girls said that her head teacher said there was fighting in town, and it was possible the fighting would soon spread to the village" (p. 182). The nature of this "fighting" in Bridgetown is unclear to those in Creighton village: "Mr. Foster was vague. He said something might have been happening, but he wasn't in the city and therefore he couldn't say. Some people met at the corner to ask one another what would happen, but it was useless. No one knew what was happening. There was fighting in town and the fighting would soon spread to the village. They returned to their houses and waited" (p. 182).

When Mr Foster visits the local police station to find out what is happening, he returns only to tell those assembled anxiously at his house that the station is closed, since the police have left to help attend to the situation in the city. The widespread threat of violence is perhaps suggested in the reaction of the villagers to this news, which, even in its lack of detail, forebodes an unspeakable scale of uprising: "The people returned home and waited. From one end of the street to the other the houses were closed. The doors were locked or bolted, and the occupants peeped out through the jalousies or under the windows which were prised open now and again" (p. 182). When "the sun came out and dispersed the rain clouds", what might have been a symbol of clemency and natural order is now a very literal threat of meteorologically facilitated summer riot. The idea that this riot might be political, however, is beyond the comprehension of the collectively focalized villagers, who, locked terrified in their houses,

> had never heard of anything like it before. They had known a village fight, and they were used to fights between boys and girls. Sometimes after the cricket competition one village team for various reasons might threaten to fight with the opponent. These fights made sense, but the incidents in the city were simply beyond them. There was fighting in the city. And the fighting would soon spread to the village. That was all that was clear. And they couldn't say they understood that. (p. 183)

Thus, Lamming seeks to produce a narrative capturing that initial sense of shock among a community for whom the idea, and event, of anti-colonial violence is alien and threatening rather than supported. He does so to document that anti-colonial struggles rarely originate in the movement of the masses but in a select portion of the overall population.

Castle is not just a novel of its protagonist's education. It is more than an accurate depiction of the impact of anti-colonial violence on the collective consciousness of an unsuspecting community. It is a novel with a prescriptive, educational element of caution for its audience. It implicitly advises its readership of the pitfalls in late-colonial society of a newfound political awareness. Its pedagogy is conveyed through Lamming's representation of Mr Slime, the capitalistic traitor of Creighton village, which provides a narrative mimesis of the concept of the pitfalls of emerging anti-colonial consciousness.

As described above, Mr Slime is first introduced in the novel as the teacher of class 5 of the village school: he is present in the school assembly during the ceremonies of Empire Day. Via focalization, the narrative presents the head teacher's scrutiny of the young, well-dressed Slime; the head teacher considers there to be "something a little flamboyant, almost vulgar, about his dress" (p. 50).

As an index of social ambition, Slime's polished nails and brilliant ties show an ostentatious self-regard that extends almost preposterously beyond the dress and social codes of the village school environment: they imply Slime's vanity and grasping wish to elevate his status far beyond its current parameters. For the head teacher, who has reached the highest level of his own professional potential, although Slime works well, his dress signifies crude aspirations beyond the scope of the current socioeconomic and professional context.

Slime demonstrates his highly questionable morality very early in the novel. He has an envelope containing compromising photographs – apparently of himself – with the head teacher's wife, which he means to show to the class 4 teacher. Through an unfortunate accident, the envelope is dropped when Slime leaves the assembly in an attempt to pass the material on surreptitiously to his colleague. A schoolboy picks it up; the head teacher notices; the boy is asked to bring the envelope to him; the head teacher opens the envelope and is confronted by its contents. The novel leaves any confrontation between the head teacher and Slime as a gap in the narrative, but when he is next seen in the text, he has left the village school and his ambition continues apace.

Chapter 4 of *Castle* presents as playtext the scripted dialogue of an interchange between two village elders, known to all as Ma and Pa. The employment of playtext in this chapter is significant. In eschewing any kind of diegetic narrative voice more typical of the prose novel, such as G.'s first-person narrative or passages of omniscient third-person narration, Lamming does not proclaim to affect any form of ideological containment or superior historical or intellectual knowledge over the two veteran characters in this depicted scene, as they debate Mr Slime's rise to prominence. Pa and Ma, representatives of a continuum of ancient Afro-Barbadian ideas and traditions, are allowed to speak for themselves on the topic of Slime. If Pa disagrees with Ma's scepticism on the matter of Mr Slime's radical charisma and capacity to deliver his people into freedom, their dialectic stands without narratorial obtrusion as authoritative viewpoints.

The two characters and their opinions are thus integral to themselves and one another, without the interference of a third narratorial party. Lamming wishes to present a mimetic rendering of the social reality of the impact of Mr Slime's public influence in Creighton village, as it is realized and articulated by the people, in the immediacy of that present moment. A narrator, framing that moment in the past tense and employing intervening instances of "Ma said" or "Pa said", would mediate excessively between the Creighton village elders and the reader: the reader would not gauge an accurate sense of Slime's effect on his community at the precise moment of his ascendancy. The playtext of Pa and Ma's discussion of Slime provides a clear window into the opinions of the elders in the village on this subject.

Pa, a veteran of the construction of the Panama Canal, has seen much Barbadian history and marvels at the ascendancy of Slime in the life of the village community. Slime is now a businessman: he has moved on from instructing children to educating the local population about how they might attain self-sufficiency and a measure of economic independence by investing in his new ventures. Pa advises Ma,

> Now look what he go an' do. He open a Friendly Society an' a Penny Bank, an' in the twinklin' of an eye, Ma, before you says Jack Robinson, he has them all two both flyin'. A year before we never ever hear' bout such things, an' now there ain't a single soul in all Creighton's village who ain't in Society an' Penny Bank all two at the same said time. Everybody puttin' they pennies one by one week after week, an' only God knows what that sort o' thing'll lead to. (p. 69)

Slime's rise is so fast that Pa equates him to modern-day Moses, who "rise up when nobody wus least expectin' to take his people out of the land of Egypt" (p. 69). Pa motions to Ma, a deeply religious woman, and appeals that Slime is a prophet for his people, as endorsed by God as the seers of the Old Testament and thus having moral authority over the village patriarch, Creighton. Pa has been so seduced by Slime's oratory, and by the village's reaction to him, that "[w]hen I hear the way the men an' women welcome him the night he speak his speech 'bout the future an' what an' what the future got in store for us how we'd be much better off when he wus finish doin' what he say he would, I says to myself 'twus Moses all over again" (p. 70). Slime's prophetic charisma charms the village with promises that one day the land will be theirs. Historically, there is indeed a context for Slime's Friendly Society: investors could hope to own land of up to an acre.[15] Now, in readiness for the Promised Land, the villagers invest in their deliverance:

> They all got they bank book, how little it is, an' they got the Society card, an' they know for certain if they in compliance they will get a decent an' proper funeral when 'tis time for them to go 'bout they business. An' that ain't all, 'cause the way he say in the speech he speak the other night how he goin' to make us owners o'

this land. I couldn't sort o' catch my breath when I hear it, but 'tis a big thing to expect, an' they all tell him in turn, an' 'twus only fair o' them to tell him, that he wus they chief an' they'll follow him till they die. (p. 71)

When the Bridgetown riots of July 1937 spread to Creighton village, Mr Slime defuses a tense standoff in the middle of the road between armed city workers, full of murderous intent, and the landlord. His plan to assume Creighton's power is not at fruition, and so more years pass before Slime usurps his colonial authority in the village. The Penny Bank and Friendly Society eventually outgrow the village's needs. Creighton and his sick wife eke out a few more years at their estate. Yet news of their departure from the village, and the circumstances in which Slime inherits the village, reveal his self-serving, traitorous, acquisitive capitalistic mentality at the expense of the trust of his own people.

Slime in many respects proves James Connolly's 1897 warning about the pitfalls of Irish national consciousness, but in a Caribbean late-colonial context. The boys of the village had envisaged the idea of the shadow king, a figure of Barbadian life who orchestrates the duties and administration of colonial life for the real king in England. Slime, for all his posturing as a liberator of the people, has been enslaving them through the very banking system that Connolly had argued would ensure that Ireland could never be free of British rule. The village is informed by a stranger – the former chief sanitary inspector and another "shadow" of the power structure – that he now part-owns the property (with Slime), and that residents must vacate their tenancies forthwith and move elsewhere.

The village refuses to believe this news until a posted public notice by Creighton's solicitors confirms the transition of power and land and announces that any queries should be addressed to Slime, the "Managing Director on behalf of the Penny Bank" and the ironically named "Help Your Brother Friendly Society". Shocked, the village cannot comprehend how and why Slime might betray them in such a manner. They can only mumble in a traumatized stupor, "It say we got to see Mr. Slime. See Mr. Slime. Mr. Slime. Mr. Slime. Mr. Slime" (p. 238).

Therefore, as a shadow agent of capitalist colonialism, Slime anticipates Frantz Fanon's discussion of national bourgeoisies in *The Wretched of the Earth*. Lamming wishes to warn future Slimes that he knows they have no real power;

they merely ride on the back of a banking system that belongs to the very colonial force that they pretend to replace:

> The national middle class which takes over power at the end of the colonial regime is an under-developed middle class. . . . [It] is not engaged in production, not in invention, not building, nor labour [but i]ts innermost vocation seems to be to keep in the running and to be part of the racket. The psychology of the national bourgeoisie is that of the businessman, not that of a captain of industry; and it is only too true that the greed of the settlers and the system of embargoes set up by colonialism has hardly left them any other choice.
> . . . Seen through its eyes, its mission has nothing to do with transforming the nation; it consists, prosaically, of being the transmission line between the nation and a capitalism, rampant though camouflaged, which today puts on the masque of neo-colonialism.[16]

Slime produces nothing to sustain the people of Creighton village come the withdrawal of the old landlord from the village. In accordance with Fanon's description of the national bourgeoisie, he enters into a capitalistic racket: the Penny Bank and the Friendly Society. Under the system of embargoes in Barbados, where capitalists maintain a monopoly and workers' rights are oppressed, Slime has had very little alternative opportunity to succeed in life except through an ascendancy within the class system that has been set in place by the British before him. Slime dons the mask of neo-colonialism, and inherits the tasks of British capitalism in further exploitation of his own peoples. He embodies the fundamental pitfall of national consciousness as described by Fanon in *The Wretched of the Earth*.

Ostensibly, *Tears*, an Irish novel, accords fairly closely with the model of the British *Bildungsroman*. It is a semi-autobiographical narrative about an eleven-year-old Leinster boy, Martin Matthew Reilly. Martin is orphaned and is now living, not altogether happily, with his "citizen merchant" uncle, John, and aunt, Eileen, in a small (fictive) town called Glenkilly, not far from Dublin. Yet delving more closely into the novel's specificities of setting, historical context and narrative, one sees that *Tears*, like *Castle*, subverts conventions of the English novel. It traces the complex path to adulthood of a protagonist whose conflicted background is the product of a history of colonial rule. Martin, like G., grows up in a period of anti-colonial violence and upheaval, and struggles to forge a sense of identity while negotiating communities and mindsets across Britain and his colonized island.

If one is to presume some semi-autobiographical basis for Glenkilly, then the setting is at least loosely based on Farrell's native Carlow Town. Martin is introduced at the start of the novel in the Redmondite, pre-Troubles era of Irish political nationalism in 1910. Within the interior space of the Reilly homestead itself are clues as to the very class to which the family belongs, at least at this time, prior to the Anglo-Irish War. This citizen-mercantile, Catholic family constitutes a powerful middle-class, Redmondite voting core. It has expendable (and thus politically investable) income. It can afford to employ house servants. Its support of Home Rule rather than Republican Irish independence might situate it ideologically as what was called at the time "Castle Catholic": in other words, like Redmond, it adheres to the idea of a self-governing Ireland administered from Dublin Castle as per before the Act of Union in 1800 and still subject to the British Crown. This considerable detail depicts daily life as it was lived not in the English middle-class homestead but in the decidedly individual and nuanced context of an Ireland still under British rule and leaning towards non-Unionist ideas of nationalist self-determination. The Reilly household might be much more financially comfortable than G.'s at the start of *Castle*, but as the first setting for the exposition of a *Bildungsroman*, it is similar to *Castle* in portraying a society under, rather than unambiguously one with, British rule.

Just as G. tries to find out his heritage from his mother by asking about absent relatives whose fortunes were determined by British colonial economy, Martin tries to construct a sense of identity based on scraps of knowledge of forebears whose lives were tied up in a history of combat against British forces. He writes in his diary:

> I have [the name] Matthew from my father, that was his name, he was Aunt Mary's favourite brother. I don't know where I have Martin from. My father and mother are dead. I never saw them. One of my ancestors was Colonel Reilly who sailed away to fight for France with Sarsfield and The Wild Geese after the Treaty of Limerick which the English broke. He died at Blenheim, fighting for France, King Louis, the Fleur-de-Lis and Ireland. God save Ireland. (p. 31)

We see Martin trying to compensate for his lack of information regarding his parents – particularly his mother – by alluding to an ancestral Colonel Reilly, who fought for Catholic France against British troops at the Battle of Blenheim in 1704, during the Nine Years' War. This point is of proleptic significance to the novel, in that in his formative Irish Catholic education Martin tries to situate a sense of his historical identity by perceiving fellowship between Catholic Ireland and France against English Protestantism. What distinguishes Martin, from the outset of the novel, is that his familial relations are characterized by absence. His parents are dead, and he tries to reconstruct instead a narrative of heredity via a burgeoning nationalist, anti-British Protestant discourse (implicitly acquired via his uncle John Reilly).

We have seen that in *Castle*, G. acquires a narrative of memory from his mother, who, coincidentally and ironically, cannot remember her relations either, since they left Barbados when she was two years old. This is a motif of the postcolonial *Bildungsroman*: we also see a very comparable motif in *Tears*. Martin's narrative about Colonel Reilly is likely handed down generationally. G., G.'s mother and Martin all seek to recreate a sense of their origins from a past marked by the devastating social influence of historical forces upon families. The nature of, and reasons for, Martin's parentage being a taboo subject, cloaked in mystery, is a line of inquiry that he must pursue throughout the novel in order to complete a narrative of selfhood. As clues and snippets of information appear to Martin, they problematize his early attempt to fashion for himself a Catholic Irish identity. They show the hand of Irish colonial history and sectarian difference at every turn.

Tears portrays the impotent rage and violence of provincial teachers in Martin's local environment with such evident correspondence in key respects to *Castle* that it appears that Farrell, like Lamming, is aiming to portray a particular crisis in late-colonial society. In the despondence of frustration, low-level Irish Catholic educational professionals resent British rule but remain subservient, instead taking out their pathetic anger on children from their own caste. They resemble the teachers of Creighton village, right down to the unnatural beatings that they administer.

Farrell sets the stage for his interrogation of the provincial Irish education system in chapter 2 of *Tears*. We see the young Martin sitting in a local Glenkilly shop and hearing a veteran of Fenian campaigns against the British, a Mr Burns, argue that "a Protestant – aye a pagan – rebel is worth twenty Catholic slaves". Martin witnesses Burns admonish the divisive, self-serving tendency of "the good Catholics . . . the ah, the Slave-Hearts!" (p. 60). Burns believes that for all their "shoddy" patriotism, many Catholics play into British hands by making the idea of a free Ireland impossible. The new "Catholic University" (University College Dublin) and thus Catholic education in Ireland, in his view, has caused division. Through its sectarianism, exclusivity and prejudice, it has proven the fool to British interests in severing a nationalist movement in which Catholics and Protestants should be united nationwide. By chapter 4, Martin has adopted Burns's views, and he comes to despise the Faithful Brothers who teach him at his first school.

The Brothers reserve their anger not for those in control of their fates, but for their schoolboys. Martin wonders why the Brothers are so sadistic to the boys:

> Once again, he pondered the question: why, when boys were formed in a half-circle before the chair, did Brother Kirwan so often swing his foot, so that the toe of a boot kicked into a thigh? Boys were always arguing about what caused the sharp pain as opposed to the feel of the kick itself. Some maintained that the frayed state of the toe of his right boot was because of pushing pins between the sole and the upper; others claimed actually to have seen the pin. (p. 92)

Martin soon finds himself in an altercation with a particularly aggressive teacher, Brother Finnegan. Yet what emerges from the scene is not just Finnegan's brutality but a suggestion of Finnegan's own insecurity regarding his lack of status; it is possible that the former is predicated upon the latter. Finnegan accuses Martin of "stopping to titivate [him]self in the gangway" prior to the lesson. Martin questions Finnegan and takes a blow to the head as a result. Finnegan's follow-up outburst is elliptical, and telling: " 'Maybe that'll teach ye not to be impertinent. You're the worst-mannered boy I ever met. "By what, by what." ' The long lips sneered as they mimicked Martin's voice. 'Ye think yourself too good for everyone but you've no manners at all yerself. Talking out to me as if I were . . . as if I were . . . !' " (p. 94). As if he were what? As if he were only the tool of an education system deferential to two masters, the British Crown and Rome? Finnegan is a cog in the wheel of state and church repression, manipulated into impotence and rage but having more in common with the boys whom he teaches and attacks than with his superiors.

The Faithful Brothers of *Tears* are based upon the Christian Brothers, an institute created in 1802 following the efforts of a widowed citizen-merchant of Waterford, Ireland, Edmund Ignatius Rice, to improve Catholic education.

Following the repeal of the Anglo-Irish Protestant Ascendancy's penal laws against Irish Catholics, including a reversal on a ban on Catholic education in 1782, Rice sought to reverse the tide of discrimination against the majority population in Ireland and improve the numeracy and literacy of the young. While Rice's school was, at first, staffed by secular teachers, the Christian Brothers founded a monastery in Waterford in 1803. Over the course of the next few decades, the institute expanded to open schools around the country and beyond to England.[17] Following the Catholic Emancipation Act of 1829, the Christian Brothers' schools had a strong measure of legitimacy in Ireland, although their pupils only totalled around 10 per cent of Ireland's total population. The Christian Brothers' schools had left the British-instituted National schools system in 1838 and therefore struggled to maintain the funding needed to keep up an exclusive syllabus founded on tenets of Irish nationalism and Catholic values. In 1878, the British government offered the Christian Brothers "payment by results": if a sizeable quota of pupils passed their Intermediate Exams, funding would ensue. The Christian Brothers were thus under enormous pressure, and were fearfully subservient to the purse of the very masters whom they hoped to replace, in order to achieve results in the classroom. As the stress of keeping the schools afloat mounted, it has been proposed that Christian Brothers became more extreme in their discipline in order to produce academic successes.[18]

It is ironic that Rice, in his vision for a new Catholic nationalist education system in Ireland, had originally instructed teachers not to enforce corporal punishment upon children.[19] Under a British financial "incentive", conditions in Christian Brothers' schools became so violent that it is unsurprising that in *Tears*, Martin sees these teachers as "Slave-Hearts" to the colonial-capitalist god of money, at the expense of all decency towards one's fellow countrymen.

The Christian Brothers schools of Ireland are historically specific in relation to British colonial educational practices, in that they operated with a significant degree of relative autonomy from the main British hegemonic system of education founded under British law and administered throughout its domains and territories. They are answerable to, and dependent upon, British powers inasmuch as they depend on their financial assistance in order for their schools to survive. This is one of the root causes of their violent repression of their pupils in pursuit of "results" and funding, along with resentment at being a link in the chain of their own subordination. Martin moves on to a Catholic boarding school, Dunslane; he is still being taught by the clergy. It is around this time, however, that he acquires a taste of a very different form of education system in Ireland, administered to the Protestant Anglo-Irish Ascendancy and in the name of imperial Britain. The effect that this alternative schooling has on Martin is similar to that experienced by G. at the High School in *Castle*. Soon after starting at Dunslane, Martin is visited by his maternal aunt, Kathleen Vincent. Kathleen is a Protestant: she is monied, genteel and tolerant. She invites him to stay with her at Keelard, in a large Anglo-Irish property very much in the model of the Ascendancy Big House with its expansive gardens. Martin spends his summer months with his new extended family. With his cousins Peggy and Sally, he is taught by an English governess, Miss Clare, at home. The violent intolerance and frustration of the Faithful Brothers could not be more opposed to Miss Clare's gentility. Miss Clare instructs Martin in a matter that counters his younger preconceptions. Martin had once written in his diary about the confederacy of the Catholic Irish "Wild Geese" and France against the English in the Nine Years' War. Now, Miss Clare shifts his paradigm for him, by aligning France with England due to their status as imperial powers. (Implicitly, it was, after all, Anglo-Norman colonists who first settled in Ireland and began hundreds of years of English rule in the country.) She says,

> "Every man has two fatherlands, his own and France." The English genius for tolerance; the French genius for civilization. The two greatest peoples the world had ever known.
> "Greater than Greece? Than Rome?"
> "Than Rome – certainly. Than Greece – not greater, just more developed. France and England are the grandchildren of the Hellenic spirit." (pp. 169–70)

Martin fantasizes about Ireland one day being a free, equal power in relation to these two nations, yet the implication in Miss Clare's lesson is different. Ireland as a country is the child of an Anglo-Norman, colonial father. Miss Clare is of a tradition rooted in Anglo-Norman history. In her view, every Irish person's spiritual identity is ultimately born of Norman English conquest. Ireland, in essence, is a little England.

Miss Clare might "rule the classroom with all the authority of a martinet", but this is in marked difference to the seething chaos of the Brothers, whose authority appears in question at any given moment. Moreover, "Martin liked her. She was comfortably reassuring. She suggested all the stability and security of accepted principles" (p. 175). Unlike the nervous and vitriolic Brothers, who are, in spite of their autocratic classroom tyranny, deferential to foreign masters, Miss Clare rigorously believes in her own English power. Martin desires this self-assurance; it was his own confidence in questioning the Brothers that led to beatings. Martin feels plural in identity, and certainly different from the one-dimensional, Gaelic Catholic construction of Irishness. While at Keelard, Martin even toasts the king. These developments have considerable postcolonial implications. Michael Farrell is examining in fictional form how the protagonist Martin begins to realize the pitfalls of excessive native sympathies to an anti-colonial, Catholic Ireland. The suggestion present in the narrative is that a truly successful post-independence Ireland must take heed of the already oppressive tendency of those members of anti-colonial society who would seize power at the first opportunity in a new, Catholic state. If they are so quick to beat children, they would not stop at browbeating and repressing the general public.

There is some nuance of difference in techniques by which the narrative voices of *Castle* and *Tears* convey to readers G.'s and Martin's attitudes as young adults receiving colonial educations. *Castle* is largely written from the retrospective position of G.'s adult, authorial voice; G. reflects upon and critiques his younger self's exposure to what is in many respects a Little English high school system. However, *Tears* is voiced from an omniscient narratorial perspective, in the third person. The narrator of *Tears* is at liberty to plunge into Martin's boyhood consciousness and reveal his enthusiasms for aspects of his education under Miss Clare as opposed to the Faithful Brothers. However, the narratorial voice itself is of a heterodiegetic speaker outside the chronotope of the textual *fabula*, who speaks and reflects on his own account, at the level of narrating the text, rather than at the level of the narrated text. He is, according to this simple logic, thus never able to offer a first-person account of an adult Martin looking back on his life. (One could argue tentatively for some authorial self-reflexivity between the narrative voice in the text and an adult Martin, or one could propose a degree of internal dialogism between the omniscient narrator and the various boyhood and adult "Martins" in the novel, but in basic structural narratological terms, this would be difficult to establish convincingly.) One could then decide from this the following distinction between the novels. G. comes to try to reconcile his British colonial and native intellectual selves by tearing himself away from the strongest tendencies of British education in order to construct the subject in close mimicry of the imperial model. G. takes elements of his education but refuses to lose himself in the image of an Englishman. In Bhabhalian terms, G. repeats with a difference the educational precepts of British rule; he adapts his education in his own people's image. Martin's route to reconciliation of his native Irish and British attributes and educational experiences remains more enigmatic since we do not have full access to presentation of his first-person, direct thought – whether as a young adult or as an authorial, reflective adult. In Fanonian terms, Martin is still at a stage in his development and self-erudition where he risks psycho-affective injury by being both Irish and English rather than being able to tear away from his colonial past in pursuit of an emancipatory future. He also is not yet at a stage when he can learn to negotiate his contradictory influences towards a sense of resolved selfhood. *Castle* and *Tears*, in spite of these differences, both show their protagonists at variant stages of an effort towards coping with polarized colonial and non-colonial education systems and constructions of identity and imagined community.

Tears, like *Castle*, is a historically mindful work of semi-autobiography. In addition, *Tears* bears close resemblance to *Castle* in the ways in which it narrates the shocking impression of an explosion of anti-colonial violence upon everyday local communities not involved in riot or rebellion. It makes a similar point to *Castle*: that anti-colonial revolt does not necessarily originate within the general populace, but often derives from the actions of select few.

There are some differences in the historical contexts of anti-colonial rebellion between *Castle* and *Tears*. The 1937 Bridgetown riots were largely spontaneous and not a concerted act of paramilitary revolution. In their wake, there were fourteen fatalities, forty-seven injuries and three hundred convictions for rioters of up to ten years.[20] In the hope of quelling the rioting, British powers immediately promised a full report into the causes of the disturbances; this led in time to the Moyne Report that sought to reform working conditions, collective bargaining rights, health and education in the region. This is in marked contrast with the counterproductive severity of General John Maxwell's punishment of the Irish rebellion leaders, which in turn precipitated the increase in Republican combat against overstretched British forces, and the escalation of the Anglo-Irish War from 1916 until the Anglo-Irish Treaty of 1921. However, these events are violent, shocking turning points in the histories of Barbados and Ireland respectively. Farrell, like Lamming, wishes to demonstrate in his novel just how taken unawares the general population was by the outbreak of rebellion which was to change their country's history forever.

This is demonstrated particularly in the form in which this violence is narrated. In the two texts, information regarding the shock of rebellion in the capital city filters out to the suburban districts or villages as scattered, confused and incomplete indexical acts of signification for the bewildered population on the periphery to try to piece together and understand. These acts of violence are almost unprecedented in their size, suddenness and impact: *Tears* and *Castle* register the initial uproar, fear and strangeness of events seemingly without form or purpose, using strikingly parallel narrative strategies.

In *Tears*, on the date of Easter Monday 1916, the sixteen-year-old Martin is depicted as staying for the holiday period with his Protestant warden, Miss Peters (his Aunt Kathleen having left for England and died in an accident). Martin is given leave to go out bathing for the day, and he is given a pound as an extra Easter gift to buy food. Martin by this stage in the novel has been raised to find greater gentility and familial affection among Protestants than Catholics: he even reads the *Irish Times*, a newspaper noted for its Protestant sympathies.

Martin's inklings that there is anything extraordinary about the unfolding events of the day come to him in dribs and drabs of information. The first signs of unusual activity on Easter Monday are provided as events and dialogue without superfluous narratorial interjection, the significance of which the historically aware reader, rather than the oblivious Martin, will be able to decipher as unusual. Martin makes his way to his bathing spot, and spies "a group of Volunteers marching down and emerging on to the main road from one of the long roads that led in from the hills. They belonged, he saw, to that 'cranky' minority who, refusing to support England in the war, had broken away from the majority in the Volunteer movement and from Mr. Redmond" (p. 303).

Martin has no way of knowing that the Volunteers are planning to converge in rebellion, and Farrell, being a superior writer, certainly offers no unnecessary commentary to emphasize the dramatic irony of Martin's lack of awareness as to what is about to happen. Historian Peter Cottrell explains the rise of the Republican Volunteer movement in Ireland prior to the Easter Rising as follows. In 1915, British intelligence was alerted to the involvement of a former colonial diplomat, Dublin-born Sir Roger Casement, in Irish Republican negotiations with Germany to employ combined military attacks against Britain. Casement was a Gaelic League member and founding force in the Irish Volunteers. On 18 April 1916, Casement departed from Germany on the U-boat *Aud* carrying ammunition for distribution in Ireland; he was arrested in Dublin on 22 April.[21] Although the following day (Easter Sunday) British powers at Dublin Castle instructed the Royal Irish Constabulary to arrest leading members of the Volunteers and Sinn Féin in an attempt to contain increasingly coordinated paramilitary activity against the Crown, this directive lacked intelligence of the imminent planned uprising in Dublin. Thus, arrests were not carried out in time to prevent the surprise rebellion. The insurrection had been planned for Easter Sunday – whereupon Volunteers mobilized from Cork would converge on Dublin and receive armaments from the *Aud* – but Casement's arrest stalled mobilization of Volunteers until Easter Monday.[22] It is this mobilization that Martin witnesses in *Tears*, unaware of its intent.

Martin encounters Seumas Conroy, a former Dunslane school peer whom he had noted for his pious obsession with a Gaelic, Catholic Irish nationalism. Conroy is leading the Volunteer parade. Conroy speaks in elliptical phrases: he explains to Martin that the Volunteers are marching into Dublin. "You should be with us", Conroy advises him. Conroy finds it amusing that Martin should be venturing to engage in an activity as banal as going for a bath, "While – while – but I forgot. Of course people will be going to places just as on any Easter Monday." Martin, of course, has no way of foretelling his peripheral role in what is planned by the Volunteers as a turning point in Irish history. Easter Monday 1916 is just another day, and while the reader observes Conroy's words as signposts to an armed political uprising, they are mysterious to Martin. Martin mocks Conroy for his revolutionary zeal, and ridicules him, quipping, "Tell me, Seumas – you're not thinking of blowing up Dublin Castle today, are you?" (p. 303).

Returning from bathing, and heading towards a train to take him to Dublin, Martin is met on the road by more fragmentary, indexical signifiers of the violence in the capital:

> But when he turned into a side-road towards a railway station he met groups straggling aimlessly in the half-light, then larger groups talking excitedly by the ditch where their womenfolk hushed weary infants.

> "If it's for the train you're looking, you can save your legs," they called to him in cantankerous satisfaction.
> "What do you mean?"
> "There's red murder in the city." (p. 312)

Martin is confronted by so much hearsay and speculation that it is hard for him to gauge any pattern of cohesive events from the flurry of revelations presented to him:

> Every sort of rumour was offered him. The Germans had landed at Cork, the Americans had declared war on behalf of Irish Independence. A Spanish admiral called de Valera was "blowing hell out of everything in Ringsend". In any event there would be no train to Dublin.
> "But what's wrong?" he asked.
> "Oh, nothing at all! Only the biggest insurrection ever. Only all Dublin captured behind our backs. Only roaring murder and arson, that's all. Nothing to speak of. Nothing much at all." (p. 312)

Thus, if *Castle* can be said to provide a template for a postcolonial historical novel in which an aspiring few seek rebellion while the greater majority are stunned and forever changed by discovering the reasons for the anger and suddenness of such anti-colonial revolt, then *Tears* very much accords to this model and should be read in a postcolonial comparative context. Slow and relatively passive as the events following the Barbadian riots are, events in *Castle* incorporate the inevitable withdrawal of a plantocracy and its replacement by a new bourgeois elite. In *Tears*, similar events transpire, albeit with more alacrity and bloodshed. Moreover, *Tears* matches *Castle* in its extensive, near-Fanonian representation of this emergent bourgeoisie and its deep flaws.

As we have seen, in *Castle*, Lamming creates Mr Slime as his composite of a self-serving, mendacious, capitalistic bourgeoisie riding on the coattails of anti-colonial feeling and pocketing the spoils of a spirit of emergent self-determination by guile and cunning. The population of Creighton village is hypnotized by his rhetoric: they fall victim to his promises of a better, post-plantocratic society when he evicts them from their rented property. In many ways, *Tears* features an identical figure, whom Farrell creates to serve as an embodiment of capitalistic, late-colonial self-interest that preys upon the goodwill of an emergent national consciousness.

In *Tears*, the character Tim Corbin constitutes a capitalist, self-aggrandizing shadow king of colonial power masquerading as a man of his people. He is a member of the national bourgeoisie whose affectation of Gaelic Irish Catholic Republican sympathies disguises competitive interest for himself only: he embodies the class warned against by Connolly and also portrayed by Slime in Lamming's novel. Just as the village school's head teacher in *Castle* had been suspicious of Slime's ostentatiousness, the Fenian veteran Mr Burns in *Tears* expresses distaste at the "shoddy patriots, the play-boys", of which he identifies Corbin as a prime example: "Aye, you have them here in Glenkilly and you know them. They're swarming over Ireland now. Look at that fellow Tim Corbin, over in Ballow. A fine Catholic, they call him, a nice Party-man, a fine patriot. Tim Corbin of Ballow! Aye, a fine Slave-Heart!" (p. 60).

Further parallels between Slime and Corbin emerge throughout *Tears*. Just as Slime, early in *Castle*, relishes unsavoury relations with the head teacher's wife, Corbin shows his unpleasantness in his pleasure in scandal. In chapter 6 of *Tears*, Martin is sent by his Dunslane schoolmaster Jimmy Curran on an errand, with his friend Norman Dempsey, to deliver a letter in Ballow. They visit the Royal Leinster Hotel, where they encounter an altercation between Corbin and Martin's Uncle John, Martin being the object of the dispute.

Corbin's predilection for tittle-tattle and potential scandal, and arguably thus his demonstration of a questionable moral rectitude, comes to light when he makes sarcastic inferences regarding the mystery of Martin's parentage. He follows his facetious query to John regarding Martin's mother, "Tell me, John, by the way, was it a Dublin lady now she was, or from where?" with the overheard aside, "Wouldn't it be a good one now if the pure and holy Reillys, God's first-prize Catholics, had a skeleton in the cupboard all the time! I've sometimes wondered whether there wasn't something a bit fishy . . ." (pp. 134–35).

This remark earns Corbin a blow to the jaw, but no providential check to his ascendancy as the novel progresses. In *Castle*, Slime precedes his socioeconomic ascendancy and betrayal of the people of Creighton village by displaying interest in, or even directly causing, the more embarrassing personal affairs of his peers and superiors. In *Tears*, Corbin also seems perversely interested in finding skeletons in professional competitors' cupboards. This trait is the mark of one who thrives within an acquisitive bourgeois nationalist ideology of achieving a monopoly, at whatever cost, over one's perceived rivals in the community. This ideology itself stems from the legacy of capitalist private enterprise.

Corbin, like Slime, rises to prominence in the political as well as business life of his community. Corbin visits Dunslane school, where he is invited by the encouraging Dean and Father MacTaggarty to deliver a lecture, "Catholic Principles in Public Life". The staff consider Corbin a man who plays "a part in the big affairs of the world", and "one of the most prominent Catholic figures in the county" (p. 221). While the schoolboys hearing the speech suspect him of humbug, Corbin has nonetheless "bamboozled" the priests with his rhetoric, "like so many others". Corbin's oratory, and vision for a new, self-sufficient Catholic Ireland, mirrors Slime's outspoken ideal for a self-reliant Creighton village. The two men acquire keen adherents along the way.

Most significantly, Corbin parallels Slime in proving a traitor to the good faith of the people and to the cause of transcending subjection to colonial land ownership. Martin, now an atheist at twenty-one years of age, joins the Flying Column of the Irish Republican Army. He envisages a new Ireland that will no longer be betrayed, either by British rhetoric as it had been in the early days of the Great War or by the false, self-serving tenets of Catholic Irish politics (p. 439). Although his new political stance as a supporter of Sinn Féin gradually strains his correspondence and relationship with his Protestant, Keelard cousins Peggy and Sally, he maintains sincere affection for the household in which he had joined in the song of "God Save the King". His vision of a new Ireland will indeed accommodate the Anglo-Irish Big House into its ambit rather than destroy it. However, following the death of Tom Prendergast, the gardener at Keelard, during a Flying Column ambush of a Royal Irish Constabulary barracks that also claimed the life of Martin's beloved Norman, Martin pays a visit to the old Protestant homestead. He discovers to his horror that Keelard has been destroyed by the Flying Column; his beloved Aunt Kathleen's garden has been reduced to scorched earth and occasional marigolds (p. 499).

Martin quizzes a man present at the scene, who it transpires is an intelligence officer for the Flying Column: this man is in confederacy with none other than Corbin. They have torched and looted Keelard in the absence of its owners Peggy and Sally Vincent, with a view to pressuring the sisters into selling the property. Since the old Ascendancy is no longer as prosperous as before, it emerges that Corbin seeks to present himself as "a buyer in the market who would take over all the trouble of claiming malicious-injury compensation and a lot of trouble and delay" (p. 502). The very revolutionary activity in which the idealistic Martin had become involved, so as to ensure a free Ireland admitting of both Catholic and Protestant communities, has been intercepted by capitalistic, bourgeois Catholic agents in league with Corbin's characteristically avaricious objectives. Just as Slime sells his supporters out for his own gain and power, Corbin manipulates the Republican movement and its revolutionary efforts for his financial reward.

If the Vincents refuse to sell Keelard, their livestock, Martin guesses, will either be driven away or killed (p. 503). The property is to be rebuilt by Corbin for the purposes of the Faithful Brothers – that frustrated, violent band of teachers whom Martin has, via his rebellious Catholic Aunt Mary, come to deride as resembling "great black cockroaches in the sun" (p. 88). The Flying Column officer informs Martin that

> the Faithful Brothers have been having their eyes out for a place round this way to open as a boarding-school. Only, with the troubles, they'll be keeping their horns in at the moment. . . . Trust the priests or a monk to mind the dibs. But Mr. Corbin, if he got a good bargain – only of course a real good bargain – might pay cash now and build with the compensation money with an eye to the school's requirements. Then he could sell when the right times came again. (p. 504)

Martin reaches a sad reflection regarding the pitfall of Irish national consciousness, particularly endemic among the bourgeois Catholic mercantile classes to which he partly belongs: it is in league with exploitative capitalism that perpetuates the oppression of the majority by a self-aggrandizing few: "So there it all was! A few acres of ground for the Faithful Brothers around their new boarding-school; a fat profit for Corbin; fees and profit for O'Mahony; and forty or fifty acres of the farm bought up by this fellow for a song under a campaign of 'the land for the people'" (p. 504).

So, Slime and Corbin parallel one another extensively. They bear out fictively the warnings of James Connolly about the pitfalls of pre-independence nationalism, and as shadow agents of capitalist colonialism they anticipate Frantz Fanon's discussion of national bourgeoisies in *The Wretched of the Earth*.

The first section of *Tears* bears the title "White Blackbird". Martin is the paradoxical figure symbolized by this unnatural songbird. Exposure to an Anglo-Irish colonial education and family environment, and a discovery that his mother's people were of Protestant stock, render Martin a clash of internal opposites. If the blackbird is a traditional figure of an ancient Celtic songbird, present since the beginning of time and able to bear witness to the living and the dead, then Martin is an old soul in many respects. Like the blackbird, Martin sings forth and bears witness to the ravages of Irish history, of life and death. Yet Martin is a white blackbird, an anomaly and freak among his surrounding peers. If the binary opposite of the Irish spirit is the British imperial mind – and it can be symbolized as white as opposed to black – then Martin is indeed this white blackbird, a Protestant Catholic, an English Irishman. If Martin deviates from the norm, he is an outcast, an outsider from his immediate community. Martin is faced with a crisis of identity in understanding who he is, within the spheres of colonial or colonized spheres of school, home and his local environment.

In postcolonial terms, Farrell, like Lamming, employs the language of colour to describe the internal conflict at the heart of a young man with divided loyalties to British colonial and local communities and identities. This is not altogether the same as the language of physical, racial typification. In conventional racial terms, Martin is "white", but symbolically he is black, in being, as an ostensibly Irish Catholic, not-English and Other. He is a Celt, identified traditionally as the blackbird. His "whiteness" is in many respects the coat of Englishness that he learns to wear, via his intermittent "English" education by Miss Clare and the Vincents; it becomes part of him. He is a blackbird with a white coat. The significance of Martin Reilly as a postcolonial creation is to exemplify the unease and the tension at the crux of relations between colonizer and colonized. Martin is neither quite black nor white: he is faced with the challenge of forging an identity as a compromise, if not quite a hybrid, of contradictory castes. Whether or not Martin will ever be able to balance these oppositions satisfactorily remains a question unanswered at the close of *Tears*. In prison for anti-British, Republican activity at the novel's climax, Martin reads an old letter from his Aunt Kathleen for the first time. The missive informs Martin of his maternal English heritage. Martin's complex background thus becomes a matter not just of education but parentage: he is the offspring of a taboo affair between star-struck lovers of rival castes or colours, so to speak. There is a sense that Martin has far to go before he can evolve as a psychically balanced resolution of cultural and socio-political adversarial properties.

Lamming's G., it should be said, is not born into two cultures. G. realizes that even though he has had a British education, he must refuse the "white" mask of colonial identity in order to secure a safe psychic sense of selfhood. G. might assimilate the useful heritage of a European education in the formation of his erudition. Yet in every *Bildungsroman*, the protagonist is fundamentally an autodidact. In a novel that is a postcolonial *Bildungsroman*, G. teaches himself to take the best of his British education and use it to gauge a historical understanding of Creighton village, Barbados, the Caribbean, and a whole past of slavery and resistance additionally conveyed to him by his old school friend Trumper, home after years in a racially divided America. Like Shakespeare's Caliban, G. learns to use colonial language against the oppressor. G. is better placed than Martin to defend himself against the worst psychological ravages of perceiving oneself as colonial and colonized. If what Frantz Fanon called native intellectuality is fortified by awareness of one's origins – what Lamming called the castle of one's skin – then one does not need to don the "white" mask of colonialism and disguise one's true self in order to find selfhood. Martin, however, has little choice in the matter, at least by the end of *Tears*. Martin discovers that he is Irish *and* English: he personifies a sociohistorical paradox. Martin's route to self-education is arguably only beginning at the climax of *Tears*. While *Tears* may be a large novel, it is a *Bildungsroman* without a conclusion offering a glimpse of the protagonist's epiphanic point of cultural and decolonizing self-discovery. Martin *is* both the colonizer and the colonized. He cannot easily forsake one for the other, in accordance with a Fanonian formation. Yet the novel's closing words offer a hope that Martin might, as the protagonist of a postcolonial *Bildungsroman*, learn in time to modify a sense of self by neutralizing the extremes of contrary cultures. As Lamming's G. finds a sense of his own identity, history, community and reality over the course of *Castle*, the narrator begins to hope for Martin "that at long last the old hammer of reality . . . might yet ring music from the anvil of a man" (p. 592).

G. in *Castle* learns to fortify his Afro-Barbadian intellectuality within the castle of his psychic skin without masking it behind the false selfhood of British colonial identity. Martin in *Tears*, on the other hand, is born an aberrant mix of British colonizer and Irish colonized, a figurative white blackbird. While Martin has not been able to develop a decolonizing identity between or beyond the attributes of his British and Irish inheritance, the realization at last of his mother and father's story makes the reconciliation of his opposing histories and identities a possibility beyond the text of the novel.

Conclusion

IN THE INTRODUCTION TO THIS BOOK, I posed the following questions: given the resemblances between developments in novelistic formations and traditions of Ireland and the Caribbean, from the 1920s to the 1960s, just how close and firm are those parallels when one tests them? What is the significance of these correspondences? What conclusions are to be drawn from these corollaries?

In answer to the first and second questions, chapter by chapter, this study has traced robust, corresponding trajectories in the evolution of the Irish and Caribbean novel over a forty-year period. The significance of these correspondences is that the Irish novel between the 1920s and the 1960s articulated issues surrounding decolonizing processes as incisively, as comprehensively and as critically in a large number of regards as works already established in the postcolonial novelistic canon. Chapter 1's comparative examination of Alfred Mendes's *Black Fauns* (1935) and Liam O'Flaherty's *The Informer* (1925) focuses on the origin of a particular type of novel that can be said to be at least intellectually postcolonial in presenting an alternative to imperial representations, or more accurately, non-representations, of people of the colonies. Mendes and O'Flaherty had no real novelistic precedent for their attempts to represent the lives of the poor of their respective islands. Mendes wrote in a milieu of decolonizing thought that included novelist Claude McKay, whose 1933 historical novel *Banana Bottom* endeavours to examine the complex social hierarchy, education systems and ideological tensions of turn-of-the-last-century Jamaica. Yet it was Mendes, along with C.L.R. James, who was one of the first writers to try to engage with the exigencies of contemporary barrack-yard island life as its audience would have known it and recognized it, using a socio-realist novel form as their mode of expression. In *Black Fauns*, the descriptive detail and character dialogue paint a portrait of slum life in a way that expanded not only the possibilities of the novel but also other media of Caribbean cultural production. *Black Fauns*, along with C.L.R. James's *Minty Alley* (1936), made possible the lucid depictions of the realities of yard life so characteristic of novels such as V.S. Naipaul's *Miguel Street* (1959) or Earl Lovelace's *The Dragon Can't Dance* (1979). *Black Fauns*'s innovations also facilitate the possibility of shrewdly observational West Indian cinematic works such as Perry Henzell's 1973 *The Harder They Come*, for example.

In the case of O'Flaherty, his realism may have been preceded by works in the dramatic genre such as J.M. Synge's *The Playboy of the Western World* (1907). Yet O'Flaherty's conscious decision to use a slum setting within Dublin, and operate discursively within a starkly socio-realist novelistic mode of presentation from description to dialogue, paved the way for novels incorporating iconoclastic, anti-Revivalist realism, such as Patrick Kavanagh's *Tarry Flynn* (1948), Brendan Behan's *Borstal Boy* (1958), Edna O'Brien's *The Country Girls* (1960) and Michael Farrell's *Thy Tears Might Cease* (1963). All of these texts can be said to be intellectually postcolonial in their disengagement from British representations of Irish people, place or history. Liam O'Flaherty's *The Informer* is as instrumental in precipitating these postcolonial works as *Black Fauns* is to the postcolonial Caribbean novels that followed.

By the late 1920s, Irish and Caribbean novelists had begun to explore the possibilities of the European *Bildungsroman* – the novel of self-education – and applied this form to portrayals of young men and women in the declining decades of British influence in each region. Evidently, then, these writers were not just coincidentally engaged in writing *Bildungsromane*; they were making social critiques of their own societies in the light and contexts of colonial rule. Jean Rhys's *Voyage in the Dark* (1934)and Elizabeth Bowen's *The Last September* (1929), discussed in chapter 2, are certainly *Bildungsromane* of a generation of planter-settler Irish and West Indian society who were in their late twenties and early thirties at the time the novels were published. Rhys's and Bowen's novels constituted a particular kind of narrative of education. Protagonists Anna Morgan and Lois Farquar, based largely on their authorial creators, are young girls who at the cusp of adulthood realize that they are dislocated from any direct sense of colonial lineage. They are orphans and wards of alternately remote or interfering elder colonial relatives, and they do not realize that their world, and the values they hold, are about to be changed utterly. Lois and Anna struggle to synthesize a new concept of selfhood, place and identity when it is clear that their colonial era is coming to an end. They are women at the end of the collapse of a patriarchal colonial paradigm; each novel investigates how they seek to refigure identity on their own social and gender terms. Rhys and Bowen therefore constitute a second key stage in the evolution of the postcolonial novel in the Caribbean and in Ireland. They use the form of the *Bildungsroman* to analyse the effect of the end of plantocratic society on its youngest, female generations. Postcolonial critics of Irish literature could expand on the reading presented in chapter 2, and use such a reading of Bowen's work and see it in relation to a development, over the course of the first few post-independence decades, in Irish women's writing that responded in part to processes of decolonization. In particular, Bowen's finely realized exploration into the mind of a young, modern Irish female consciousness largely makes Edna O'Brien's interrogations of patriarchal Irish society possible, by way of her representations of Kate Brady and Baba Brennan in *The Country Girls*.

Rhys and Bowen were not the only writers to take the *Bildungsroman* form and use it to give voice to the youth bearing witness to decolonizing movements in Caribbean or Irish histories. Neither were they the only novelists to consider the gendered dimensions of detachment from British colonial patriarchy. C.L.R. James's *Minty Alley* and Patrick Kavanagh's *Tarry Flynn*, which I compared in chapter 3, are on the face of things novels of principally male protagonists' education and erudition. However, the lesson learned by Haynes in *Minty Alley* and Tarry in *Tarry Flynn* is not about their own potential socio-economic or cultural individuation in society, but rather the role that women in menial occupations play in providing their privileges. James and Kavanagh effectively turn the *Bildungsroman* form on its head, empowering not even their central characters so much as those women who previously lived on the fringes of patriarchal structures founded by a British power. Mrs Rouse and Mrs Flynn are hardly background subalterns or silent peripheral fixtures. They speak; moreover, they dictate the course of Haynes's and Tarry's roads to social consciousness. Postcolonial critics of Irish literature can take the example of representations of matriarchal society and economy in *Tarry Flynn* and scrutinize the novel's innovative position, as a book written by a man, within the context of male fiction that questions the role that women play in an ostensibly patriarchal, post-independence, Catholic Ireland. John McGahern's *Amongst*

Women (1990) would be one later male-authored Irish novel possibly deserving of postcolonial analysis from the gendered perspective demonstrated in chapter 3 of this book. *Amongst Women* depicts Rose Brady Moran, a middle-aged woman who maintains quiet pride and subtle matriarchal power as a wife and stepmother, even in the face of domestic tyranny from her husband Michael: a man whose psyche and deep masculine insecurities have been shaped by the violent anti-colonial struggle of the Anglo-Irish War of Independence.

The texts examined in chapter 4 trace psychological and intellectual paths of education as well as conveying the incidents and scenery of the physical voyage. For this reason, it is not surprising that a novel of migration will be another form of *Bildungsroman*. In the context of colonial history, though, the education that the protagonist of the migrant novel receives will significantly relate to their comprehension of the vicissitudes of dislocation, often from the colonial periphery to the imperial core. Sam Selvon's 1956 novel *The Lonely Londoners*, which I considered alongside Samuel Beckett's 1938 novel *Murphy* in chapter 4, is a multi-perspectival, dialogic expression of West Indian migration to England that captures a whole generation's effort to negotiate the psychological effects of leaving one's former British colonial island, understanding one's origins in the context of colonial history, and arriving and settling in a strange, inhospitable London that bears little resemblance to one's preconceptions or experience. There are characters in the novel with comical, romantic nicknames such as Sir Galahad or more Biblical names such as Moses (named after a man who led his people out of slavery to the Promised Land). Their quest is often futile, and they discover that it is in being caught between places and mental spaces of origin and destination that they will find identity and community. Samuel Beckett's darkly comic *Murphy*, like *The Lonely Londoners*, seeks to analyse how a migrant tries to negotiate a sense of self between the uncertainties of colonial island origin and British imperial destination. *Murphy*, like Selvon's novel, features a protagonist lacking provenance or target who tries to construct a new kind of selfhood in existential statelessness. In *The Lonely Londoners*' case, it is through ballad, kiff-kiff laughter, oldtalk, story and the synthesis of a new migrant Caribbean voice in Britain. In *Murphy*'s case, it is via a form of meditative self-hypnosis that detaches the protagonist's mind from his uncertain surroundings, past and future.

If *Murphy*, a novel not ordinarily read in postcolonial terms, can be read as such, this then opens up an exciting challenge to readers of Irish fiction.

For example, could novels such as Flann O'Brien's *At Swim-Two-Birds* (1938) be read as postcolonial? If so, then how? *At Swim-Two-Birds* could be said to deconstruct the Irish myths of Finn Mac Cool and Mad King Sweeney in a way that suggests a parody of the earnest fetishism of the Anglo-Irish Ascendancy in the Celtic Twilight era for the Gaelic aristocratic heroes of an imagined past. In critiquing the construction of an Irish national culture, and having the lofty Finn Mac Cool converse intertextually with characters from cheap paperback westerns, O'Brien could be said to use the novel to disengage from an earlier generation of writers from the colonial classes who wanted to use Gaelic myth to their own separatist-nationalist ends. The titular, doomed hod-carrier Finnegan of James Joyce's *Finnegans Wake* (1939) may not only allude to the deceased protagonist of a 1850s music hall song but could also be a play on Finn Mac Cool, here diminished from king to navigator and destined for an unpleasant end toiling for colonial economic gain.

George Lamming's *In the Castle of My Skin* (1953) and Farrell's *Thy Tears Might Cease*, considered as *Bildungsromane* in chapter 5, constitute a new stage in the attempt to adapt the postcolonial novel of education in the Caribbean and Ireland. By the 1950s and 1960s, what would later be called postcolonial theory had become much more sophisticated. Lamming uses the *Bildungsroman* to explore the effect of these issues on the growing consciousness of his own generation as they were experienced in the course of British Barbadian history. Farrell's novel, published in 1963, was mainly drafted over a thirty-year period but largely consolidated around the 1950s, when themes of intellectual as well as political decolonization were central to current affairs, arts and literature. Farrell used the *Bildungsroman* form and in the process, like Lamming, he intellectualized upon and then fictionalized themes relevant to his own generational experience of an Ireland starting to break away from the prevailing influence of British colonial power.

In essence, the Caribbean and Irish postcolonial novel began in the 1920s and 1930s with broad socio-realist examinations of the lives of the poor, and then progressed in the succeeding decades to use the format of the *Bildungsroman* to investigate experiences of the decline of colonial power across the West Indies and Ireland from a variety of perspectives, inclusive of the plantocracy, the poor, the migrant and the provincial. Postcolonial novel forms are supremely democratic in their reach of social classes and, thus, represented voices. They can narrate a sequence of events of relevance to colonial history, and explore how these events impressed themselves upon the psyches of a range of portrayed characters across an archipelago of socioeconomic and cultural communities. The postcolonial Caribbean novel and the postcolonial Irish novel alike exemplify the attempt to realize deconstructive and alternative colonial voices and histories, using the devices of the chronotope as well as the revolutionary, destabilizing and decolonizing power of the dialogic imagination.

Therefore, in answer to the third question posed in the introduction, one can conclude that between 1925 and 1965, Irish writers in English employed a series of narrative strategies to document, through the novel form, clearly identifiable elements of detachment from the legacy and structures of British colonial power and history. The people of the slum acquire a self-determining voice. The planter-colonial vocally questions her status and destiny in a crumbling Big House society. Working women are shown finding pride and dignity in spite of poverty and marginalization by patriarchal colonial economics; younger women venture further to emigrate from such restrictive conditions. Migrants arrive in the imperial motherland of London and find it difficult to determine identity, place and purpose. The youth of local societies fraught by anti-colonial uprisings experience lost illusions about the protective or benign influence of British rule; they also learn to distrust self-appointed, business-minded representatives of their own class who claim to wish to operate in the interests of a new, autonomous society. Novels produced in Ireland between 1925 and 1965 differ vastly in historical and geographical settings, vastly apart from Caribbean novels of the same period. However, the formal and thematic narrative currents of Irish and Caribbean novels in English at this time cross and become richly confluent in portraying a decolonizing world that writes right back to the heart of the British Empire.

After the American Revolution, Britain's (second) imperial and colonial mission across the globe grew, largely unchallenged, for over a century, as the British Empire became the dominant world power. By the close of the nineteenth century, as Empress Queen Victoria passed fifty and then sixty years of her reign over territories within a range of countries in the Americas, Europe, Africa and Australasia, writers in Ireland began to find ways to establish art forms in order to disengage from the dominant hegemonic structures of centuries of British rule. The Irish Literary Revival from the 1880s saw writers such as W.B. Yeats, Lady Augusta Gregory, Douglas Hyde and George Russell ("AE") attempt to affect a renaissance of what they imagined as a golden age of pre-colonial Celtic Irish culture, arts and literature. Yeats in particular throughout his life appropriated the high cultural form of poetry as a way of re-establishing the ancient bardic tradition, and to proclaim an indomitable Irishry in the face of British cultural oppression. In 1897, Yeats, Gregory and Edward Martyn devised the *Manifesto for the Irish Literary Theatre*. They proposed that the new Irish theatre would be a high cultural expression of a distinctly Irish national art that channelled the idealism of the old Gaelic order and thus corrected misrepresentative English stereotypes of the Irish as sentimental buffoons. The Revivalists thus prepared much of the intellectual grounds of Irish independence, which came about at the end of 1922.

The development of an Irish national consciousness had not come about without its pitfalls. After independence, the new Cumann na nGaedheal government of the Irish Free State (1923–32) did little to reverse the British colonial policy of running Ireland as an agricultural economy, and as a consequence there was increased mass-migration from the island to America and Britain. A new Catholic Irish bourgeoisie ran the country, with the church having a frequently dictatorial influence in matters of state from contraception to censorship; Irish writers realized that political independence had not necessarily brought about a decolonization of the Irish mind from the dominant systems of oppression and social inequalities left by Britain. Novelists in Ireland from the 1920s were especially poised to use the advantages of a socio-realist longer prose fictive genre to investigate and critique many of the consequences of the independence, which had left Ireland, in many aspects of its lived ideology, still as it was in the late-colonial era.

Since Ireland was the first British territory since the Thirteen Colonies to achieve independence from Britain, its relative political successes and vicissitudes after 1922 became a template not only for emulation but also some caution. This is the reason why writers from other British colonies in the 1920s and 1930s, such as the Caribbean island of Trinidad, began writing, often in the socio-realist form of the novel, to address themes and issues surrounding their societies in relation to British power structures.

The first postcolonial critics tended to write about the political, national, cultural and literary processes and activities that were closest to them: this is why much early postcolonial study was concerned with works by writers from recently independent areas of Africa such as Nigeria, or from India, or the Caribbean. It was only by the late 1980s that critics began to address other regions in relation to postcolonial studies, such as Australia and, eventually, Ireland. This book has applied tools of comparative postcolonial study and revisited the Irish novel of the 1920s intertextually with the Caribbean novel of the same period. What it has shown is that while writers from these two regions might not have had the theoretical language or the hindsight to interpret the issues of their period in terms of various complex processes of decolonization, they used their literary skill and the form of the socio-realist novel to render a detailed account of peoples' reactions to social forces, tensions and events as they occurred. In 2016, a postcolonial comparative reading of Irish and Caribbean novels between 1925 and 1965 can show how writers from Ireland and the British West Indies used the novel to critique and disengage intellectually from seeing themselves and their societies in the once-dominant cast of an England of the mind.

This study has therefore suggested how the established canon of Irish postcolonial literatures might be expanded by consideration of the postcolonial significance of the post-independence Irish novel. It does not try to correct the efforts of *Field Day*, *Inventing Ireland* or *Irish Classics*, nor does it try to establish a canon per se. It does, however, pinpoint the importance of the Irish novel, between the 1920s and the 1960s, to the development of a decolonizing Irish voice. It has identified those Irish novels which have most comprehensively paralleled the key postcolonial aims and themes of what have over time come to be seen as the seminal postcolonial novels of the Caribbean in that same era. It paves the way for future scrutiny of the postcoloniality of Irish literatures, and in particular the novel, in English.

Notes

INTRODUCTION

1. Bill Ashcroft, Gareth Griffiths and Helen Tiffin, eds., *The Empire Writes Back: Theory and Practice in Post-Colonial Literatures* (London: Routledge, 1989), 4–5.
2. Bart Moore-Gilbert, *Postcolonial Theory: Contexts, Practices, Politics* (London: Verso, 1997), 11.
3. Peter Hulme, "Including America", *ARIEL: A Review of International English Literature* 26, no. 1 (January 1995): 117–23.
4. Jerry W. Ward and Robert J. Butler, eds., *The Richard Wright Encyclopedia* (Westport, CT: Greenwood, 2008), 198–99.
5. "Fiftieth Anniversary of the First International Congress of Black Writers and Artists (Paris, 19–22 September 2006); Declaration of Paris", accessed 18 November 2014, http://ocpa.irmo.hr/resources/docs/Paris_Declaration-en.pdf.
6. James Currey, "Ngũgĩ, Leeds and the Establishment of African Literature", *African Studies Bulletin* 74 (December 2012): 48–62, accessed 14 November 2014, http://lucas.leeds.ac.uk/article/ngugi-leeds-and-the-establishment-of-african-literature-james-currey.
7. George Padmore Institute, "*New Beacon Review*: Collection One (1968)", accessed 12 November 2014, http://www.georgepadmoreinstitute.org/the-pioneering-years/gallery-of-publications/new-beacon-review-collection-one-1968.
8. Kenneth Ramchand, *The West Indian Novel and Its Background* (1970; repr., Kingston: Ian Randle, 2005).
9. A switch from Commonwealth studies to postcolonial studies, around the mid-1980s, is evidenced by the title of Britta Olinder's edition of the proceedings of a conference on Commonwealth literature, which was published in 1984 as *A Sense of Place: Essays in Post-Colonial Literatures* (Gothenburg: Gothenburg University Commonwealth Studies, 1984).
10. Kenneth Ramchand, "An Introduction to This Novel", in Sam Selvon, *The Lonely Londoners* (London: Longman, 1985), 3–21.

11. *Jean Rhys Review* was first published biannually in 1986 in New York. It recognized a rise in critical interest in Rhys's work, and was the first dedicated undertaking to provide a substantial body of scholarship that addressed the West Indian as well as European dimensions of Rhys's writings. Pierrette Frickey's *Critical Perspectives on Jean Rhys* (Washington: Three Continents Press, 1990) is a fresh attempt to read Rhys in relation to the Caribbean aspects of her work and biography, as is Theresa F. O'Connor's *Jean Rhys: The West Indian Novels* (New York: New York University Press, 1991).
12. Caribbean writers have also contributed to an attempt to theorize the novel of their region, sometimes comparatively in relation to other cultural forms with a possible origin in African societies. For example, as early as 1967, E.K. Brathwaite discussed the improvisatory and oral folktale elements of West Indian prose narrative as an Afrocentric phenomenon, similar in its compositional approach to African-American jazz. See E.K. Brathwaite, "Jazz and the West Indian Novel [1967]", in *The Post-Colonial Studies Reader*, ed. Bill Ashcroft, Gareth Griffiths and Helen Tiffin, 327–31 (London: Routledge, 1995).
13. *The Empire Writes Back* is a good index of the global reach of postcolonial studies by the end of the 1980s. It speaks at some length about the centrality of Caribbean literatures to postcolonial scholarly and critical interests, but also broadens out its scope to discuss writers and works from other former colonial regions, inclusive of Africa, the former British India and Australia. See Ashcroft, Griffiths and Tiffin, *Empire Writes Back*.
14. Seamus Deane, introduction to *Nationalism, Colonialism and Literature* by Terry Eagleton, Fredric Jameson and Edward W. Said (Minneapolis: University of Minnesota Press, 1990), 6.
15. Seamus Deane, ed., *The Field Day Anthology of Irish Writing: In Three Volumes* (London: Faber and Faber, 1991).
16. Angela Bourke et al., eds., *The Field Day Anthology of Irish Writing*, vols 4 and 5, *Irish Women's Writing and Traditions* (Cork: Cork University Press, 2002).
17. Declan Kiberd, *Inventing Ireland: The Literature of the Modern Nation* (London: Vintage, 1995).
18. Ibid., 6.
19. David Lloyd's *Anomalous States: Irish Writing and the Post-Colonial Moment* (Durham, NC: Duke University Press, 1993) is notable as another early attempt to consider the unique position of Ireland within the emerging context of postcolonial studies.
20. Declan Kiberd, *Irish Classics* (London: Granta, 2000).
21. Maria McGarrity, *Washed by the Gulf Stream: The Historic and Geographic Relation of Irish and Caribbean Literature* (Newark: University of Delaware Press, 2008).

22. Alison Donnell, Maria McGarrity and Evelyn O'Callaghan, eds., *Caribbean Irish Connections: Interdisciplinary Perspectives* (Kingston: University of the West Indies Press, 2015). Conor Carville's *The Ends of Ireland: Criticism, History, Subjectivity* (Manchester: Manchester University Press, 2011) is another important text that attempts to broaden the theoretical orthodoxy of 1980s and 1990s works to place Irish writing within postcolonial studies.
23. Joan FitzPatrick Dean, "The Freedom of the Theatre in the Irish Free State 1922–1929; or, The Bullet Dodged", *The South Carolina Review* 33, no. 2 (Spring 2001): 135–42.
24. Maud Ellmann, "The Irish Novel, 1914–1940", in *The Oxford History of the Novel in English*, vol. 4, *Reinvention of the British and Irish Novel 1880–1940*, ed. Patrick Parrinder and Andrzej Gąsiorek (Oxford: Oxford University Press, 2011), 464.

CHAPTER 1

1. It should not, of course, be assumed that the *Beacon* authors were the first Trinidadian authors of interest to Caribbeanists and/or postcolonialists. Scholars such as Bridget Brereton have drawn attention to the lives and works of nineteenth-century and early twentieth-century Trinidadian authors such as Michel Maxwell Philip and Stephen N Cobham. See Brereton, *Race Relations in Colonial Trinidad* (Cambridge: Cambridge University Press, 2002), and the edition of Stephen N. Cobham, *Rupert Gray: A Tale in Black and White* (1907; repr., Kingston: University of the West Indies Press, 2007) edited by Lise Winer and with annotations by Bridget Brereton, Rhonda Cobham, Mary Rimmer and Lise Winer.
2. Ramchand, *West Indian Novel*.
3. Philippa Ireland, "Laying the Foundations: New Beacon Books, Bogle L'Ouverture Press and the Politics of Black British Publishing", *E-rea* 11, no. 1 (December 2013), accessed 8 October 2014, http://erea.revues.org/3524.
4. Rhonda Cobham, introduction to *Black Fauns*, by Alfred Mendes (1935; repr., London: New Beacon, 1984), i. Further references are given parenthetically in the text.
5. Reinhard W. Sander, *The Trinidad Awakening: West Indian Literature of the Nineteen-thirties* (New York: Greenwood, 1988).
6. Stewart Brown, introduction to *The Oxford Book of Caribbean Short Stories*, ed. Stuart Brown and John Wickham (Oxford: Oxford University Press, 1999), xx–xxi.
7. The Trinidadian *Beacon* novels of the 1930s paved the way for the socially conscious Jamaican slum novels of the 1950s, such as Roger Mais's *The Hills Were Joyful Together* (1953) and Orlando Patterson's *The Children of Sisyphus* (1964).
8. Michael Anthony, *The Making of Port-of-Spain: Volume One* (Port of Spain: Key Caribbean, 1978), 65.

9. Michèle Levy, ed., *The Autobiography of Alfred H. Mendes 1897–1991* (Kingston: University of the West Indies Press, 2002), 65.
10. Ibid., 77.
11. Émile Zola, *Germinal*, trans. Peter Collier (1885; repr., Oxford: Oxford World's Classics, 2008).
12. Émile Zola, *The Experimental Novel and Other Essays*, trans. Belle M. Sherman (New York: Cassell, 1893).
13. Dorrit Cohn, *Transparent Minds: Narrative Modes for Presenting Consciousness in Fiction* (Princeton: Princeton University Press, 1984).
14. See Homi K. Bhabha, "On Mimicry and Man: The Ambivalence of Colonial Discourse", in *The Location of Culture* (London: Routledge, 1994).
15. Jane Austen, *Northanger Abbey* (1817; repr., Oxford: Oxford World's Classics, 1990).
16. The major studies of O'Flaherty thus far were published between the early 1970s and the mid-1990s. They include J.H. O'Brien, *Liam O'Flaherty* (Lewisburg, PA: Bucknell University Press, 1973); John Zneimer, *The Literary Vision of Liam O'Flaherty* (Syracuse: Syracuse University Press, 1970); and James M. Calahan, *Liam O'Flaherty: A Study of the Short Fiction*, Twayne's Studies in Short Fiction, 23 (Boston: Twayne, 1991). There has yet to be a book-length, dedicated study of O'Flaherty from a postcolonial perspective. This chapter presents the first comparative study of *The Informer* to investigate the significance of its treatment of a post-independence but still effectively late-colonial economy.
17. Liam O'Flaherty, *The Informer* (1925; repr., Harmondsworth: Penguin, 1935), 8. Further references are given parenthetically in the text.
18. Cormac Ó Gráda, *A Rocky Road: The Irish Economy since the 1920s* (Manchester: Manchester University Press, 1997), 175.
19. Donal Corcoran, "Public Policy in an Emerging State: The Irish Free State 1922–25", *Irish Journal of Public Policy* 1, no. 1 (December 2009), accessed 28 March 2014, http://publish.ucc.ie/ijpp/2009/01/corcoran/05/en.
20. Enda Delaney, *Demography, State and Society: Irish Migration to Britain, 1921–1971* (Liverpool: Liverpool University Press, 2000), 58.
21. Liam O'Flaherty, *Two Years* (New York: Harcourt, Brace, 1930). See also Jennifer Malia, "Liam O'Flaherty's Disillusionment with Irish Revolutionary Martyrdom in *The Informer* and *The Assassin*", in *Pacific Coast Philology* 44, no. 2, *Violence and Representation* (2009): 191–204.
22. E.H. Mikhail, ed., *The Abbey Theatre: Interviews and Recollections* (Lanham, MD: Rowman and Littlefield, 1988), 149.
23. Charlie McGuire, *Roddy Connolly and the Struggle for Socialism in Ireland* (Cork: Cork University Press), 2008.

24. James Connolly, "Socialism and Nationalism (1897): From Shan Van Vocht, January 1897", accessed 27 March 2014, https://www.marxists.org/archive/connolly/1897/01/socnat.htm.
25. Brown, introduction, xx.
26. Levy, *Autobiography*, 75.

CHAPTER 2

1. Jean Rhys, *Voyage in the Dark* (1934; repr., Harmondsworth: Penguin, 2000), 8. Further references are given parenthetically in the text.
2. Sylvie Maurel, *Women Writers: Jean Rhys* (Basingstoke: Macmillan, 1998), 81–82.
3. Émile Boonzaier, Candy Malherbe, Andy Smith and Penny Berens, *The Cape Herders: A History of the Khoikhoi of Southern Africa* (Claremont: David Philip, 1996).
4. Letter from Jean Rhys to Evelyn Scott, 18 February 1934, cited in Francis Wyndham and Diana Melly, eds., *Jean Rhys Letters 1931–1966* (London: André Deutsch, 1984), 21–22.
5. Ibid., 171.
6. Symington Grieve, *Notes upon the Island of Dominica (British West Indies) Containing Information for Settlers, Investors, Tourists, Naturalists, and Others; with Statistics from the Official Returns, also Regulations Regarding Crown Lands and Import and Export Duties* (London: A. and C. Black, 1906), 34–35.
7. Jean Rhys, *Smile Please: An Unfinished Autobiography* (1979; repr. Harmondsworth: Penguin, 1981), 21.
8. James Anthony Froude, *The English in the West Indies or The Bow of Ulysses* (London: Longmans, Green and Co., 1888).
9. Ibid., 129.
10. Cf. Max Nordau, *Degeneration* (1892; repr., New York: D. Appleton and Co., 1895).
11. Cf. John Beddoe, "Spain, Italy, and the British Isles", in *The Anthropological History of Europe* (Paisley: Alexander Gardner, 1912), 124–46. It can also be noted that in 1895 the Royal Irish Academy measured the heads of living peasant farmers and their families in the County Mayo villages around the district of Ballycroy, and assessed their nigrescence. This observation points to the extent to which this practice of scientific racism was established with the dominant imperial discourse of British society, and the degree to which Hester's thinking reflects ideological norms of the period. See Charles R. Browne, "The Ethnography of Ballycroy, County Mayo", in *Proceedings of the Royal Irish Academy, Third Series, Vol. IV, No. 1* (Dublin: Academy House, 1896), 74–111.
12. Delia da Sousa Correa: "Phrenology's view of the mind as consisting of separate

faculties vying for fulfilment resulted in a model of the individual as made up of perpetually warring physical forces. These energies could be productively directed. Alternatively, individual 'propensities' could rage out of control, spilling over into madness and excess.... [In *Jane Eyre*,] Bertha herself, Rochester records, was subject to 'giant propensities' (3.1; p. 306)"; Delia da Sousa Correa, ed., *The Nineteenth-Century Novel: Realisms* (London: Routledge/Open University, 2000), 124.

13. Bridget Brereton, *An Introduction to the History of Trinidad and Tobago* (Oxford: Heinemann, 1996), 90.
14. Ibid., 89.
15. Jean Rhys, *Wide Sargasso Sea* (1966; repr., Harmondsworth: Penguin, 1968).
16. Louis James, "Sun Fire – Painted Fire: Jean Rhys as a Caribbean Novelist", in *Critical Perspectives on Jean Rhys*, ed. Pierrette M. Frickey (Washington, DC: Three Continents Press, 1990), 118–28. See also Kenneth Ramchand, "Terrified Consciousness", *Journal of Commonwealth Literature* 7 (1969): 8–19.
17. Elizabeth Bowen, *The Last September* (1929; repr., London: Vintage, 1998). Further references are given parenthetically in the text.
18. Hermione Lee, introduction to Elizabeth Bowen, *Bowen's Court and Seven Winters* (1942; repr., London: Vintage, 1999), x.
19. Elizabeth Bowen, cited in Eibhear Walshe, ed., *Elizabeth Bowen's Selected Irish Writings* (Cork: Cork University Press, 2011), 7.
20. Wilson Harris, "The Limbo Gateway", in *Post-Colonial Studies Reader*, ed. Ashcroft, Griffiths and Tiffin (London: Routledge, 1995), 378–82.
21. Phyllis Lassner, *Women Writers: Elizabeth Bowen* (Basingstoke: Macmillan, 1990), 36.
22. Elizabeth Bowen, *Bowen's Court and Seven Winters* (London: Vintage, 1984).
23. Lassner, *Women Writers*, 27.
24. Hermione Lee, *Elizabeth Bowen: An Estimation* (London: Vision Press, 1981), 50–51.
25. Michael McConville, *Ascendancy to Oblivion: The Story of the Anglo-Irish* (London: Quartet, 1986).
26. Ibid., 243.

CHAPTER 3

1. C.L.R. James, *Minty Alley* (1936; repr., London: New Beacon, 1971), 22. Further references are given parenthetically in the text.
2. Rhoda E. Reddock, *Women, Labour and Politics in Trinidad and Tobago: A History* (London: Zed, 1994), 92.
3. Ibid., 93.

4. Ibid.
5. Ibid., 92.
6. Ibid., 94.
7. Ibid., 81.
8. Ibid., 84.
9. Ibid., 50.
10. Ibid., 92.
11. Ibid., 52.
12. Antoinette Quinn, *Patrick Kavanagh: A Biography* (Dublin: Gill and Macmillan, 2001), 11–13.
13. Delaney, *Demography, State and Society*.
14. Patrick Kavanagh, *Tarry Flynn* (1948; repr., London: Penguin, 1978), 5. Further references are given parenthetically in the text.
15. Reddock, *Women, Labour and Politics*, 71.
16. Ibid.
17. In the period between the First and Second World Wars, it has been noted that "most of the migrants settled not far away from where they were born, and whilst internal migration was of some consequence, it tended to occur between contiguous counties with the distance of movement usually being relatively short". Delaney, *Demography, State and Society*, 39.

CHAPTER 4

1. Susheila Nasta, "Case Study 1: Writing the Caribbean in Britain: The Migrant Voice", in *A430: Post-Colonial Literatures in English: Readings and Interpretations: Study Guide*, ed. Robert Fraser et al. (Milton Keynes: Open University, 2003), 13.
2. Roydon Salick, *The Novels of Samuel Selvon: A Critical Study* (Westport, CT: Greenwood, 2001), 5.
3. Alison Donnell, *Twentieth-Century Caribbean Literature; Critical Moments in Anglophone Literary History* (London: Routledge, 2006), 119.
4. C.J. Ackerley, *Demented Particulars: The Annotated* Murphy (Edinburgh: Edinburgh University Press, 2010), 11. See also Hugh Kenner, *Samuel Beckett: A Critical Study* (New York: Grove Press, 1961); Ruby Cohn, *Samuel Beckett: The Comic Gamut* (New Brunswick, NJ: Rutgers University Press, 1962).
5. Kenner, *Samuel Beckett*, 35.
6. Ibid., 21.
7. Ackerley, *Demented Particulars*, 11.
8. See Aidan Arrowsmith, "Inside-Out: Literature, Cultural Identity and Irish

Migration to England", in *Comparing Postcolonial Literatures: Dislocations*, ed. Ashok Bery and Patricia Murray (Houndsmills: Macmillan, 2000), 59–69. See also Patrick Bixby, *Samuel Beckett and the Postcolonial Novel* (Cambridge: Cambridge University Press, 2009).
9. Delaney, *Demography, State and Society*, 46.
10. Sam Selvon, *The Lonely Londoners* (1956; repr., London: Longman, 1985), 47. Further references are given parenthetically in the text.
11. Ramchand, "Introduction to This Novel", 15.
12. Harris, "Limbo Gateway", 26.
13. Samuel Beckett, *Murphy* (1938; repr., London: Faber and Faber, 2009), 13–14. Further references are given parenthetically in the text.
14. David Brooke, "The Railway Navvy: A Reassessment", *Construction History* 5 (1989): 35–45. See also Renaissance London, "Irish London", accessed 25 March 2013, http://www.20thcenturylondon.org.uk/irish-london; Alistair Hennessy, "Workers of the Night: West Indians in Britain", in *Lost Illusions: Caribbean Minorities in Britain and the Netherlands*, ed. Malcolm Cross and Han Entzinger (London: Routledge, 1988), 36–53.

CHAPTER 5

1. Ngũgĩ wa Thiong'o, "Foreword: Freeing the Imagination: Lamming's Aesthetics of Decolonisation", in *Caribbean Reasonings: The George Lamming Reader: The Aesthetics of Decolonisation*, ed. Anthony Bogues (Kingston: Ian Randle, 2011), xi.
2. Bogues, *Caribbean Reasonings*.
3. Michael Farrell, *Thy Tears Might Cease* (1963; repr., London: Arena, 1984). Further references are given parenthetically in the text. Hereafter referred to as *Tears*.
4. Brendan Kennelly, "*Thy Tears Might Cease* by Michael Farrell", *Hermathena: A Dublin University Review* 99 (Autumn 1964): 97–98.
5. Peter Costello, *The Heart Grown Brutal: The Irish Revolution in Literature from Parnell to the Death of Yeats, 1891–1939* (Dublin: Gill and Macmillan 1977), 93–123.
6. Franco Moretti, *The Way of the World: The Bildungsroman in European Culture* (London: Verso, 1987).
7. Charlotte Brontë, *Jane Eyre* (1847; repr., Oxford: Oxford World's Classics, 2008).
8. George Lamming, *In the Castle of My Skin* (1953; repr., London: Longman, 1986), 4. Further references are given parenthetically in the text.
9. Mary Chamberlain, "Memories of Race and the Formation of Nation: Barbados 1937–1967" (paper presented to the Memory and Narrative Symposium, "Diversity" in an International Context, University of California, Berkeley, 2006), 8.

10. Anthony Layne, "Educational Reform in Barbados in the Post-War Period", in *Educational Reform in the Commonwealth Caribbean*, ed. Errol Miller, accessed 2 January 2014, http://www.educoas.org.
11. Keith A.P. Sandiford, *Cricket Nurseries of Colonial Barbados: The Elite Schools, 1865–1966* (Kingston: University of West Indies Press, 1998), 1–8.
12. Frantz Fanon, *The Wretched of the Earth*, trans. Constance Farrington (1961; repr., Harmondsworth: Penguin, 1967), 175.
13. Bhabha, "On Mimicry and Man", 85–92.
14. Hilary Beckles, *A History of Barbados: From Amerindian Settlement to Nation-State* (Cambridge: Cambridge University Press 1990), 165.
15. Hilary Beckles: "Between 1907 and 1910 at least 110 societies were established, a remarkable increase over previous years. . . . These black organisations attracted the attention of the legislature for the principal reason that the large sum of capital they collected could be used against the interests of the white community if properly mobilised. For example, societies could purchase land on behalf of members and influence the pattern of land distribution." Ibid., 151.
16. Fanon, *Wretched of the Earth*, 120–23.
17. John Luke Slattery, "Christian Brothers of Ireland", *The Catholic Encyclopedia*, vol. 3 (New York: Robert Appleton Co., 1908), accessed 1 January 2014, http://www.newadvent.org/cathen/03710b.htm.
18. Daire Keogh, "Ireland Owes More Than It Will Ever Realize to the Christian Brothers", *Irish Independent*, 9 June 2006, accessed 1 January 2014, http://www.independent.ie.
19. Patrick Barkham, "The Brothers Grim", *Guardian*, 28 November 2009, accessed 1 January 2014, http://www.theguardian.com.
20. Mary Chamberlain, *Empire and Nation-Building in the Caribbean: Barbados, 1937–66* (Manchester: Manchester University Press, 2010), 5.
21. Peter Cottrell, *The Anglo-Irish War: The Troubles of 1913–1922* (Oxford: Osprey, 2006), 33.
22. Carlton Younger, *Ireland's Civil War* (1968; repr., London: Fontana, 1986), 33.

Selected Bibliography

Abbott, H. Porter. *The Fiction of Samuel Beckett: Form and Effect*. Berkeley: University of California, 1973.
Ackerley, C.J. *Demented Particulars: The Annotated* Murphy. Edinburgh: Edinburgh University Press, 2010.
Adshead, Maura, and Michelle Millar. *Ireland as Catholic Corporatist State: A Historical Institutional Analysis of Healthcare in Ireland*. Limerick Papers in Politics and Public Administration, No. 5. Limerick: Department of Politics and Public Administration, University of Limerick, 2003.
Ahmad, Aijaz. *In Theory*. London: Verso, 1987.
Allen, Richard, and Harish Trivedi, eds. *Literature and Nation: Britain and India, 1800–1990*. London: Routledge, 2000.
Anderson, Benedict. *Imagined Communities: Reflections on the Origin and Spread of Nationalism*. London: Verso, 1983.
Angier, Carole. *Jean Rhys: Life and Work*. London: André Deutsch, 1990.
Anthony, Michael. *The Making of Port-of-Spain: Volume One*. Port of Spain: Key Caribbean, 1978.
Arensberg, Conrad, and Solon T. Kimball. *Family and Community in Ireland*, 2nd ed. 1940. Reprint, Cambridge, MA: Harvard University Press, 1968.
Arrowsmith, Aidan. "Inside-Out: Literature, Cultural Identity and Irish Migration to England". In *Comparing Postcolonial Literatures: Dislocations*, edited by Ashok Bery and Patricia Murray, 59–69. Houndsmills: Macmillan, 2000.
Ashcroft, Bill, Gareth Griffiths and Helen Tiffin. *The Empire Writes Back: Theory and Practice in Post-Colonial Literatures*. London: Routledge, 1989.
———, eds. *The Post-Colonial Studies Reader*. London: Routledge, 1995.
Athill, Diana. Foreword to *Smile Please: An Unfinished Autobiography*, by Jean Rhys. 1979. Reprint, Harmondsworth: Penguin, 1981.
Attridge, Derek, Geoff Bennington and Robert Young, eds. *Post-Structuralism and the Question of History*. Cambridge: Cambridge University Press, 1987.
Austen, Jane. *Northanger Abbey*. 1817. Reprint, Oxford: Oxford World's Classics, 1990.

Bakhtin, Mikhail M. *The Dialogic Imagination: Four Essays*. Translated by Caryl Emerson and Michael Holquist. Austin: University of Texas, 1981.

Baucom, Ian. *Out of Place: Englishness, Empire, and the Locations of Identity*. Princeton: Princeton University Press, 1999.

Beckett, Samuel. *Murphy*. 1938. Reprint, London: Faber and Faber, 2009.

Beckles, Hilary. *A History of Barbados: From Amerindian Settlement to Nation-State*. Cambridge: Cambridge University Press, 1990.

Beddoe, John. "Spain, Italy, and the British Isles". In *The Anthropological History of Europe*, 124–46. Paisley: Alexander Gardner, 1912.

Behan, Brendan. *Borstal Boy*. 1958. Reprint, London: Arena, 1990.

Berman, Art. *From the New Criticism to Deconstruction: The Reception of Structuralism and Post-Structuralism*. Chicago: University of Illinois, 1988.

Bery, Ashbok, and Patricia Murray. Introduction to *Comparing Postcolonial Literatures*, edited by Ashbok Bery and Patricia Murray, 1–17. Houndmills: Macmillan, 2000.

Bhabha, Homi K. "On Mimicry and Man: The Ambivalence of Colonial Discourse". In *The Location of Culture*, 85–92. London: Routledge, 1994.

———, ed. *Nation and Narration*. London: Routledge, 1990.

Bixby, Patrick. *Samuel Beckett and the Postcolonial Novel*. Cambridge: Cambridge University Press, 2009.

Boehmer, Elleke, ed. *Empire Writing: An Anthology of Colonial Literature 1870–1918*. Oxford: Oxford University Press, 1998.

Bogues, Anthony, ed. *Caribbean Reasonings: The George Lamming Reader – The Aesthetics of Decolonisation*. Kingston: Ian Randle, 2011.

Bonaccorso, Richard. *Sean O'Faolain's Irish Vision*. Albany: State University of New York Press, 1987.

Boonzaier, Émile, Candy Malherbe, Andy Smith and Penny Berens. *The Cape Herders: A History of the Khoikhoi of Southern Africa*. Claremont: David Philip, 1996.

Bostock, William. "Language Grief: Its Nature and Function at Community Level". *Language, Society and Culture* 1, no. 2. Hobart: University of Tasmania, 1997. http://eprints.utas.edu.au/1631/1/Bostock.html.

Bourke, Angela, et al., eds. *The Field Day Anthology of Irish Writing*. Vols 4 and 5: *Irish Women's Writing and Traditions*. Cork: Cork University Press, 2002.

Bowen, Elizabeth. *Bowen's Court and Seven Winters*. 1942. Reprint, London: Vintage, 1999.

———. *The Last September*. 1929. Reprint, London: Vintage, 1998.

Bradbury, Malcolm, and James McFarlane, eds. *Modernism: A Guide to European Literature 1890–1930*. Harmondsworth: Penguin, 1976.

Brathwaite, E.K. "Jazz and the West Indian Novel". In *The Post-Colonial Studies Reader*, edited by Bill Ashcroft, Gareth Griffiths and Helen Tiffin, 327–31. London: Routledge, 1995.

Brereton, Bridget. *A History of Modern Trinidad: 1783–1962*. Kingston: Heinemann, 1981.

———. *An Introduction to the History of Trinidad and Tobago*. Oxford: Heinemann, 1996.

———. *Race Relations in Colonial Trinidad*. Cambridge: Cambridge University Press, 2002.

Brontë, Charlotte. *Jane Eyre*. 1847. Reprint, Oxford: Oxford World's Classics, 2008.

Brooke, David. "The Railway Navvy: A Reassessment". *Construction History* 5 (1989): 35–45.

Brown, Janet, Patricia Anderson and Barry Chevannes. *Report on the Contribution of Caribbean Men to the Family: A Jamaican Pilot Study*. Kingston: University of the West Indies, 1993.

Brown, Stewart. Introduction to *The Oxford Book of Caribbean Short Stories*, editd by Stewart Brown and John Wyndham, xx–xxi. Oxford: Oxford University Press, 1999.

Browne, Charles R. "The Ethnography of Ballycroy, County Mayo". In *Proceedings of the Royal Irish Academy, Third Series, Vol. IV, No. I*, 74–111. Dublin: Academy House 1896.

Bryan, Patrick. "Book Reviews: *Panama Money in Barbados, 1900–1920* by Bonham C. Richardson". *Caribbean Quarterly* 33, nos. 1–2, "Pluralism Revisited" (March–June 1987): 98–100.

Calahan, James M. *The Irish Novel*. Dublin: Gill and Macmillan, 1988.

———. *Liam O'Flaherty: A Study of the Short Fiction*. Twayne's Studies in Short Fiction, 23. Boston: Twayne, 1991.

Carter, R.W.G., and A.J. Parker, eds. *Ireland: Contemporary Perspectives on a Land and Its People*. London: Routledge, 1989.

Carville, Conor. *The Ends of Ireland: Criticism, History, Subjectivity*. Manchester: Manchester University Press, 2011.

Chamberlain, Mary. *Empire and Nation-Building in the Caribbean: Barbados, 1937–66*. Manchester: Manchester University Press, 2010.

———. "Memories of Race and the Formation of Nation: Barbados 1937–1967". Paper presented to the Memory and Narrative Symposium, "Diversity" in an International Context. University of California, Berkeley, 2006.

Chappell, William. *The Ballad Literature and Popular Music of the Olden Time*. London: Chappell and Co., 1859.

Chatman, Seymour. "Story and Discourse". In *Literature in the Modern World: Critical Essays and Documents*, edited by Dennis Walder, 105–15. Oxford: Oxford University Press, 1990.

Childs, Peter, ed. *Post-Colonial Theory and English Literature: A Reader*. Edinburgh: Edinburgh University Press, 1999.

Clarke, Edith. *My Mother Who Fathered Me: A Study of the Families in Three Selected Communities of Jamaica*. 1957. Reprint: Kingston: The Press, West Indies University Press, 1999.

Cleary, Joe. "Irish Studies, Colonial Questions: Locating Ireland in the Colonial World".

In *Outrageous Fortune: Capital and Culture in Modern Ireland*, 14–46. Dublin: Field Day, 2007.

Cobham, Rhonda. Introduction to *Black Fauns*, by Alfred Mendes, i–xvi. 1935. Reprint, London: New Beacon, 1984.

Cobham, Stephen N. *Rupert Gray: A Tale in Black and White*. 1907. Reprint, Kingston: University of the West Indies Press, 2007.

Cohn, Dorrit. *Transparent Minds: Narrative Modes for Presenting Consciousness in Fiction*. Princeton, NJ: Princeton University Press, 1984.

Cohn, Ruby. *Samuel Beckett: The Comic Gamut*. New Brunswick, NJ: Rutgers University Press, 1962.

Connolly, Clare, ed. *Theorizing Ireland*. Basingstoke: Palgrave Macmillan, 2003.

Connolly, Cyril, ed. *Horizon: A Review of Literature and Art: Irish Number* 5, no. 1 (January 1942).

Connolly, James. "Socialism and Nationalism (1897): From Shan Van Vocht, January 1897". Accessed 27 March 2014. http://www.marxists.org/archive/connolly/1897/01/socnat.htm.

Connor, Steven. "Beckett and Bion". Accessed 26 October 2012. http://www.stevenconnor.com/beckbion.

Coogan, Tim Pat. *Ireland in the Twentieth Century*. London: Hutchinson, 2003.

Corcoran, Donal. "Public Policy in an Emerging State: The Irish Free State 1922–25". *Irish Journal of Public Policy* 1, no. 1 (December 2009). Accessed 28 March 2014. http://publish.ucc.ie/ijpp/2009/01/corcoran/05/en.

Corrigan, Karen P. "Regional Variation and the Local Standard for Irish English". In *Dialects of English: Irish English*. Vol. 1: *Northern Ireland*, 153–55. Edinburgh: Edinburgh University Press, 2010.

Costello, Peter. *The Heart Grown Brutal: The Irish Revolution in Literature from Parnell to the Death of Yeats, 1891–1939*. Dublin: Gill and Macmillan, 1977.

Cottrell, Peter. *The Anglo-Irish War: The Troubles of 1913–1922*. Oxford: Osprey, 2006.

Cronin, Anthony. *Samuel Beckett: The Last Modernist*. London: Harper Collins, 1996.

Cross, Malcolm, and Han Entzinger, eds. *Lost Illusions: Caribbean Minorities in Britain and the Netherlands*. London: Routledge, 1988.

Crowley, Tony. *The Politics of Language in Ireland 1366–1922: A Sourcebook*. London: Routledge, 2000.

Culler, Jonathan. *Structuralist Poetics: Structuralism, Linguistics and the Study of Literature*. London: Routledge, 1975.

Currey, James. "Ngugi, Leeds and the Establishment of African Literature". *African Studies Bulletin* 74 (December 2012): 48–62. Accessed 12 November 2014. http://lucas.leeds.ac.uk/article/ngugi-leeds-and-the-establishment-of-african-literature-james-currey.

Da Sousa Correa, Delia, ed. *The Nineteenth-Century Novel: Realisms*. London: Routledge/ Open University, 2000.

Dean, Joan FitzPatrick. "The Freedom of the Theatre in the Irish Free State 1922–1929; or, The Bullet Dodged". *The South Carolina Review* 33, no. 2 (Spring 2001): 135–42.

Deane, Seamus, ed. *The Field Day Anthology of Irish Writing: In Three Volumes*. London: Faber and Faber, 1991.

———. Introduction to *Nationalism, Colonialism and Literature*, by Terry Eagleton, Fredric Jameson and Edward W. Said, 3–19. Minneapolis: University of Minnesota Press, 1990.

Delaney, Enda, *Demography, State and Society: Irish Migration to Britain, 1921–1971*. Liverpool: Liverpool University Press, 2000.

Delaney, Enda, and Donald M. MacRaild, eds. *Irish Migration, Networks and Ethnic Identities since 1750*. London: Routledge, 2007.

Donnell, Alison. *Twentieth-Century Caribbean Literature; Critical Moments in Anglophone Literary History*. London: Routledge, 2006.

Donnell, Alison, and Sarah Lawson Welsh, eds. *The Routledge Reader in Caribbean Literature*. London: Routledge, 1996.

Donnell, Alison, Maria McGarrity and Evelyn O'Callaghan, eds. *Caribbean Irish Connections: Interdisciplinary Perspectives*. Kingston: University of the West Indies Press, 2015.

Dorney, John. "The Big House and the Irish Revolution". Accessed 7 July 2011. http://www.theirishstory.com/2011/06/21.

Douglass, Frederick. *Narrative of the Life of Frederick Douglass, an American Slave*. 1845. Reprint, Harmondsworth: Penguin, 2014.

Dunne, Catherine. *An Unconsidered People: The Irish in London*. Dublin: New Island, 2003.

Eagleton, Mary, ed. *Feminist Literary Criticism*. London: Longman, 1991.

Eagleton, Terry, and Drew Milne, eds. *Marxist Literary Theory: A Reader*. Oxford: Blackwell, 1996.

Ellmann, Maud. "The Irish Novel, 1914–1940". In *The Oxford History of the Novel in English*. Vol. 4: *The Reinvention of the British and Irish Novel 1880–1940*, 451–72. Oxford: Oxford University Press, 2011.

Estévez Forneiro, Reyes. "Hiberno-English: The Result of a Language Contact Situation". Galicia: Universidade de Vigo, 1997. Accessed 8 July 2012. http://webs.uvigo.es/ssl/actas1997/05/Estevez1.pdf.

Fanon, Frantz. *Black Skin, White Masks*. Translated by Charles Lain Markmann. 1952. Reprint, London: Pluto, 2008.

———. *The Wretched of the Earth*. Translated by Constance Farrington. 1961. Reprint, Harmondsworth: Penguin, 1967.

Farred, Grant, ed. *Rethinking C.L.R. James*. Oxford: Blackwell, 1996.

Farrell, Michael. *Thy Tears Might Cease*. 1963. Reprint, London: Arena, 1984.
Fehsenfeld, Martha Dow, and Lois More Overbeck, eds. *The Letters of Samuel Beckett Volume I: 1929–1940*. Cambridge: Cambridge University Press, 2009.
"Fiftieth Anniversary of the First International Congress of Black Writers and Artists (Paris, 19–22 September 2006); Declaration of Paris". Accessed 18 November 2014. http://ocpa.irmo.hr/resources/docs/Paris_Declaration-en.pdf.
Fitzpatrick, David. *The Two Irelands: 1912–1939*. Oxford: Oxford University Press, 1998.
Fletcher, John. *The Novels of Samuel Beckett*. London: Chatto and Windus, 1964.
Foster, R.F. *Modern Ireland: 1600–1972*. Harmondsworth: Penguin, 1999.
Foucault, Michel. *Madness and Civilization: A History of Insanity in the Age of Reason*. New York: Random House, 1965.
Frame, Robin. *Colonial Ireland 1169–1369*, 2nd ed. Dublin: Four Courts Press, 2012.
Fraser, Robert, et al. *A430 Post-Colonial Literatures in English: Readings and Interpretations: Study Guide*. Milton Keynes: Open University, 2003.
Frickey, Pierrette, ed. *Critical Perspectives on Jean Rhys*. Washington: Three Continents Press, 1990.
Froude, James Anthony. *The English in the West Indies or The Bow of Ulysses*. London: Longmans, Green and Co., 1888.
Fumagalli, Maria Cristina. *The Flight of the Vernacular: Seamus Heaney, Derek Walcott and the Impress of Dante*. Amsterdam: Rodolpi, 2001.
Genette, Gérard. *Narrative Discourse: An Essay in Method*. Translated by Jane E. Lewin. Ithaca: Cornell University Press, 1980.
George Padmore Institute. "*New Beacon Review*. Collection One (1968)". Accessed 8 October 2014. http://www.georgepadmoreinstitute.org.
Gilroy, Paul. *There Ain't No Black in the Union Jack: The Cultural Politics of Race and Nation*. London: Routledge, 1987.
Gontarski, S.E., ed. *A Companion to Samuel Beckett*. Chichester: Wiley-Blackwell, 2010.
Gordon, Lois. *The World of Samuel Beckett 1906–1946*. New Haven: Yale University Press, 1996.
Graddol, David, Dick Leith and Joan Swann, eds. *English: History, Diversity and Change*. London: Routledge/Open University, 1996.
Grattan, Henry. "Declaration of Irish Rights, April 19, 1780". In *The Speeches of the Right Hon. Henry Grattan*. Accessed 6 July 2011. https://archive.org/details/speechesofright hoogratiala.
Graver, Lawrence, ed. *Samuel Beckett: The Critical Heritage*. London: Routledge, 1979.
Grene, Nicholas. *The Politics of Irish Drama: Plays in Context From Boucicault to Friel*. Cambridge: Cambridge University Press, 1999.
Grieve, Symington. *Notes upon the Island of Dominica (British West Indies) Containing Information for Settlers, Investors, Tourists, Naturalists, and Others; with Statistics from*

the *Official Returns, also Regulations Regarding Crown Lands and Import and Export Duties*. London: A. and C. Black, 1906.

Hall, Stuart. "Race, the Floating Signifier". Accessed 10 June 2011. http://www.mediaed.org/assets/products/407/transcript_407.pdf.

Harlow, Barbara, and Mia Carter, eds. *Imperialism and Orientalism: A Documentary Sourcebook*. Oxford: Blackwell, 1999.

Harmon, Maurice, *Sean O'Faoláin: A Critical Introduction*. Notre Dame, IN: University of Notre Dame Press, 1967.

Harris, Clive, and Winston James. *Inside Babylon: The Caribbean Diaspora in Britain*. London: Verso, 1993.

Harris, Wilson. "The Limbo Gateway". In *The Post-Colonial Studies Reader*, edited by Bill Ashcroft, Gareth Griffiths and Helen Tiffin, 378–82. London: Routledge, 1995.

Hart, Keith, ed. *Women and the Sexual Division of Labour in the Caribbean*. Kingston: Canoe Press, 1989.

Harte, Liam. *The Literature of the Irish in Britain: Autobiography and Memoir, 1725–2001*. London: Palgrave Macmillan, 2009.

Hennessy, Alistair. "Workers of the Night: West Indians in Britain". In *Lost Illusions: Caribbean Minorities in Britain and the Netherlands*, edited by Malcolm Cross and Han Entzinger, 36–53. London: Routledge, 1988.

Hickey, Raymond. "Irish English Resource Centre". Accessed 13 October 2012. http://www.uni-due.de/IERC.

———. *A Sound Atlas of Irish English*. Berlin/New York: Mouton de Gruyter, 2004.

Hickling, Frederick W., and Vanessa Paisley. "Issues of Clinical and Cultural Competence in Caribbean Migrants". *Transcultural Psychiatry* 49, no. 2 (April 2012): 223–44.

Hindley, Reg. *The Death of the Irish Language: A Qualified Obituary*. London: Routledge, 1990.

Honychurch, Lennox. *The Dominica Story: A History of the Island*. Roseau: The Dominica Institute, 1975.

———. *Jean Rhys Biography: For The Jean Rhys Tour*. Accessed 6 March 2012. http://www.lennoxhonychurch.com/jeanrhysbio.cfm.

Hulme, Peter. "Including America". *ARIEL: A Review of International English Literature* 26, no. 1 (January 1995): 117–23.

———. "Islands and Roads: Hesketh Bell, Jean Rhys and Dominica's Imperial Road". *Jean Rhys Review* 11, no. 2 (Spring 2000): 23–51.

Ireland, Philippa. "Laying the Foundations: New Beacon Books, Bogle L'Ouverture Press and the Politics of Black British Publishing". *E-rea* 11, no. 1 (December 2013). Accessed 8 October 2014. http://erea.revues.org/3524.

James, C.L.R. (as "J.R. Johnson"). "Ireland and the Revolutionary Tradition of Easter Week". *Labor Action* 5, no. 14 (April 1941): 3.

———. *Minty Alley*. 1936. Reprint, London: New Beacon, 1971.

James, Louis. "Sun Fire – Painted Fire: Jean Rhys as a Caribbean Novelist". In *Critical Perspectives on Jean Rhys*, edited by Pierrette M. Frickey, 118–28. Washington, DC: Three Continents Press, 1990.

Johnson, Jean Bassett. "A Clear Case of Linguistic Acculturation". *American Anthropologist* 45, no. 3 (July–September 1943): 427–34.

Johnson, Nuala C. *Ireland, the Great War and the Geography of Remembrance*. Cambridge: Cambridge University Press, 2003.

Joyce, James. *The Restored Finnegans Wake*. 1939. Reprint, Harmondsworth: Penguin, 2012.

———. *Ulysses*. 1922. Reprint, Harmondsworth: Penguin, 2000.

Kavanagh, Patrick. *The Complete Poems*. Newbridge: Goldsmith, 1972.

———. *Tarry Flynn*. 1948. Reprint, London: Penguin, 1978.

Kennelly, Brendan. "*Thy Tears Might Cease* by Michael Farrell". *Hermathena: A Dublin University Review* 99 (Autumn 1964): 97–98.

Kenner, Hugh. *Samuel Beckett: A Critical Study*. New York: Grove Press, 1961.

Kenny, Kevin, ed. *The Oxford History of the British Empire Companion Series: Ireland and the British Empire*. Oxford: Oxford University Press, 2004.

Keogh, Daire. "Ireland Owes More Than It Will Ever Realize to the Christian Brothers". *The Irish Independent*, 9 June 2006. Accessed 1 January 2014. http://www.independent.ie.

Kiberd, Declan. *Inventing Ireland: The Literature of the Modern Nation*. London: Vintage, 1995.

———. *Irish Classics*. London: Granta, 2000.

Kincaid, Andrew. "Review: Ireland and Postcolonial Theory. Edited by Clare Carroll and Patricia King. University of Notre Dame Press, 2003". *E-Keltoi: Journal of Interdisciplinary Celtic Studies* 1, no. 1 (2005). Accessed 12 November 2014. https://www4.uwm.edu/celtic/ekeltoi/bookreviews.

Lamming, George. *In the Castle of My Skin*. 1953. Reprint, London: Longman, 1986.

Lassner, Phyllis. *Women Writers: Elizabeth Bowen*. Basingstoke: Macmillan, 1990.

Layne, Anthony. "Educational Reform in Barbados in the Post-War Period". In *Educational Reform in the Commonwealth Caribbean*, edited by Errol Miller. Accessed 2 January 2014. http://www.educoas.org.

Ledgister, F.S.J. "A Region for Itself". *Caribbean Review of Books* 23 (2010). Accessed 21 January 2013. http://caribbeanreviewofbooks.com.

Lee, Hermione. *Elizabeth Bowen: An Estimation*. London: Vision Press, 1981.

———. Introduction to *Bowen's Court and Seven Winters*, by Elizabeth Bowen, vii–xv. 1942. Reprint, London: Vintage, 1999.

Levy, Michèle, ed. *The Autobiography of Alfred H. Mendes 1897–1991*. Kingston: University of the West Indies Press, 2002.

Lloyd, David. *Anomalous States: Irish Writing and the Post-Colonial Moment*. Durham, NC: Duke University Press, 1993.
Lloyd, Trevor. *Empire: The History of the British Empire*. London: Hambledon and London, 2001.
Loomba, Ania. *Colonialism/Postcolonialism*. London: Routledge, 1998.
Macardle, Dorothy. *The Irish Republic*. 1937. Reprint, London: Corgi, 1968.
MacLean, Carl, Catherine Campbell and Flora Cornish. "African-Caribbean Interactions with Mental Health Services: Experiences and Expectations of Exclusion as (Re)productive of Health Inequalities". *Social Science and Medicine* 56, no. 3 (2003): 56–59. Reprint, 2005. Accessed 20 July 2012. http://eprints.lse.ac.uk/180/1/african-caribbean_interaction.pdf.
Malia, Jennifer. "Liam O'Flaherty's Disillusionment with Irish Revolutionary Martyrdom in *The Informer* and *The Assassin*". *Pacific Coast Philology* 44, no. 2, *Violence and Representation* (2009): 191–204.
Matthews, Kelly. "Something Solid to Put Your Heels On: Representation and Transformation in *The Bell*". *Éire-Ireland* 46, nos. 1–2 (Spring–Summer 2011): 106–27.
Maurel, Sylvie. *Women Writers: Jean Rhys*. Basingstoke: Macmillan, 1998.
Maurer, Noel, and Carlos Yu. *What Roosevelt Took: The Economic Impact of the Panama Canal, 1903–37*. Accessed 16 March 2013. http://www.hbs.edu/faculty/Publication%20Files/06-041.pdf.
McConville, Michael. *Ascendancy to Oblivion: The Story of the Anglo-Irish*. London: Quartet, 1986.
McGarrity, Maria. *Washed by the Gulf Stream: The Historic and Geographic Relation of Irish and Caribbean Literature*. Newark: University of Delaware Press, 2008.
McGuire, Charlie. *Roddy Connolly and the Struggle for Socialism in Ireland*. Cork: Cork University Press, 2008.
McLellan, David, ed. *Karl Marx: Selected Writings*, 2nd ed. Oxford: Oxford University Press, 2000.
McLoughlin, Michael, ed. *Great Irish Speeches of the Twentieth Century*. Dublin: Poolbeg, 1996.
Mendes, Alfred. *Black Fauns*. 1935. Reprint, London: New Beacon, 1984.
Mikhail, E.H., ed. *The Abbey Theatre: Interviews and Recollections*. Lanham, MD: Rowman and Littlefield, 1988.
Millette, James. *Society and Politics in Colonial Trinidad*. 1970. Reprint, London: Zed, 1985.
Milroy, James, and Lesley Milroy. *Authority in Language: Investigating Language Prescription and Standardisation*. London: Routledge, 1985.
Montaño, John Patrick. *The Roots of English Colonialism in Ireland*. Cambridge: Cambridge University Press, 2011.
Moore-Gilbert, Bart. *Postcolonial Theory: Contexts, Practices, Politics*. London: Verso, 1997.

Moretti, Franco. *The Way of the World: The Bildungsroman in European Culture*. London: Verso, 1987.
Nasta, Susheila. "Case Study 1: Writing the Caribbean in Britain: The Migrant Voice". In *A430: Post-Colonial Literatures in English: Readings and Interpretations: Study Guide*, edited by Robert Fraser et al., 13. Milton Keynes: Open University, 2003.
———, ed. *Critical Perspectives on Sam Selvon*. Washington: Three Continents Press, 1988.
Newton, Darrell Motley. "Calling the West Indies: The BBC World Service and *Caribbean Voices*". Accessed 22 March 2013. http://www.open.ac.uk/socialsciences/diasporas.
Newton, Velma. *The Silver Men: West Indian Labour Migration to Panama 1850–1914*. Kingston: Institute of Social and Economic Research, University of the West Indies, 1984.
Nordau, Max. *Degeneration*. 1892. Reprint, New York: D. Appleton and Co., 1895.
O'Brien, Flann. *At Swim-Two-Birds*. 1938. Reprint, Harmondsworth: Penguin, 2000.
O'Brien, J.H. *Liam O'Flaherty*. Lewisburg, PA: Bucknell University Press, 1973.
O'Connor, Kevin. *The Irish in Britain*. London: Sidgwick and Jackson, 1972.
O'Connor, Theresa F. *Jean Rhys: The West Indian Novels*. New York: New York University Press, 1991.
O'Flaherty, Liam. *The Informer*. 1925. Reprint, Harmondsworth: Penguin, 1935.
———. *Two Years*. New York: Harcourt, Brace, 1930.
Ó'Gráda, Cormac. *A Rocky Road: The Irish Economy since the 1920s*. Manchester: Manchester University Press, 1997.
Ó Siadhail, Mícheál. *Learning Irish: An Introductory Self-Tutor*. New Haven: Yale, 1980.
Ohlmeyer, Jane H. "A Laboratory for Empire? Early Modern Ireland and English Imperialism". In *The Oxford History of the British Empire Companion Series: Ireland and the British Empire*, edited by Kevin Kenny, 26–60. Oxford: Oxford University Press, 2004.
Oireachtas. "Seanad Éireann – Volume 122 – 19 April 1989, National Development Plan, 1989–1993: Motion". Accessed 13 October 2012. http://oireachtasdebates.oireachtas.ie.
Olinder, Britta, ed. *A Sense of Place: Essays in Post-Colonial Literatures*. Gothenburg: Gothenburg University Commonwealth Studies, 1984.
Onega, Susana, and José García Landa. *Narratology: An Introduction*. London: Longman, 1996.
Paquet, Sandra Pouchet. *Caribbean Autobiography: Cultural Identity and Self-Representation*. Madison: University of Wisconsin Press, 2002.
———. *The Novels of George Lamming*. London: Heinemann, 1982.
Phillips, Mike, and Trevor Phillips. *Windrush: The Irresistible Rise of Multi-Racial Britain*. London: Harper Collins, 1998.
Pilling, John, ed. *The Cambridge Companion to Beckett*. Cambridge: Cambridge University Press, 1994.

Pizzichini, Lillian. *The Blue Hour: A Portrait of Jean Rhys*. London: Bloomsbury, 2009.
Power, Orla. "Beyond Kinship: A Study of the Eighteenth-Century Irish Community at Saint Croix, Danish West Indies". *Irish Migration Studies in Latin America* 5, no. 3 (November 2007): 207–14.
Punter, David. *Postcolonial Imaginings: Fictions of a New World Order*. Edinburgh: Edinburgh University Press, 2000.
Quinn, Antoinette. *Patrick Kavanagh: A Biography*. Dublin: Gill and Macmillan, 2001.
———. *Patrick Kavanagh: Born-Again Romantic*. Dublin: Gill and Macmillan, 1991.
Ramchand, Kenneth. "An Introduction to This Novel". In Sam Selvon, *The Lonely Londoners*, 3–21. London: Longman, 1985.
———. "Terrified Consciousness". *Journal of Commonwealth Literature* 7 (1969): 8–19.
———. *The West Indian Novel and Its Background*. 1970. Reprint, Kingston: Ian Randle, 2005.
Reddock, Rhoda E. *Women, Labour and Politics in Trinidad and Tobago: A History*. London: Zed, 1994.
———. "Women and the Sexual Division of Labour, Historical and Contemporary Perspectives: The Case of Trinidad and Tobago". In *Women and the Sexual Division of Labour*, edited by Keith Hart, 54–71. Kingston: Canoe Press, 1989.
Rhys, Jean. *Smile Please: An Unfinished Autobiography*. 1979. Reprint, Harmondsworth: Penguin, 1981.
———. *Voyage in the Dark*. 1934. Reprint, Harmondsworth: Penguin, 2000.
———. *Wide Sargasso Sea*. 1966. Reprint, Harmondsworth: Penguin, 1968.
Richardson, Bonham. "The Impact of Panama Money in Barbados in the Early Twentieth Century". *New West Indian Guide/Nieuwe West-Indische Gids* 59, nos. 1–2 (1985): 1–26.
Rimmon-Kenan, Shlomith. *Narrative Fiction: Contemporary Poetics*. London: Routledge, 1988.
Roots. "'Cognitive Mapping' and History in the Barrack-Yard Novel". In *Long Way From Home: Fragments and Correspondence* [blog], edited by Aaron Love. Accessed 14 March 2012. http://fragments-correspondence.org. Site now archived at http://archive.is/fragments-correspondence.org.
———. "In the Castle of My Skin, the Caribbean Novel, and the Historical Conjuncture of the 1930s". In *Long Way From Home: Fragments and Correspondence* [blog], edited by Aaron Love. Accessed 20 January 2013. http://fragments-correspondence.org. Site now archived at http://archive.is/fragments-correspondence.org.
Royal Irish Academy. *The Doegen Records Project (Tionscadal Gréasáin Chiernínì Doegen)*. Accessed 9 July 2012. https://www.doegen.ie/.
Ryan, Louise, Gerard Leavey, Anne Golden, Robert Blizard and Michael King. "Depression in Irish Migrants Living in London: Case-Control Study". *British Journal of Psychiatry* 188 (2006): 560–66.

Said, Edward W. *Culture and Imperialism*. London: Vintage, 1993.
———. *Orientalism: Western Conceptions of the Orient*. Harmondsworth: Penguin, 1978.
———. "Yeats and Decolonization". In *Literature in the Modern World: Critical Essays and Documents*, edited by Dennis Walder, 34–41. Oxford: Oxford University Press/ Open University, 1990.
Salick, Roydon. *The Novels of Samuel Selvon: A Critical Study*. Westport, CT: Greenwood, 2001.
Sander, Reinhard W. *The Trinidad Awakening: West Indian Literature of the Nineteen-thirties*. New York: Greenwood, 1988.
Sandiford, Keith A.P. *Cricket Nurseries of Colonial Barbados: The Elite Schools, 1865–1966*. Kingston: University of the West Indies Press, 1998.
Scott, David. "The Sovereignty of the Imagination: An Interview with George Lamming". *Small Axe* 6, no. 2 (2002): 72–200.
Sebba, Mark, and Shirley Tate. "'Global' and 'Local' Identities in the Discourses of British-Born Caribbeans". *International Journal of Bilingualism* 6, no. 1 (2002): 75–89.
Selvon, Sam. *A Brighter Sun*. New York: Viking, 1953.
———. *The Lonely Londoners*. 1956. Reprint, London: Longman, 1985.
———. *Ways of Sunlight*. 1957. Reprint, London: Longman, 1979.
Shepherd, Verene, Bridget Brereton and Barbara Bailey, eds. *Engendering History: Caribbean Women in Historical Perspective*. Kingston: Ian Randle, 1995.
Sherwood, Rae. *The Psychodynamics of Race: Vicious and Benign Spirals*. Brighton: Harvester, 1980.
Shiel, Michael. *The Quiet Revolution: The Electrification of Rural Ireland*. Dublin: O'Brien, 2003.
Slattery, John Luke. "Christian Brothers of Ireland". *The Catholic Encyclopedia*, vol. 3. New York: Robert Appleton Co., 1908. Accessed 1 January 2014. http://www.newadvent.org/cathen/03710b.htm.
Smyth, Gerry. *Decolonisation and Criticism: The Construction of Irish Literature*. London: Pluto, 1998.
Stokes, Eric. *The English Utilitarians and India*. Oxford: Clarendon Press, 1959.
Swift, Roger, and Sheridan Gilley, eds. *The Irish in Britain 1815–1939*. Savage: Barnes and Noble, 1989.
Talib, Ismail S. *The Language of Postcolonial Literatures*. London: Routledge, 2002.
Tannehill, I.R. "Tropical Disturbances, September 1936". *Monthly Weather Review* 64, no. 9 (1936): 297.
Thiong'o, Ngũgĩ wa. "Foreword: Freeing the Imagination: Lamming's Aesthetics of Decolonisation". In *Caribbean Reasonings: The George Lamming Reader: The Aesthetics of Decolonisation*, edited by Anthony Bogues, xi. Kingston: Ian Randle, 2011.
Toolan, Michael J. *Narrative: A Critical Linguistic Introduction*. London: Routledge, 1988.

Walder, Dennis, ed. *Literature in the Modern World: Critical Essays and Documents*. Oxford: Oxford University Press, 1990.

———. *Post-Colonial Literatures in English: History, Language, Theory*. Oxford: Blackwell, 1988.

Wall, Maureen. "The Rise of a Catholic Middle Class in Eighteenth-Century Ireland". *Irish Historical Studies* 11, no. 42 (September 1958): 91–115.

Walshe, Eibhear, ed. *Elizabeth Bowen's Selected Irish Writings*. Cork: Cork University Press, 2011.

Ward, Jerry W., and Robert J. Butler, eds. *The Richard Wright Encyclopedia*. Westport, CT: Greenwood, 2008.

White, Lawrence William. "Peadar O'Donnell, 'Real Republicanism' and *The Bell*". *The Republic: Culture in the Republic* 4 (2005). Accessed 18 March 2013. http://theireland institute.com/republic/04/pdf/white004.pdf.

Williams, Patrick, and Laura Chrisman, eds. *Colonial Discourse and Post-Colonial Theory: A Reader*. Harlow: Prentice Hall, 1993.

Wood, Donald. *Trinidad in Transition: The Years after Slavery*. 1968. Reprint, Oxford: Oxford University Press, 1987.

Wyke, Clement H. *Sam Selvon's Dialectal Style and Fictional Strategy*. Vancouver: University of British Columbia, 1991.

Wyndham, Francis, and Diana Melly, eds. *Jean Rhys Letters 1931–1966*. London: André Deutsch, 1984.

Younger, Carlton. *Ireland's Civil War*. 1968. Reprint, London: Fontana, 1986.

Zneimer, John. *The Literary Vision of Liam O'Flaherty*. Syracuse: Syracuse University Press, 1970.

Zola, Émile. *The Experimental Novel and Other Essays*. Translated by Belle M. Sherman. New York: Cassell, 1893.

———. *Germinal*. Translated by Peter Collier. 1885. Reprint, Oxford: Oxford World's Classics, 2008.

Index

Abbey Theatre (Dublin), 9–10
Achebe, Chinua, 4
Ackerley, Chris, 101
African Writers' Series (Heinemann), 4
Amongst Women (John McGahern), 157
Angier, Carole, 48–49
Anglo-Irish Ascendancy, 32, 37, 44, 56, 62, 65–67, 150–51
Anglo-Irish War, 56, 62
Anthropology (Edward Burnett Tylor), 53
Arrowsmith, Aidan, 101
Ashcroft, Bill, 1
At Swim-Two-Birds (Flann O'Brien), 158
Atlee, Clement, 102

Bakhtin, Mikhail, 116
Baldwin, James, 3
Bank of Ireland, 32
Barrack yard, 17–18, 70–72, 78–86
The Beacon (1930s periodical), 15–16, 41, 71, 97
Beckett, Samuel, 8, 10, 13, 99–123, 157
Beddoe, John, 53
Behan, Brendan, 155
Bell, Henry Hesketh, 50
Bhabha, Homi K., 132, 145
Bildungsroman, 13, 85, 125–53, 155–59
Bixby, Patrick, 101

Black Arts Movement (USA, 1960s), 3
Black Fauns (Alfred Mendes), 5, 11, 15–43, 154–55; characters: Estelle, 22–31, 34–35, 38–40, 43; Ethelrida, 18–19, 21–31, 34, 36; Ma Christine, 18, 22–31; Mamitz, 24–31, 34–35, 38–40, 43; Mannie, 21, 36; Martha, 22–31; Miriam, 18–31, 33; Mr de Pompignon, 17, 22; Snakey, 25–31
Bogues, Anthony, 124
Borstal Boy (Brendan Behan), 155
Bowen, Elizabeth, 10, 11–12, 44–69, 99, 155
Brereton, Bridget, 54
Bridgetown Riots 1937 (Barbados), 145–48
A Brighter Sun (Sam Selvon), 100, 117
Brown, Stewart, 16, 42

Calling the West Indies (BBC), 100
Canboulay, 54–55
Caribbean Artists' Movement, 3
Caribbean Irish Connections (2015 book), 8–9
Caribbean novel, 2–3,
Caribbean Voices (BBC), 3, 100
Caribbean Writers' Series (Heinemann), 5,

Casement, Roger, 146–47
In the Castle of My Skin (George Lamming), 2–6, 13, 100, 124–53, 158; characters: G., 125–53; G.'s mother, 126–27; Ma and Pa, 135–37; Mr Foster, 133; Mr Slime, 128–51; Trumper, 131, 152
Cathleen Ní Houlihan (W.B. Yeats), 120–21
Celtic Twilight, 158
Césaire, Aimé, 3
Chamberlain, Mary, 129,
Christian Brothers, 140–44
Cipriani, Captain Arthur, 17–19,
Cobham, Rhonda, 5, 16, 29–30, 71
Cohn, Dorrit, 28, 74–75
Cohn, Ruby, 101
The Colonizer and the Colonized (Albert Memmi), 124
Committee on Evil Literature, 9
Conference of Commonwealth Literature, 4
Connolly, James, 41, 137
Connolly, Roddy, 41
Corentyne Thunder (Edgar Mittelholzer), 5
Cosgrave, W.T., 9
Costello, Peter, 124–25
Coterie of Social Workers (Trinidad and Tobago), 81
Cottrell, Peter, 146
The Country Girls (Edna O'Brien), 155–56
Crick Crack, Monkey (Merle Hodge), 131
Cronin, Anthony, 101
Cúchulainn, 120
Cumann na nGaedheal, 9, 32, 102, 160

Darwin, Charles, 130
David Copperfield (Charles Dickens), 126

Deane, Seamus, 7
Degeneration (Marx Nordau), 52
Descartes, Rene, 110
Diamond Jubilee 1897, 19
Dickens, Charles, 126
Donnell, Alison, 2, 9, 100
The Dragon Can't Dance (Earl Lovelace), 155

Eagleton, Terry, 7
Easter Rising 1916 (Ireland), 145–53
Education Code 1935 (Trinidad and Tobago), 73
Ellison, Ralph, 3
Ellmann, Maud, 10
The Empire Writes Back (Ashcroft et al.), 1
The English in the West Indies (James Anthony Froude), 52

Fanon, Frantz, 3, 124, 131–32, 148, 151, 153
Far from the Madding Crowd (Thomas Hardy), 22
Farrell, Michael, 10, 13, 124–53
Field Day, 7, 161
The Field Day Anthology of Irish Writing, 7
Film Act 1970 (Ireland), 9
Finnegans Wake (James Joyce), 158
First International Congress of Black Writers and Artists (Paris, 1956), 3–4
Freud, Sigmund, 53
Froude, James Anthony, 52

Gaelic League, 147
Garvey, Marcus, 3
The George Lamming Reader (ed. Anthony Bogues), 124
Germinal (Émile Zola), 20–21, 86

Geulincx, Arnold, 101
Gibbons, Luke, 7
Goethe, Johann Wolfgang, 126
Gomes, Albert, 18
Grattan, Henry, 65
Great Expectations (Charles Dickens), 126
Gregory, Lady Augusta, 120, 160
Grieve, Symington, 51
Griffiths, Gareth, 1

The Harder They Come (Perry Henzell), 155
Hardy, Thomas, 22
Harlem Renaissance, 3, 4
Harrington, John P., 101
Harris, Clive, 102
Harris, Wilson, 4, 58
Heaney, Seamus, 7
The Heart Grown Brutal (Peter Costello), 124–25
Henzell, Perry, 155
Hodge, Merle, 131
Housewifization (Trinidad and Tobago), 81
Huggins, John, 102
Hulme, Peter, 2
Hyde, Douglas, 160

The Informer (Liam O'Flaherty), 11, 15–43, 154–55; characters: Connemara Maggie, 39–40; Dan Gallagher, 33–43; Frankie McPhillip, 34–43; Gypo Nolan, 33–43; Katie Fox, 34, 38–40; Louisa Cummins, 38–39
Inventing Ireland (Declan Kiberd), 8, 161
Invisible Man (Ralph Ellison), 3
Ireland: 1169 Norman landings, ix; 1800 Act of Union, ix, 139

The Irish Beckett (John P. Harrington), 101
Irish Classics (Declan Kiberd), 9, 161
Irish Free State, 9, 32, 96, 119, 160
Irish novel, 2–3,
Irish Revival, 9, 37, 43, 120, 159–60
Irish University Review, 124
An Island Is a World (Sam Selvon), 100

James, C.L.R., 5, 12–13, 15–16, 42, 70–98, 99, 155, 157–58
James, Ida (C.L.R. James's mother), 86–87
Jameson, Frederic, 7
Jane Eyre (Charlotte Bronte), 53, 56, 126–27
Jones, Eldred, 4
Journal of Commonwealth Literature, 4
Joyce, James, 43, 158

Kavanagh, Bridget (Patrick Kavanagh's mother), 86
Kavanagh, Patrick, 8, 12–13, 70, 86–98, 99, 157–58
Kennelly, Brendan, 124
Kenner, Hugh, 101
Khoikhoi, 47–48
Kiberd, Declan, 7–8
Kiely, Benedict, 10
Kristeva, Julia, 46–47

La Rose, John, 4,
Labour Leader (Trinidad and Tobago), 96
Lamming, George, 3, 13, 100, 124–53, 158
Lassner, Phyllis, 61, 63–64
The Last September (Elizabeth Bowen), 11–12, 44–69, 155; as a "Big House" novel, 44, 56, 61–63, 143, 150, 159;

The Last September (Elizabeth Bowen) *(continued)*
  characters: Anna Partridge, 65; Betty Vermont, 60, 65; Francie Montmorency, 57, 59; Gerald Lesworth, 61, 67; Hugo Montmorency, 57, 59, 61; Laura Farquar, 57; Laurence, 66; Leslie Hawe, 62; Lois Farquar, 56–68, 155–56; Marda Norton, 62; Michael Connor, 61; Mrs Boatley, 66; Mrs Carey, 60; Myra Naylor, 57, 60, 64–68; Richard Naylor, 57, 59; Walter Farquar, 57
Layne, Anthony, 129
"Leda and the Swan" (W.B. Yeats), 10
Lee, Hermione, 56
The Lonely Londoners (Sam Selvon), 5, 99–123, 157; characters: Cap, 107–22; Daniel, 116; Galahad, 102–22; Moses Aloetta, 99–122; the Austrian girl, 111–15
Longman Drumbeat series, 5
Loomba, Ania, 2
Lovelace, Earl, 155

Mac Cool, Finn, 158
Manifesto for the Irish Theatre (Yeats, Gregory, Martyn), 160
Married Women's Property Act 1882 (Crown Colony Law), 81
Married Women's Property Act 1893 (Crown Colony Law), 81
Marson, Una, 3
Martyn, Edward, 160
Maurel, Sylvie, 46–47
Maxwell, General John, 145
McConville, Michael, 65
McGahern, John, 157
McGarrity, Maria, 8

McKay, Claude, 3–4
Memmi, Albert, 124
Mendes, Alfred, 5, 11, 15–43, 71, 81–82, 99, 154–55
Miguel Street (V.S. Naipaul), 155
The Mimic Men (V.S. Naipaul), 131
Minty Alley (C.L.R. James), 5, 12–13, 15–16, 19, 70–98, 155, 157–58; characters: Aucher, 78–79; Benoit, 80–81; Ella, 72–78, 87, 89, 95, 97; Haynes, 71–85, 89–92, 156; Maisie, 82–85, 96; Miss Atwell, 84–85; Mrs Haynes, 72–78, 89–90; Mrs Rouse/"Ma" Rouse, 78–85, 89, 95–97; Nurse Jackson, 82; Philomel, 83–84
Mittelholzer, Edgar, 5
Moore-Gilbert, Bart, 2
Morgenstern, Johann Karl Simon, 126
Murphy (Samuel Beckett), 10, 13, 99–123, 157; characters: Austin Ticklepenny, 115–16; Celia Kelly, 112–22; Miss Counihan, 119–22; Mr Endon, 115; Murphy, 110–23; Neary, 110–22; Wylie, 121–22

Naipaul, V.S., 3, 131, 155
Nana (Émile Zola), 46
Nasta, Susheila, 100
Nationalism, Colonialism and Literature (1990), 7
New Beacon Books, 4, 15–16, 71
New Beacon Reviews, 4
Nordau, Max, 52
Notes upon the Island of Dominica (British West Indies) (Symington Grieve), 51

O'Brien, Edna, 155–56
O'Brien, Flann, 158

O'Callaghan, Evelyn, 8
O'Casey, Sean, 10
O'Flaherty, Liam, 10, 11, 15–43, 154–55

Paquet, Sandra Pouchet, 2, 6
Parnell, Charles Stewart, 125
Paulin, Tom, 7
Payne, Clement, 133
Pearse, Padraig, 120
The Playboy of the Western World (John Millington Synge), 155
The Plough and the Stars (Sean O'Casey), 10

Quinn, Antoinette, 86

Ramchand, Kenneth, 2–6, 15–16, 71, 105
Ramsaran, Gladys, 72–73
Reddock, Rhoda E., 72–86, 96
Redmond, John, 125, 139, 146
Report of the West India Royal Commission (Moyne Report), 145
Rhys, Jean, 4, 6, 11–12, 44–69, 99, 155
Russell, George ("A.E."), 160

Said, Edward, 7, 66
Salick, Roydon, 100
Samuel Beckett and the Postcolonial Novel (Patrick Bixby), 101
Sander, Reinhard W, 16
Sandiford, Keith A.P., 130
Scott, Evelyn, 49
Selvon, Sam, 3, 13, 31, 99–123, 157
Sheppard, Oliver, 120
Sinn Féin, 147, 150
Synge, John Millington, 155

Tarry Flynn (Patrick Kavanagh), 12–13, 70–98, 155–57; characters: Aggie Flynn, 98; Bridie Flynn, 93–98; Father Daly, 93; Mary Flynn, 95–98; Mrs Callan, 94; Mrs Flynn, 87–98; Tarry Flynn, 87–98, 156
The Teachers' Association (Trinidad and Tobago), 83
Teachers' Journal (Trinidad), 83
Thy Tears Might Cease (Michael Farrell), 13, 124–53, 155, 158; characters: Colonel Reilly, 140; Jimmy Curran, 148; Martin Matthew Reilly, 138–53; Miss Clare, 143–44, 152; Mr Burns, 140; Norman Dempsey, 149; Seumas Conroy, 147; the Faithful Brothers, 140–44, 150–51; the Vincents, 143–52; Tim Corbin, 148–51
Tiffin, Helen, 1
Times Literary Supplement, 120
The Tower (W.B. Yeats), 9–10
Trinidad (1929–1930 periodical), 15–16
Trinidadian water riots 1903, 19
Tylor, Edward Burnett, 53

Ulysses (James Joyce), 124

Voyage in the Dark (Jean Rhys), 6, 44–69, 100, 155; characters: Anna Morgan, 44–56, 67–68, 155–56; Bo Costerus, 53, 68; Gerald Morgan, 45, 50–53; Hester Morgan, 45, 50–53, 64–65, 67–68; Maillotte Boyd, 50, 54; Maudie, 47; Vincent, 54; Walter Jeffries, 47–48; as plantation novel, 44, 51–52, 55, 68

Walcott, Derek, 3
Washed by the Gulf Stream (Maria McGarrity), 8

The West Indian Novel and Its Background (Kenneth Ramchand), 4–5, 15–16, 71
White, Sarah, 4
Wide Sargasso Sea (Jean Rhys), 55–58
William Meister's Apprenticeship (Johann Wolfgang Goethe), 126
Williams, David, 5
Williams, Eric, 4

The Wretched of the Earth (Frantz Fanon), 124, 131–32, 151, 153
Wright, Richard, 3
Wyndham, Francis, 49

Yeats, W.B., 9, 120–21, 160

Zola, Émile, 20, 33, 43, 46

www.ingramcontent.com/pod-product-compliance
Lightning Source LLC
Chambersburg PA
CBHW021842220426
43663CB00005B/363